Praise fo

"*Beyond Faery* is an essential and intriguing look at the wide variety / animals and creatures which humans may encounter. Reminiscent of Katherine Briggs' *Fairies in Tradition and Literature*, Kruse's work looks at groups of fairies and thoroughly discusses their qualities, motifs, and stories in a way that engages readers. Highly recommended for anyone with an interest in British folklore or fairies; even if you consider yourself knowledgeable on the topic you will learn something here."

—Morgan Daimler, author of *A New Dictionary of Fairies* and *Fairies: A Guide to the Celtic Fair Folk*

"The creatures of the woodland, waterways, and oceans are brought to life for the modern reader in this engaging, well-researched new work. It is packed with stories, anecdotes, and folklore accounts, making it a satisfyingly rich read."

—Christina Oakley Harrington, Treadwell's Bookshop of London

BEYOND

FAERY

About the Author

John Kruse is a writer and blogger on faery themes. His professional interests are law and legal history, but in recent years he has brought his research skills to a subject that has fascinated him since his late teens. In 2016 he began to write the *British Fairies* blog on WordPress. In 2017 he published *British Fairies* with Green Magic Publishing and he has several other books on faery and faery beasts forthcoming.

To Write to the Author

If you wish to contact the author or would like more information about this book, please write to the author in care of Llewellyn Worldwide Ltd. and we will forward your request. Both the author and publisher appreciate hearing from you and learning of your enjoyment of this book and how it has helped you. Llewellyn Worldwide Ltd. cannot guarantee that every letter written to the author can be answered, but all will be forwarded. Please write to:

John T. Kruse
℅ Llewellyn Worldwide
2143 Wooddale Drive
Woodbury, MN 55125-2989

Please enclose a self-addressed stamped envelope for reply,
or $1.00 to cover costs. If outside the U.S.A., enclose
an international postal reply coupon.

Many of Llewellyn's authors have websites with additional
information and resources. For more information,
please visit our website at http://www.llewellyn.com

BEYOND FAERY

Exploring the World of Mermaids, Kelpies, Goblins & Other Faery Beasts

Llewellyn Publications
Woodbury, Minnesota

JOHN T. KRUSE

FIRST EDITION
First Printing, 2020

Book design by Samantha Penn
Cover design by Kevin R. Brown
Cover illustration by Dominick Finelle
Interior illustrations by Wen Hsu

Llewellyn Publications is a registered trademark of Llewellyn Worldwide Ltd.

Library of Congress Cataloging-in-Publication Data
Names: Kruse, John T. author.
Title: Beyond faery : exploring the world of mermaids, kelpies, goblins &
    other faery beasts / John T. Kruse.
Description: First edition. | Woodbury, Minnesota : Llewellyn Publications,
    [2020] | Includes bibliographical references. | Summary: "This book
    explores some of the more fearsome beasts that have been known to meddle
    in human affairs. The author reveals the secret lives of merfolk and
    meremaids, river sprites and kelpies, hags and banshees as well as hobs,
    goblins, bogies daemon dogs, and many more. These are the magical
    creatures that tend to terrify instead of help, and learning their ways
    may be just what readers need to survive an encounter with one of these
    other-world beasts"—Provided by publisher.
Identifiers: LCCN 2020030013 (print) | LCCN 2020030014 (ebook) | ISBN
    9780738766102 (paperback) | ISBN 9780738766355 (ebook)
Subjects: LCSH: Animals, Mythical.
Classification: LCC GR825 .K73 2020 (print) | LCC GR825 (ebook) | DDC
    398.24/54—dc23
LC record available at https://lccn.loc.gov/2020030013
LC ebook record available at https://lccn.loc.gov/2020030014

Llewellyn Publications
A Division of Llewellyn Worldwide Ltd.
2143 Wooddale Drive
Woodbury, MN 55125-2989
www.llewellyn.com

Printed in the United States of America

Other Books by John Kruse

British Fairies
Faery

For Sue, for her love and support, Rhiannon,
Fliss, and the Lady of the Elder Tree.

CONTENTS

Part 1

WATER BEASTS

Part 2

 ⌣ ⌣

LAND BEASTS

ACKNOWLEDGMENTS

I wish to thank my publishers for giving me the idea to write this book in the first place. The core of the text represents material cut from my book on Faery. Separating it and focusing on the subject of faery beasts alone has deepened my knowledge of this vast and fascinating subject.

I would also like to acknowledge the valuable resource that is the Paranormal Database, a huge catalogue of hauntings and mysteries across the British Isles. I should also admit my debt to Katharine Briggs. Her *A Dictionary of Fairies* is very often the point of departure for my research, and she supplied many valuable clues for developing this book. Not least amongst these was her decision to interpret "faeries" as broadly as possible: her inclusion of such a variety of beasts encouraged me to be equally bold in my approach to the subject.

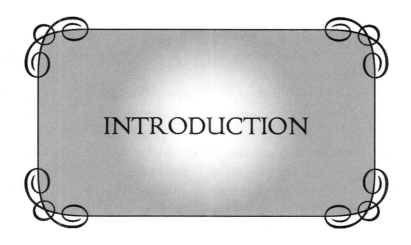

INTRODUCTION

English author Maurice Hewlett, in his 1913 novel *Lore of Proserpine*, called for a book that described the physical laws under which faery life lives. He even suggested a title for it, "The Natural History of the Preternatural," donated to whoever felt up to the task of supplying what Hewlett felt to be lacking. This present book may not be a complete natural history of all of faery kind, but it offers readers a "field guide" to the faery beasts, describing their habitats and their habits.[1]

Definitions

What is a faery? What *isn't* a faery? At the far boundary of supernatural beings, it can be very hard to make firm distinctions, and it is a difficulty that we humans have had for many hundreds of years. As I'll describe later, whether a creature like a "boggart" is a faery or a ghost, for example, was a question never fully settled in Lancashire. In this book, I'll be dealing with a spectrum of preternatural or spirit beings that fit less easily into the category of "faery."

---

1. Maurice Hewlett, "The Secret Commonwealth," in *Lore of Proserpine* (New York: Charles Scribner, 1913), 62.

In the recent book *Magical Folk*, faeries are defined as "magical, living, resident humanoids."[2] If we accept this, we would certainly incorporate in our list all the spirits that people would immediately imagine if they heard the word "faery." Winged flower faeries, gnomes, brownies, elves—goblins even—would all be included.

What about mermaids though? They're humanoid, definitely, but they are also part fish and live mostly in the sea, although they can survive perfectly well on land. Are they faeries in the narrow sense of the word? Probably they're not, but they are amongst the host of creatures associated with the faery realm—sharing many of its features and magical properties—and which fascinate the many people who are attracted by faeries as well. We need a broader definition of the word "faery," it would appear, and, fortunately, that is not far to seek. "Faery" derives ultimately from the Latin word *fata*, the name of the Fates. In medieval French, this became *fée*, meaning magical or enchanted. In turn, this produced *fayerie*, a state of enchantment, a word which itself evolved to denote a place and then the people living within it—our faeries. If we use *faery* and *fae* in that older, wider sense, it is very suitable for talking about the beasts I am going to discuss. They are not "faeries" but they are "faery"—enchanted or invested with glamour.

My purpose in this book, therefore, is to properly examine these "fae-beasts," to understand how they live and how they interact with human beings. As the book progresses, the beings described get less and less human-like in appearance and behaviour. Increasingly, their relationship to humans is not one of close similarity in conduct and looks, but rather one of alien, inscrutable threat.

A second key question may be: why faery *beasts*? Are mermaids or hobgoblins truly beast-like? Given the humanoid qualities of several of the supernatural beings that I propose to discuss in this book, this objection may seem like a fair one, but I think there are good reasons for differentiating "true" faeries from other magical beings. Everyone shares a standard image of a faery—a humanlike being, perhaps winged, perhaps with pointed ears, but essentially and recognisably similar to ourselves. This is not an inaccu-

2. Simon Young and Ceri Houlbrook, eds., *Magical Folk: British and Irish Fairies: 500 AD to the Present* (London: Gibson Square, 2018), 12.

rate convention. Variations in height, skin tone, or the colour of eyes and hair don't detract from their close resemblance to humans. In contrast, the faery beasts to be covered in this book all diverge more or less sharply from this. Merfolk are an obvious example: partly human, of course, but also part fish. The hobs and hags I shall describe, again, resemble people in many ways, but by their size, hairiness, or some even more unusual feature—such as a single eye or fangs—they are marked out as different. Towards the end of this book, there will be little doubt that we are discussing "beasts" in the proper sense of the word in the form of supernatural dogs, bulls, and horses. My choice of "faery beasts," therefore, marks the fact that we will be concerned with classes of creatures materially distinct from ourselves and from the great family of beings (brownies, elves, and pixies) that we can label simply "faery."

Scary Monsters

There can be a strong presumption nowadays that faeries are benign and friendly beings. Folklore indicates that this is very far from the truth. The faeries are, at the very least, reserved and secretive. At worst, they are positively dangerous for humans. In this book, I will examine the side of supernatural beings that we are less ready to acknowledge but still must respect.

The prevalent idea that all faeries are pretty and pleasant does Faery itself a disservice. It divests it of diversity and reduces it to a limited number of types—noble warrior elves and butterfly faeries, principally. There seems to be no space for monsters now. Traditional faery beliefs allowed for considerably more diversity—in fact, for a complex wealth of faery forms—and this book is, in part, my attempt to restore that variety.

Whilst the creatures and beings to be described have "faery" nature in the sense that they are mystical, magical, and sometimes inexplicable, they are in many ways unlike the more humanoid faeries that we tend to envisage when the word "faery" is used. Faeries have communities and a culture; there are lots of them, and they interact in many complex ways (emotionally and economically, for example) with each other and with humans. They are constantly in contact with our world, interested in our food, our possessions, and even in sexual relationships with us; there's a lot to say about them. The faery beasts that are the subject of this book are far fewer in number to begin with, and they tend to relate to humans in a far simpler and far more predictable manner. In fact, to be brutally honest, the main mission of a lot of these beings is either to terrify us or to devour us. For that reason, a lot of our descriptions are going to be much shorter and less involved because there's generally a lot less detail to examine and a lot less scope for interaction between our worlds.

Common Characteristics

Another reason for treating these beasts and beings as "faery" is the fact that they share so many traits and patterns of behaviour with the more conventional faery. For those readers acquainted with my other books on faeries, you may already be familiar with the preferences and habits which I'm now going to describe.[3]

Faeries are known from time to time to change their shape and their size; faery beasts do the same, but far more frequently—so regularly, in fact, that it is one of their distinguishing features. Faeries often only appear at night, and this is just as true (if not more so) for most of the creatures to be described in this book. The more humanoid mermaids are probably the main exception to this. Sometimes, too, the only way of seeing a supernatural being is to be blessed with the second sight—or to be in the company of a person who is, whom you may touch and so share their gift for as long as you are in contact. The same applies to some of the faery beasts: for instance, Geldeston in Norfolk was cursed by the presence of a bogle, variously called the "hateful thing," the "hellhound" or "churchyard beast," which would appear as a large dog and harass travellers and drag children along the road. One day, three people were walking along the road when one heard a dog padding along behind them. Her companions heard nothing, but they decided to speed up anyway. Accordingly, they linked arms—and then the older woman of the three was also able to hear and see the dog, which accompanied them a little further before disappearing into the churchyard wall.

Faeries are associated from time to time with locating or protecting buried treasure, and faery beasts quite often have a similar function. Just as faeries can object to the building or siting of certain churches, so, too, can the beasts—the best example of this being the buggane on the Isle of Man

---

3. See my *Faery* (2020), especially chapter 2 section 4, and *British Fairies* (2017).

who objected to the building of St. Trinian's Church on the slopes of Greeba Mountain. As a sign of its displeasure, the buggane destroyed the roof of the new building three times. Given the beasts' predilection for mischief, and the trouble that they can cause if they feel that they are being ignored or thwarted, another very common practice is for people to make offerings of food and drink to them, just as happens with the brownies of Northern England and Lowland Scotland and other domestic faeries.

There is a persistent link between supernatural beings and the weather. Faeries may be able to cause bad weather or may appear only in certain conditions, and the same applies to faery beasts. They are often blamed for tempests—especially mermaids—or they may be able to foresee them and give warnings (if they're so inclined).[4]

This is just an outline, and a few examples, of the common likes and dislikes of faery beasts, which make it clear that they are just as much a part of Faery as the faeries and elves with whom many readers may be more familiar. I'll now focus on two shared traits which are of particular interest, but many more detailed illustrations of the issues just covered will follow throughout the book.

Faery Beasts & Water

There is a very close relationship between most of the faery beasts described in this book and water, whether that is still or flowing fresh water or the sea. Mermaids and sea-trows live in the ocean, of course, which is part of the reason why the book has been divided between sea and land beasts. Unfortunately, the situation is by no means as clear cut as this; most of the riverine and marine creatures are actually amphibian. The kelpies, water horses, and water bulls I shall describe all have their abode in water, but most of their activities involving humans are conducted on land—although victims will very likely be dragged off to the water to be devoured. Mermaids come onto the shore voluntarily to relax, but they can be forced to live on land permanently without it proving fatal. Turning to the "land" beasts that I shall catalogue, many of these are still closely linked to water in some way—for example, by haunting wells, springs, or watercourses.

---

4. See my *Faery* (2020) chapter 6.

What does this affinity mean? Part of it, I think, is a physical manifestation of what separates human beings from the otherworld. Whilst conventional faeries may use magic to disappear—whether or not that involves simply becoming invisible or switching to a different dimension—for the faery beasts, the boundary between us is tangible and real. They can disappear below the water surface where we can't follow them. Travelling to faeryland is always risky and, in the case of the faery beasts, it can be directly perilous if Faery is an environment in which we cannot breathe. Another aspect of the faery beasts' association with water is the link that exists with a force of nature and a source of life. The beasts are a controlling factor in our environment, often having influence over the weather and releasing water upon us from the sky as well, as I just noted. Water is vital to human beings—and yet it is also dangerous. This might, indeed, be a good summary of our interactions with the supernatural beings that fill the natural world around us.

Curiously, though, and just like faeries, many faery beasts are unable to cross flowing water. Of course, as I've already stated, several of these creatures live in water, but, even then, there may be some sort of antipathy: for example, a marine creature may not be able to tolerate fresh water. This anomalous situation is a puzzle, but its explanation may be that nature inherently puts limits upon all its elements. Curbs exist to restrain the unbounded power of all natural forces so that everything is held in balance.

Faeries and Death

As has already been suggested, and as I shall illustrate in detail later, there is a persistent link between death and the faery beasts. This is to be seen in the apparent preference of black dogs to lurk in and around graveyards, the belief that the "wild hunts" heard in the skies are often in pursuit of lost souls, or the fact that meetings with barguests and banshees are regularly preludes to misfortune or mortality. More particularly, as will be remarked repeatedly in this book, the faery beasts are quite often the bringers of death to unlucky humans.

It's indisputable that, as well as the banshees, some faery beasts serve as harbingers of death. For example, a clergyman out walking near his home on the Isle of Man heard a bull bellowing. He knelt and prayed and soon a bull larger than any normal one passed him by, shaking the ground as it went.

It disappeared towards a cottage and, when the priest went to the house, he found that the owner had died that very minute. In this case the supernatural bull, the *tarroo ushtey*, acts as a herald of death—or even its deliverer.[5]

Nonetheless, there is a very longstanding theory within the study of folklore that faeries may represent the souls of deceased ancestors and that faeryland is, as a consequence, the land of the dead in some form. It is indisputable that the conventional faeries have a close relationship to death, although the exact nature of that interaction is ambiguous and hard to define. For example, on the Isle of Man it was believed that a mock funeral procession, acted out by the faeries, would precede a death in the human community. Further, in 1847, it was reported in the local newspaper *Mona's Herald* that after an islander had ploughed up some waste ground, the windows of his house had been broken by the fae because he had disturbed an old fairy graveyard. A very similar story comes from Benbecula in the Outer Hebrides. Against the advice and warnings of his neighbours, a man built a house on a spot where a body had been buried. A spirit called a *bocan*, similar to a poltergeist, entered the new house, throwing fuel for the fire around and hitting people's feet with a stick. This went on for a year—despite an effort to lay the spirit—and then ceased. In Fife it was said that the faeries had pulled down a house in which a murder had been committed, and that they would not let the owner rebuild and nightly would demolish anything constructed during the day. Lastly, at Largs in Ayrshire, a man abducted by the faeries and taken to a revel reported that a headless man danced all night with them.[6]

Turning to the faery beasts that are the subject of this book, very many types of bogie, as well as daemon dogs and fae animals, are known to frequent, or to haunt, churchyards, graveyards, and other sites where bodies are interred or murders or suicides have occurred. What ties these padfoots,

5. George Waldron, *The History and Description of the Isle of Man: viz. Its Antiquity, History, Laws, Customs, Religion and Manners of Its Inhabitants [...]* (Douglas: Manx Society, 1731), 34.

6. Waldron, *The History and Description*, 38; Arthur W. Moore, *The Folk-Lore of the Isle of Man Being an Account of Its Myths [...]* (London: D. Nutt, 1891), chapter III; John L. Campbell and Trevor H. Hall, *Strange Things: The Story of Fr. Allan McDonald, Ada Goodrich-Freer and the Society for Psychical Research's Enquiry into Highland Second Sight* (Edinburgh: Birlinn Ltd., 2006), 261; *County Folk-lore*, vol. 7, 32; John Gregorson Campbell, *Superstitions of the Highlands & Islands of Scotland: Collected Entirely from Oral Sources by John Gregorson Campbell* (Glasgow: James MacLehose and Sons, 1900), 77.

rses, and hounds to these sites? Do they memorialise where a body lies by their appearances, or are they the ad, albeit in nonhuman form?

The Scottish and Manx examples just cited certainly portray faery kind as being very protective of the dead, and this is perhaps a good way of conceiving the relationship of many faery beasts to death. Often, phantom dogs and similar creatures are seen at places not only where a body is concealed or a forgotten burial lies, but where a murder was committed, a suicide occurred, or where a person died whose body was never recovered—for example by drowning. The fae animals involved in such cases may not be the troubled souls of the deceased but might instead be understood as guardians or remembrances of those who died.

Even so, we must confront the question of the degree of difference (if any) that exists between some faery beasts and ghosts. The distinction is not always clear nor fixed. For example, boggarts are often associated with locations where murders or suicides are known to have taken place, or where burials have been discovered, but at the same time, the correlation is not necessarily direct. Two ancient skeletons may be exhumed, but there will only be one boggart haunting the spot; two orphans may have been murdered at an old house, but only one boggart haunts the ruined site where it stood. A difference definitely exists between the two supernatural forms, and I have therefore tried to exclude from my evidence experiences which involve beings that conform to our conventional idea of a ghost: a pale, transparent human figure resembling the dead person. For that reason, too, I have chosen to use the word "sprite" to denote a supernatural being in preference to "spirit," which is too suggestive of souls of departed people and too potentially confusing.

Fellow faery writer Richard Sugg has wrestled with this same problem and, in his 2018 book, *Fairies*, he often draws a line between "real ghosts" and faeries.[7] There are several shared characteristics, undoubtedly. Many faery beasts, just like ghosts, will frequent or haunt a specific location. Several types of faery beast can be banished, or "laid," with a religious or magi-

---

7. Richard Sugg, *Fairies: A Dangerous History* (London: Reaktion Books, 2018), 14–5, 141–8, 150–3.

cal ceremony, exactly as can be done with troublesome ghosts. At the same time, there seem to me to be clear differences as well. My own feeling is that whilst faery beings will have a personality and purpose that is their own, ghosts are different because they're related to the life, appearance, and conduct of a deceased human. Ghost manifestations occur at a time and place that relates to the deceased's former existence, whereas faery beasts have a mission unconnected with any individual human experience. The beasts may well be connected to a particular site, but this is for reasons different from those which oblige a ghost or ghoul to linger around a once familiar spot.

Remedies & Protections Against Faery Beasts

Faery beasts can be dangerous and deadly, but we are not without defences against them. Some of these derive from Christian religion, but many are far older.

For most of recorded history, faery creatures have coexisted with humans who have been members of the Christian church. Given the strength and pervasive nature of religious belief over centuries, it was inevitable that people would turn to the ritual and symbols of Christianity to provide them with measures against faery threats. As shall be described repeatedly throughout the book, holy words, pieces of scripture, and holy symbols have all been relied upon to repel and defeat supernatural dangers.

Even so, readers will also observe that other measures are regularly deployed as well: people will rely upon iron, salt, fire, the wood of the rowan tree, and "lucky" gestures to keep the faeries at bay. Even though these materials may well be arranged in a Christian fashion, usually by making the shape of a cross, the primary power resides in the substance itself. Faery beasts, just like faeries, have an aversion to a wide range of things. For example, they can both be held at bay or kept away from human homes and property using stale urine. Branches of rowan (or mountain ash) are also regarded as very effective. Why is not clear, but the fact that the tree's berries are red may be the reason; in fact, anything that is red, such as pieces of cloth, can be protective, perhaps because they are the colour of blood. There are numerous Highland Scottish stories of *glaistigs* and other hags fended off with blades. One of their common tricks is to ask a man for a pinch of snuff, hoping that he will hold out his hand and thereby become vulnerable to being snatched away. Offering the snuff on the tip of a dagger will keep the fearsome female at arm's length—although this may have to be sustained throughout a whole night![8]

There is very obviously nothing inherently Christian about a burned coal or peat or a steel blade. These defences rely on a much older magic and on beliefs that long predate the arrival of Christianity. As I suggested in the section on water, within nature we will find protections and counterweights to the powers of the faery beasts. Water drawn from particular streams or from certain wells is another tested defence, confirming that there are natural powers that will prove to be efficacious against faery peril.

The faery beasts are not repelled by Christian ritual as such; they are not demonic forces from hell. Instead, whether it is a person praying and crossing themselves or drawing a circle on the ground with a knife, faery power is being tried against a different sort of magic. With the right skill and determination, a person can fend off the threats these beings can pose, whether they are a devout churchgoer or not.

A Note on Sources

This book draws on a wide range of British folklore sources, primarily from the eighteenth and nineteenth centuries. At this time, whilst many faery beliefs were still widely known within communities, enthusiastic amateurs went out and collected stories and accounts. Most of these collectors were men, and many were church ministers or school masters indulging a hobby, or university professors with a professional interest in folklore.

These folklorists saved for us many beliefs and tales that might otherwise have been forgotten, but we must still recognise that there may have been much that they chose not to record, or that they "tidied up" for public consumption. Stories that seemed too amoral or which, at least, didn't offer a suitable moral lesson might well have been rejected. The Faery that has been preserved for us in these books and journals can be very white and very straight. I don't think there's any reason to assume that (for example) all mermaid love affairs had to be with fishermen, rather than fisherwives, nor should we too readily take for granted that all humanoid faeries were Caucasian.

---

8. James MacDougall, *Folk Tales and Fairy Lore in Gaelic and English: Collected from Oral Tradition by Rev. James MacDougall,* ed. George Calder (Edinburgh: John Grant, 1910), 227, 243, 259.

Earlier centuries were just as accepting of diverse sexualities—you only have to read the Marquis de Sade or John Cleland's *Fanny Hill* to discover that—but those same churchmen, teachers, and professors who collected the faery lore also made up the establishment that suppressed just that sort of material. Likewise, if we go back to Shakespeare's time, we'd find a ready acceptance that faeries could well be of African or Asian origin (or that they might even have quite unhuman skin tones), but this diversity has been largely forgotten since.

In conclusion, then, I am working with the evidence preserved for me, and that data was collected within an almost exclusively Christian, heterosexual, and unmixed society. Don't take it for granted that this is the whole story, though.

Plan of the Book

As I have already explained, the book is split broadly into two parts, dealing first with those supernatural beings that live in and close to water. These are the various types of merfolk, the "meremaids" of inland bodies of water, river sprites, a range of water monsters, and the fearsome water horses and bulls of Scotland, the best known of which is the kelpie.

The second part of the book examines the faery beasts that reside solely on land. These include the hags, banshees, and the hobgoblins, all of which are more or less humanlike in their appearance. Then I turn to the bogies, boggarts, and bogles, supernatural beings of astonishing variety in form and behaviour. Many of these can appear as dogs or cows, but I then turn to discuss those faery beasts that will *only* be encountered in four-legged form: the "daemon dogs" and the fae animals, a group which includes enchanted donkeys, cats, calves, and hares. I conclude the book with a chapter on wills of the wisp, a type of supernatural being that often lacks any recognisable shape or body at all.

Part 1
WATER BEASTS

As I said in the introduction, a simple (although far from conclusive or exact) division of faery beasts is to separate them into those that dwell on land and those that dwell in water. The latter never confine themselves to the rivers, lakes, or sea where they have their main abode, but they will still spend a large part of their lives feeding, sleeping, and mating beneath the waves. Over and above any ferocity in their temperaments, the fact that they belong in a different element is part of the reason they can be so dangerous to us.

Water beasts take many forms: they can resemble humans, they can look like familiar farm animals, such as horses and cattle, or they can be out and out monsters. The humanlike forms are found in several species or types: there are some that dwell in saltwater and some that dwell in fresh. Some of the latter live in lakes (what I've called meremaids), whereas others are found in rivers and springs (what I've referred to as water sprites). What unites all the water beasts is the fact that for many of their significant interactions with humankind they will come out of the water to find us.

The main occupation of many of these creatures is seducing mortals and luring them to their doom. (Mermaids, it's true, might sometimes accidentally drown their lovers, but it is not generally their intention, unlike most of the water beasts discussed in chapters 2 to 6.) Poet Joseph Rodman Drake in his verse "To a Friend" described travellers being terrorised by "the kelpie's fang."[9] In Charles Mackay's 1851 ballad "The Kelpie of Corryvreckan" a handsome stranger on a horse rides off with lovestruck Jessie but then plunges beneath the waves with her so that she is found drowned the next day.[10] Many of the stories of water beasts, like that of Jessie, have a moral element, which may be more or less explicit. Jessie's want of caution with a handsome stranger might be read as a warning to virgins everywhere. In other accounts, the message concerns violation of a Sunday or a festival like Easter: children who ought to be at church are instead playing by a lakeside and Satan seems to come in the guise of a pretty pony to seize their souls.[11]

---

9. Joseph Rodman Drake, "To a Friend," in *The Culprit Fay and Other Poems* (New York: George Dearborn, 1836), 43.

10. Charles Mackay, "The Kelpie of Corryvreckan," in *Legends of the Isles and Other Poems* (London: Charles Gilpin, 1851), 56.

11. For example, at Loch Venachar—John Leyden, *Journal of a Tour in the Highlands and Western Islands of Scotland in 1800,* ed. James Sinton (Edinburgh: William Blackwood, 1903), 13–14.

Chapter 1

MERFOLK

Merfolk, mermaids, and mermen are human-sized and humanlike beings who live in the saltwater of the oceans around our coasts. Because they are so similar to us, and because they will approach people out at sea or will come onto dry land, humans have had a long relationship with them.

Although merfolk may sometimes take on another form and appear as seals, and their bodies may only be part human, most of the time we can speak to them and interact with them as we would with other humans and, for that matter, with other faeries. Merfolk have communities and a society that we can understand and relate to quite easily. Of course, because they live in water and all their food comes from the sea, their way of life is a great deal simpler than either ours or that of the terrestrial faeries. Under the sea, there's no need of clothes, money, or any great hierarchies; it follows from this that, often, their interactions with people will be limited to sex, food, and conflict.

Types of Merfolk

There are broadly three types of sea supernatural:

- the merfolk, including the familiar mermaids of popular culture and the finfolk of Orkney
- the seal-like *roane* and selkies
- assorted other types, including the Orkney sea-trows, the Cornish *bucca*, and the *fir ghorm* of the Hebrides

The well-known mermaids and mermen are part human, part fish and are found around the coasts of England, Wales (where they are named *morforwyn*), and the Isle of Man (where they are called *ben-varrey*). Secondly, there are the seal people, which comprise the selkies of Shetland and the *roane* of the Highlands and Islands. These are humanlike beings who can put on a seal-skin to move through the sea. As men and women, they are more beautiful and have more attractive characters than humans, but as seals it is only their eyes that disclose their true natures. Their skins are extremely precious to them, as each one is unique to its wearer and is irreplaceable. Capturing the skin therefore captures the wearer.

Both mermaids and selkies can assume normal human form by magically removing their marine skins, but there is some debate over how often they can effect this transformation. It may only be once a year on Midsummer's Eve, or it may be as often as every ninth night or at every "seventh stream"— that is, every spring tide.

Scottish mermaids (*maighdean mara*) are believed to be similar to the selkies in that they can take off their fins and appear on land as women. On Orkney, at least, there's some debate about the actual nature of the mermaid's tail, whether it's a real fish tail or whether it's just a petticoat that can be tightly wrapped around the legs and looks like flippers. Rather like selkies' skins, it's also said that if you are able to pull a few of the scales off a mermaid's tail, she will be forced to assume human form; if she can find where the missing scales have been hidden by her husband, she will be able to return to the sea. In due course, I'll discuss human relationships with merfolk, so it may be worthwhile pausing here to address a question of physiology. It's generally agreed that selkies are humans within a sealskin whilst mermaids are partially fish but can divest their tails. Nonetheless, on this intimate matter, some uncertainty remains: it's notable that a number of Victorian painters, at least, experimented with an alternative depiction in which their mermaids' scales began below the buttocks, leaving rather more of the body human and so resolving some difficult questions of reproduction ...[12]

The very human nature of the merfolk is revealed in an amusing account from the Isle of Skye. A member of the MacLeod clan saw a mermaid combing her hair on a rock one day when he was out hunting. He thought to shoot her and display her body for reward, but every time he raised the gun to his shoulder and took aim, he hesitated: she looked so human he feared that killing her might be regarded as murder by the authorities and that he might hang as a result. He dithered, time and again raising the gun and then fearing to pull the trigger, and this went on so long that eventually the mermaid dived off the rock into the sea and the chance was lost.[13]

We should also note a hybrid type of merman, the Cornish "sea-pisky" called the *bucca*. Cornish fishermen gave the *bucca* offerings of fish to ensure good catches. The *bucca* has a good reputation on the whole: he can bring good or bad fortune to fishing boats, depending on their respect for him, but he will also protect them in storms and guide them to shore. It's said to be good luck to see him at work on the seabed, amongst the seaweed and lobsters. Finally, mention must be made of the sea-trows of Orkney. These are other groups or species of humanoid marine dwellers that will be described at the end of this chapter.[14]

Origins & Nature

There's a variety of views as to the origins of the sea folk. One widely held theory is that they're fallen angels; another is that they're wicked souls who

---

12. Alasdair MacGregor, "The Seal-Folk," in *The Peat-Fire Flame: Folk-Tales and Traditions of the Highlands and Islands* (Edinburgh: Moray Press, 1937), n.p.

13. John A. MacCulloch, *The Misty Isle of Skye: Its Scenery, Its People, Its Story* (Edinburgh: Oliphant, Anderson & Ferrier, 1903), 244.

14. J. Henry Harris, *Cornish Saints & Sinners* (London: Clowes and Sons, 1907), chapter 31.

have been turned into seal form as a punishment. On Orkney, it's said that a person who has been cursed is turned into a selkie.[15]

The merfolk have undersea homes where they breathe air like land dwellers. According to one account from the Isle of Man, an explorer in a diving bell who descended to a great depth found a grand city of houses and pyramids made of pearl and coral arranged on streets and squares. Mermaids are quite often sighted sitting alone on rocks near to shore, whereas selkies live in groups on rocks and skerries some distance offshore. It will be noted that they live on the surface breathing air, in contrast to the merfolk.[16]

We know very little about merfolk society and habits. Inevitably there are merchildren, and scattered references to them are found. I'll describe some others in due course, but one from the Scottish island of Barra tells of a man out hunting when he saw what he thought was a sea otter eating a fish on the reef in Caolas Cumhan. He aimed his gun but realised that he was actually looking at a mermaid mother holding her baby—so he spared the pair.[17] In a second incident, two Manx merchildren were found stranded on rocks at the Calf of Man in 1810. One was already dead; the other was saved and taken into Douglas town, where it was reported to have been about sixty centimetres in length, brown in colour except for violet scales on the tail and green coloured hair.[18]

As for mermaid diet, we also know very little. There are a couple of reports of merfolk herding the faery sea cows (which implies that they have some use for milk and even meat), and we hear, too, that they seem intrigued by human food, being known to eat bread and fruit. But their main staple appears, quite predictably, to be raw fish. There is an early medieval story of a merman caught in nets at Orford in Suffolk. He was taken to the castle and kept for six months, during which time he spoke not a single word.

---

15. *County Folk-lore,* vol. 3, 120.

16. Samuel Hibbert, *A Description of the Shetland Isles, Comprising an Account of Their Scenery, Antiquities, and Superstitions* (Lerwick: T. & J. Manson, 1891), 261; *County Folk-lore* vol. 3, 170.

17. "Women with Child," Merfolk and Selkies, Paranormal Database, accessed May 7, 2020, www.paranormaldatabase.com/reports/mermaid.php.

18. "Mer Children," Isle of Man—Paranormal Database Records, Paranormal Database, accessed May 7, 2020, www.paranormaldatabase.com/isleofman/mandata.php.

He ate everything that was provided to him, but was especially keen on fish, although he had the habit of squeezing them dry before consuming them. Eventually someone left the doors unlocked, and he was able to escape back to the sea.[19]

Lastly, there's regular interaction between merfolk and humans, and they are able to converse with each other with perfect ease. In one story from South Uist, fishermen are surprised that a mermaid mother is able to speak Gaelic,[20] but all the accounts imply that the sea people have been able to pick up the dialect of the coastal dwellers.

Contemporary Ideas of Merfolk

Just like faeries, elves, and pixies, it is very notable how the popular image of mermaids has improved over the last century and a half and how they are coming to be regarded as wholly cute and attractive figures of myth.

Today, mermaids are viewed as figures suitable for children to like, draw, and to imitate, with mermaid tails being a widely available form of fun beach wear. It seems very likely that this more benign idea is derived from Hans Christian Andersen's 1837 story of "The Little Mermaid." The main character in this is presented as a model of Christian self-sacrifice and goodness, and she has doubtless had a pervasive influence commensurate with the story's popularity. For modern generations, the Disney cartoon version of the story featuring Ariel, the little mermaid, has profoundly affected popular views of marine supernaturals since its release in 1989. Other symptoms of these revised views of merfolk may be the 1984 film *Splash* starring Daryl Hannah, the popularity of Barbie mermaid dolls and their animated adventures, and the very recent appearance of female entertainers playing mermaids for parties and corporate events.

Even so, whilst terrestrial faeries have been the subject of prettification and miniaturisation since the late sixteenth century, mermaids have only been subjected to this process much more recently. The consequence is that a great deal more of the older folklore attitudes survive, both in stories and in poetry. Mermaids are still clearly supernatural creatures deserving of awe,

---

19. Ralph of Coggeshall, *Chronicon Anglicanum, De Expugnatione [...]* (English Chronicle), 1197, ed. J. Stevenson (London: Her Majesty's Stationery Office, 1875), 117–8.
20. MacGregor, *The Peat-Fire Flame*, 107.

fear, and mistrust. Kindliness was never one of the mermaid's traditional traits, and it is still not how other supernatural water beasts are perceived either. In this respect, the dependable J. K. Rowling gives us a depiction more respectfully observant of folklore in *Harry Potter and the Goblet of Fire* (the creatures there being called *grindylows*, an authentic folklore name that the author borrowed from a malevolent water sprite of Yorkshire and Lancashire lakes).

It may be easier for us to identify with and to find attractive qualities in a being that lives solely on land. Mermaids live in a different element in which a human cannot survive. What's more, although most people have a good chance of meeting a land faery, you've got to live on the coast or go there frequently to have any hope of ever seeing a mermaid. These important distinctions and differences may have helped to preserve their distance from us—and our healthy respect for that difference—for so much longer than has been the case with faeries.

Conflict with Humans

There is, of course, competition and some enmity between coastal communities and merfolk. They are competing for the same fish stocks, and the merfolk are often blamed for breaking or even stealing fishing nets—although whether this is deliberate mischief or because they have become accidentally entangled in them is another matter. This struggle for resources can lead to antagonism—and to peril for both sides. In one case from Shetland some fishermen managed to snare a mermaid. When they pulled her to the surface and realised what they'd caught, one of the crew angrily stabbed her and she fell back beneath the waves. That man never prospered again in his life and, to make matters worse, was hunted by a reproving merman.[21]

Worse than these chance encounters, humans can go out deliberately to hunt the sea folk. Mermaids have no economic value, but selkies are hunted for their commercially valuable skins and blubber. This is done with some reluctance, even so, because they are powerful and malevolent beings. Nonetheless, necessity drives the hunters, and this has led repeatedly to confrontations between the two peoples. In one story from Shetland, a storm arose

---

21. Hibbert, *Shetland Isles*, 260; John Brand, *A New Description of Orkney, Zetland, Pightland-Firth and Caithness, Wherein, [...]* (Edinburgh: W. Brown, 1883), 172.

as men were stunning and skinning seals on a skerry offshore. All but one of the group made it back to their boat, but the waves mounted so quickly and so violently that this last crew member had to be left behind on the crags to face his fate. In due course, selkies emerged from the sea to comfort their relatives who had been stripped of their magical skins. On seeing the stranded fisherman, they agreed to save him from certain drowning or exposure so long as he consented to recover the stolen skins for them.[22]

In another story, a seal hunter is visited at night by a stranger on a horse who wants him to negotiate immediately over the sale of some sealskins. The hunter readily agrees to go with the unknown rider, and they gallop off on the one horse together at great speed. Reaching a cliff, they don't stop but plunge down into the sea and sink to a great depth. There they enter an open door into rooms in which there are many seals, all talking together. The hunter is shown a knife and asked if he knows it. He does, for he'd lost it that morning stuck in a seal that escaped after he had injured but not killed it. That seal is the rider's father, and he can only be cured if the hunter will tend his wound. Given his position, the man feels he has little option but to consent to this, and he dresses the injury, which promptly heals. This done, the man is only able to return to his home if he promises to renounce seal hunting for the rest of his life—something he obviously readily consents to do. When he has been escorted back to his door, he is given a large sum in gold, which is more than compensation for his lost source of income.

In a related story from the Shetland Islands, a man stunned and skinned a seal he found on a beach. The creature regained consciousness and reentered the sea, where it met a mermaid who wanted to assist if she could. The selkie wanted its skin back, naturally. The man, meanwhile, felt very guilty and told his shipmates he'd skinned a dead seal. Sometime later, they caught the mermaid on a hook; all the crew except the remorseful hunter wanted to keep her, and the majority opinion prevailed. She was secured on deck, sitting on the skin of her selkie friend. Soon, she died of exposure to the air, and within a short time a terrible storm blew up, during which the boat sank and the whole crew perished. The seal got his skin back because of his friend's sacrifice and, ever since that time, selkies have acted as the special guardians of

---

22. Hibbert, *Shetland Isles,* 566; *County Folk-lore,* vol. 7, 182.

mermaids, bringing them special foods, warning them of approaching danger and, on occasion, protecting them.

Especially unusual in this particular story is the mermaid's inability to last long in the air out of water; this isn't a feature of most stories, in which mermaids can live for years with human husbands. There is one other story with a similar conclusion. A mermaid was cast ashore by a storm near Conway in North Wales. She begged some fishermen who found her to carry her back to the sea, but they refused to assist, even when she asked them to place her tail at least in the water. The stranded mermaid died miserably of exposure overnight on the beach. Before she expired, though, the mermaid cursed the people of Conway to be always poor, and the town is said to have struggled economically ever since. Death by exposure to the air is also typical of the asrai, a type of inland meremaid I shall consider in the next chapter.[23]

Lastly, despite the persistent antagonism between land and sea people, stories do tell of merfolk and selkies recalling and repaying good deeds. The accounts tend to be variants of the same event: a man comes across a seal and her pup on the beach and catches the young one, aiming to strip it of its soft pelt. However, seeing the selkie mother's distress, he relents and releases the pup. Some years later, the man's children are trapped on rocks as the tide comes in and face drowning, until two women in grey appear and guide them ashore, telling them that this is repayment for their father's previous kindness.[24]

Relationships with Humans

At the same time as being a valuable marine resource, female selkies and mermaids make highly desirable wives. Conversely, it is also believed that mermaids are very desirous of the love of humans and will actively pursue young men: for example, one mermaid on the Isle of Man seemingly fell for a man who wooed her by giving her apples, which she called the "sweet land

---

23. Eliza Edmonston, *Sketches and Tales of the Shetland Islands* (Edinburgh: Sutherland & Knox, 1856), chapter 7; John Rhys, *Celtic Folklore: Welsh and Manx,* vol. 1 (Oxford: Clarendon Press, 1901), 199.

24. "One Spared to the Sea," The Selkie-folk, Orkneyjar, accessed May 7, 2020, www.orkneyjar .com/folklore/selkiefolk/spared.htm.

eggs;" his kindness brought him a wish of luck from the maid.[25] At Casstruan on the same island, the mermaids were said to have been very plentiful off-shore, and the local fishermen would befriend them by throwing them bread, butter, and oatcakes.[26]

Male selkies can also be extremely desirable to human women. In the Scottish Islands, it is said that any woman who finds herself a spinster, or who is dissatisfied with her human husband, can always take a selkie lover instead. Such a thing happened with a woman of Orkney called Ursilla, who had married a farmhand for love but later tired of the poor match. She sat at the high tide mark on the beach and shed seven tears into the sea. This worked as a spell to summon a male selkie (and it is the only recorded instance of a person being able to use "magical" means to bring one of the merfolk to them). The selkie who appeared for Ursilla promised to reappear to her again after the "seventh stream" (that is, the next spring tide) when he would next be able to take human form. He then began to visit her regularly, and they had a number of children together. It should be added that, whilst they may be amorous, selkie males don't prove good partners and usually desert their earthly wives before very long.[27]

However great their physical charms—which I'll discuss soon—there is considerable peril in taking a mermaid lover. It's thought that you will fall in the power of a mermaid if you answer directly any questions that she asks you. A man met a mermaid at Black Rock in the Mersey Estuary and fell in love with her. She presented him with a gold ring and told him that they would meet again in five days' time. The youth died five days later, and it was assumed that the mermaid had stolen his spirit away to be with her.[28]

Equally serious for humans is the reverse response: refusing the merfolks' advances can be just as fatal. On the coast of Man at Ballafletcher, a mermaid fell in love with a shepherd and used to bring him bits of coral and pearls as a token of her affection. One day, as might have been predicted, she tried

---

25. Sophia Morrison, *Manx Fairy Tales* (London: D. Nutt, 1911), 71.

26. *Yn Lioar Manninagh*, vol. III, 159.

27. *County Folk-lore* vol. 3, 176.

28. Ernest Marwick, *The Folklore of Orkney and Shetland* (Edinburgh: Birlinn Ltd., 2011), 24; "Black Rock—Mermaid," Paranormal Database, accessed May 7, 2020, www.para normaldatabase.com/m/detail.php?address=1469.

to drag him into the water, but he resisted strongly and managed to escape her clutches. Angrily, she threw a stone after him and then disappeared. The blow he received was light, but he developed a severe pain in his bowels that killed him within three weeks.[29]

Marine females are almost invariably depicted as nubile, naked young women who are well aware of their allure and who cultivate their beauty with their combs and their mirrors. However, as is the case with contact with all supernatural beings, involvement with merfolk is generally risky: they come (literally) from another world, and there is an imbalance of power in any contact with them. Romantic attachments will frequently prove to be fatal; some mermaids, beautiful as they may seem, are in truth perilous beings who lure men to their deaths. This often results from a combination of accident and neglect, as portrayed in the poem "The Mermaid" by W. B. Yeats, in which the passionate female drags a boy down with her, forgetting "in cruel happiness / That even lovers drown."[30]

James Hogg's poem "The Mermaid's Song" is another good illustration of the fatal attractiveness of a merfolk lover. With the promise of a kiss on her bewitching face, the "Maid of the Crystal Wave" lures a young man to go "where man should not have been, [and to see] what man should not have seen," and it proves to be his ruin.[31] A story from the Isle of Man portrays the mermaid of Purt-le-Murrey in the same siren-like way—actuated by love rather than malicious intent, she tries to lure a man into the sea with her, but luckily for him his friends are able to counteract her charms.[32]

Why do humans take such risks, knowing the dangers and disadvantages? Seal wives are highly desirable prizes, as they can be valuable commodities for mortal men: they can be excellent household managers, they often seem very fertile and produce large families, and they provide their partners with

---

29. Waldron, *The History and Description*, 65.

30. W. B. Yeats, "The Mermaid," section III from "A Man Young and Old," in *The Tower* (New York: Macmillan, 1928), 72.

31. James Hogg, "The Mermaid's Song," *Songs by the Ettrick Shepherd: Now First Collected* (Edinburgh: William Blackwood, 1831), 87.

32. Dora Broome, *Fairy Tales from the Isle of Man* (Harmondsworth: Penguin, 1951), chapter 5; see, too, Torquil Macleod, "The Mermaid of Colonsay," in *Celtic Monthly* 7 (1897): 168–9.

skills in fishing as well as in medicine. More than that, they can have access to human wealth lost in shipwrecks. A Caernarfon mermaid provided her human lover with a chest of treasure (see later for full details of this story), and a stranded mermaid on the Isle of Man also rewarded her saviour with a hoard of antique gold. This wealth may be given as a token of love or as a reward for a good deed.

At Saundersfoot in South Wales, a mermaid had been so absorbed in combing her sea-green hair and admiring herself in her mirror that she became stranded on a rock on the beach. A poor mussel gatherer found her and agreed to carry her back to the sea, in return for which she brought him gold and silver that she found under the sea. She added to his wealth on a daily basis until he was extremely rich. Humans must use this marine wealth wisely, though. According to a local legend now preserved as a Victorian poem, there was a mermaid who frequented the coast at Reay in Caithness and acquired a young lover, in part by presenting him with pearls and jewels from the sea floor. However, he used these gifts to woo girls on land, a betrayal that the mermaid learned about. One night, she played upon his greed by promising to take him to the cave where all her wealth was hidden. He eagerly went with her—and never returned to land.[33]

Despite the material advantages they offer, merfolk partners may not be good companions: they never seem very devoted to their families, leaving them at the first opportunity to return to the sea, and they are notoriously circumspect, the little they do say being very terse. For example, a mermaid trapped on land by means of sprinkling stale urine across her path spoke only once during the week she was ashore—and that to warn a woman gutting fish: "Wash and clean well the fish, there's many a monster in the sea."[34]

Usually merfolk and humans conduct their romances on land, but, very rarely, the sea folk can become involved in love affairs with mortals which

33. Karl Blind, "New Finds in Shetlandic & Welsh Folk-lore," *Gentleman's Magazine*, no. 252 (1882): 476; James Traill Calder, "The Mermaid of Dwarwick Head," in *Poems from John o' Groats* (Wick: P. Reid, 1855), 1–17.

34. George Sutherland, *Folk-lore Gleanings and Character Sketches from the Far North*. (Wick: John O'Groat Journal, 1937), 96; Hannah Aitken, ed., *Forgotten Heritage: Original Folk Tales of Lowland Scotland* (Edinburgh: Scottish Academic Press, 1973), 23; Malcolm MacPhail, "Folklore from the Hebrides—II," section 7, *Folklore* 8 (1897): 384.

end with the human departing beneath the waves. The outcomes of these matches are seldom good, although the story of the mermaid of Zennor is a happy exception. Her chosen partner, Mathey Trewella, went to live with her under the sea, and we know that this was not fatal for him because, several years later, the skipper of a boat was hailed by a mermaid because his anchor was blocking the door to her home, something that was preventing her returning to her husband Mathey and their offspring or, in some accounts, preventing her taking her children to church. It's notable that this mermaid, at least, has no aversion to Christianity, unlike many members of the faery race. She meets her husband-to-be when she attends the church in Zennor village, where she sings beautifully during Sunday services.[35]

As for submarine relationships between mermen and human women, the sources are, again, scanty. A Welsh story mentions a merman called Jinny who seems to have held a human woman captive. They lived in a "box" under the sea but daily came to land where he would lie with his head in her lap and sleep. He seems to have been a jealous partner, with little faith in his human spouse. The slightest noise would wake him, and they would immediately return to the sea, suggesting that her prospects of escape were slim.[36]

Finally, the offspring of these matches with merfolk are generally readily identifiable. It's known that the mermaids of the Isle of Man have webbing between their fingers, and there are accounts from the Scottish Islands of this trait being passed on to children conceived with human fathers. The offspring of Ursilla and her selkie partner on Orkney had webs between their fingers and toes. She tried to trim them, but they regrew until a horny crust developed—a feature that can still be seen amongst some island people today and which can be a hindrance to them by limiting the manual tasks they can undertake. Across the west of Scotland, in fact, there are traditions of local families with selkie ancestry who still spend part of their time in human form and part of the time as seals.[37]

---

35. William Bottrell, *Traditions and Hearthside Stories of West Cornwall*, Second Series (Penzance: Beare and Son, 1873), 288.

36. Blind, "New Finds in Shetlandic," *Gentleman's Magazine*, no. 252 (1882): 477.

37. *Yn Lioar Manninagh*, vol. 3 (1897); *County Folk-lore* 3, 176 and see, too, 184 (Shetland); Lewis Spence, *The Minor Traditions of British Mythology* (London: Rider & Co., 1948), 55.

Catching a Mermaid Wife

Setting the many cautions aside, men frequently have taken mermaids as partners, and this frequently involved some degree of duress. One common way of getting a mermaid wife is by force: if they can be caught when they are unawares and some distance from their skins, they can be made to remain on dry land. For example, one man from Unst was able to steal up on a group of selkie women when they were dancing on a beach in the moonlight and seize one of the discarded skins. The Scottish story of the wife of "The Goodman of Wastness" demonstrates the typical outcome of these matches. Another selkie was captured by stealing her sealskin, which she'd shed on the beach. Despite being well treated by her human husband and having raised seven children with her captor, she never forgot her ocean home and was ever alert to retrieve her skin. Eventually, of course, she found it hidden somewhere on the farm and returned instantly to her people. A sign of her persisting selkie nature was the strange song she taught to her children that no one else could understand. In another such tale, the true nature of the mermaid's feelings for her human husband were disclosed by the fact that she often went down to the beach to talk to the seals at the water's edge.[38]

A variant upon this kind of capture of a wife concerns a Raasay fisherman. Out at sea one day, he caught a mermaid in his nets. He took her home with him, where he took off "the long thing on her legs like a fish." The usual events then followed: they had many children and seemed happy enough until the day that one of the children found the "thing like a tail" hidden in the smallholding's barn. The mother then could not be withheld from the sea. What's interesting about this account, though, is the implication of force—the mermaid is involuntarily stripped of her fins and is, essentially, raped and subdued by the human.[39]

Another means of capture is to get between the mermaid and the sea and thereby bring her within your power. Furthermore, mermaids, like Scottish faeries, have an aversion to stale urine, called *maistir* in Gaelic, a substance which once was saved for use washing clothes. Sprinkled between the mermaid and the sea, she will not be able to cross the *maistir*, although the

---

38. *County Folk-lore* 3, 172; Hibbert, *Shetland*, 565.
39. Mary Julia MacCulloch, "Folklore of the Isle of Skye," *Folklore* 33 (1922): 309.

charm is only effective so long as it is renewed daily. In one instance from the Hebrides, the responsible person forgot and as soon as the trapped mermaid realised the mistake, she was able to make a dash for the surf (taking with her some sea cows which had also been caught in the same way).[40]

Finally, a mermaid (as opposed to a selkie woman) can be caught by taking her belt and pouch, in which she keeps her comb, mirror, and (according to one story) a sort of life preserver that helps her to swim. This method was employed by a man from Lochinver who fell for a mermaid there but knew that entering her element was likely to prove fatal. As ever, the match didn't prove happy, and the unwilling wife pined continually for the sea. Eventually, one summer, she was watching some farm labourers moving a haystack when she saw her pouch again—hidden inside the rick by her captor. In an instant, she was heading for the shoreline.[41]

As these examples make clear, a greater or lesser degree of compulsion is an element in almost all of the cases in which a human male acquires a merfolk bride. In one Welsh story, in fact, there appears to be an explicit allusion to rape of the mermaid. Given that it was published in 1910, it doesn't describe the matter in so many words, but a man from Caernarfonshire is described as having "made the acquaintance" of the mermaid, who at first "screeched wildly" but later calmed down and invited him to return to see her when her brother was not nearby. The story then takes a strange turn, as she seems to give him a gift of sea treasure, visits him at night, and then appears before him dressed in human form and apparently willing to come ashore and live with him.

Eventually she consents to be his wife, but even then the match seems to be less than wholly voluntary, in that the mermaid, who is called Nefyn, surrenders to her husband a cap which she tells him to hide from her; this appears to be what she uses to be able to live underwater. The couple become well off and have five sets of twins together, but it transpires that Nefyn's reason for her self-sacrifice was to learn a song that she had heard her husband singing. Once she has acquired the tune, she returns to her merfolk family. Her husband goes with her for a while but eventually returns home, and it

---

40. MacPhail, "Folklore from the Hebrides—II," *Folklore* 8 (1897): 384.

41. Ms. Dempster, "The Folk-lore of Sutherland-shire," *Folklore Journal* 6 (1888): 165; see, too, Spence, The *Minor Traditions*, 45.

is interesting to note that the visit was expected to take a month but actually lasts a year, suggesting that (as in Faery) time under the sea may pass at a different rate to time upon the land. At first, he says nothing to his children about their mother. Eventually, he is pressed for information and provides a full account of his time away; however, the next morning he is found dead in his bed, as if betraying the merfolk's secrets was fatal (another possible parallel with faeryland).[42]

Mostly, here, I have discussed merfolk seized as partners by men and women on the land. However, fishermen and sailors may be abducted by the merfolk when they're at sea, although a lot less is heard of these couplings— either because the man drowns or because he never returns to his former home. There is, however, a story of a merchant from Dumbarton who survived a shipwreck and was taken in by a mermaid living in a cave on the island where he was stranded. She treated the man very well, bringing him food and drink every day as well as gold, silver, and jewels she found on the sea floor. Eventually, a ship rescued the merchant and he took with him all the valuables she had showered upon him. The jilted mermaid followed the ship all the way back to the River Clyde, extracting from her erstwhile partner a promise that he would bring up their son with the riches he had stolen and that he would return to her in a year and a day. A related—but simpler—version of this story from Colonsay emphasises that the man was unhappy with his mermaid lover. Although she showered him with whatever he wanted, he was not satisfied by the relationship and escaped from her when he could. She pursued him and fought with his dog, a struggle that left both dead.[43]

Mermaid Beauty

"Myreugh worth an morvoron / hanter pysk ha hanter den."
(Look at the mermaid, / half fish and half man)[44]

---

42. Rhys, *Celtic Folklore: Welsh and Manx*, vol. 1, 117–123.

43. Jennifer Westwood and Sophia Kingshill, *The Lore of Scotland: A Guide to Scottish Legends* (London, Random House, 2009), 70–7; Campbell, *Superstitions of the Highlands*, chapter 4.

44. *Passio Domini*, fifteenth century, Cornwall; see Edwin Norris, ed. and trans., *The Ancient Cornish Drama*, vol. 1 (Oxford: University Press, 1859), 414–415.

Mermaid good looks are renowned, and our convention of blonde-haired, blue-eyed beauty is continually reinforced in the media by Barbie mermaids and the like. The reality is, in fact, a good deal more complex, and the truth is that most merfolk may be considerably less good looking than the stories would have us believe.

To start, when discussing merfolk looks, it's very important to distinguish between the selkies and *roane*, who totally remove their sealskins to reveal good-looking human beings within, and the merfolk, who may only take off their fishy tails. The latter are not as consistently attractive to us as the former.

Mermaids are often to be found sitting on rocks or on beaches combing their hair; there's a strong suggestion in this of their own awareness of their beauty and allure. It's not something that they are inclined to conceal; rather, it appears to be flaunted. Unlike faeries, mermaids cannot make themselves invisible. This may simply be because there's no need: they can always move further offshore or dive below the waves in order to disappear from human sight, but it may also be the case that whilst they have fewer magical powers, they are also more amenable to being observed by humankind.

In the popular imagination, mermaids are always attractive (and naked) young women, whose hair is their greatest pride and their great beauty—it's always remarked upon, even in the 1830s case of the body of a recently deceased mermaid found on a beach on the island of Benbecula, who seems to have been killed by a stone thrown at her by a boy a few days previously. In one case from July 1826, a man at Llanllwchaiarn in Mid Wales saw a mermaid swimming just off the coast and called other members of his family to see her. The man's wife stood up and attracted the mermaid's attention so that she moved a little further out and then travelled along the shoreline, but she nonetheless remained visible for about three quarters of an hour to twelve people in total. They all confirmed that she looked like a girl of about eighteen with short dark hair and a tail.[45] Had this been a faery, she would probably have vanished the instant she realised she was being watched. Another mermaid observed at Kinlochbervie in Sutherland had long red hair. In a further incident, two Galloway youths went out exploring along the coast at

---

45. Jonathan Davies, *Folk-lore of West and Mid-Wales* (Aberystwyth: printed at the "Welsh Gazette" offices, 1911), 146.

Lagvag. They found a mermaid sitting on a rock near the water and combing her hair. She looked like a bonny lass of sixteen years, with light hair, naked to her haunches and below that a fish's tail which was, they said, not scaly but like a "pellock," in other words, a porpoise. The two nearly caught her, too, except for the fact that one made a noise which caused her to "wabble" off with some speed before diving in the water.[46]

Other descriptions of merfolk—found the length of Britain—are much less complimentary. One account, from the northeast of Scotland, depicts mermaids as looking like women but with round heads, small eyes, flat faces, thickset teeth, and long hair, which they regularly comb when out of the water.[47] A farmer of Campbeltown on the Kintyre peninsula in Argyll watched a mermaid for two hours in October 1811. He said that she had a pale upper body and a red or grey tail. Her face was humanlike, but she had deep-set eyes and a short neck. She was sitting on a rock combing her hair, and her arms seemed to be short and stubby; then she dived into the water and was observed to wash her torso.[48]

The mermaids known off the coast of Caernarfon in northwest Wales were dark brown in colour; their faces only "resembled a human face" because they had neither chin nor ears, small eyes, high foreheads, wide mouths, and very prominent noses. Their arms were small and lacked elbows, their fingers were webbed, and they had fishes' tails.[49] The mermaid glimpsed bathing in 1826 had a pale body but a black fish's tail; another spotted in the Sound of Mull was described as having coarse hair and glassy eyes.

On January 12, 1809, a mermaid in the sea at Reay, in Caithness, was watched for an hour by five observers. They said she had a round head with green, oily hair and arms that were long and slender. The Cornish *bucca*,

---

46. Alexander Carmichael, trans., *Carmina Gadelica: Hymns and Incantations […]*, vol. 2 (Edinburgh: T. and A. Constable, 1900), 305; Maria Trotter and Bruce Trotter, *Galloway Gossip: Sixty Years Ago; Being a Series […]*, ed. Saxon (Bedlington: George Richardson, 1877), 375.

47. James Reid, *Scotland, Past and Present* (London: Oxford University Press, 1959), 258.

48. "Shorted Armed Mermaid," Argyll and Bute—Paranormal Database Records. Paranormal Database, accessed May 8, 2020, www.paranormaldatabase.com/highlands/Argydata.php.

49. J. Jones, ("Myrddin Fardd"), *Llen Gwerin Sir Gaernarfon, Llen Gwerin Sir Gaernarfon* (Caernarfon: Gwmni y Cyhoeddwyr Cymreig, Swyddfa Cymru, 1908), 106.

too, is not a pretty sight, having a big head, dark face, and seaweed for hair.[50] Another authority confirms mermaid hair to be green, whilst the report of a sighting at Deerness on Orkney from 1892 describes a mermaid as having a small black head, a white body and long arms. One spotted at Birsay on the island around the same time was said to be covered in brown hair, though whether this meant long hair covering her modesty or actual fur is not wholly clear. A mermaid examined from nearby at Portgordon in Banffshire in 1814 was certainly said to have had the conventional long hair we expect from her kind.[51]

Mermen are almost always described less favourably than mermaids. A male seen from quite close quarters with the mermaid at Portgordon was said to have had dark skin, small eyes, a flattened nose, dark curly grey-green hair, a wide mouth, and very long arms—in other words, he was rather fishlike. His lower half resembled a fish's body, albeit without any scales (as with the Lagvag example earlier). In contrast to this sighting, a merman sighted off Castlemartin in Dyfed in 1782 had arms and hands that were disproportionately short and thick for the body while his nose was apparently long and narrow. The observer, a man called Henry Reynolds, at first believed he had seen a pale-skinned teenager in the water until he saw the brown tail waving about. A merman spotted in the water at the Voe of Quarff in Shetland was said to have been like an old man with a very long beard. This description in particular is interesting in light of what we know of the so-called "wild man" captured at Orford in Suffolk in about 1187, who was mentioned earlier. He was formed like an ordinary man, but very powerful, and "his beard was

---

50. Simon Young, "The Reay Mermaids: In the Bay and in the Press," *Shima* 12, no. 2 (September 2018): 26, https://pdfs.semanticscholar.org/fd62/1ef9fc15857f621e574f59ed77dd0 ba44296.pdf?_ga=2.144243061.1393131365.1588952007-252660946.1588713747; Hibbert, *Shetland Isles*, 565; Donald Rawe, *Traditional Cornish Stories and Rhymes* (Padstow: Lodenek Press, 1971), chapter 15.

51. "Monsters of the Deep," Orkneyjar, accessed May 21, 2020, http://www.orkneyjar.com /folklore/mermaids.htm; Joseph McPherson, *Primitive Beliefs in the North-East of Scotland* (London: Longmans, 1929), 73; James Mackinlay, *Folklore of Scottish Lochs and Springs* (Glasgow: W. Hodge, 1893), 168; Campbell, *Superstitions of the Highlands*, 199; William Robertson, *Historical Tales and Legends of Ayrshire* (London: Hamilton, Adams & Co., 1889), 174.

copious and pointed and he was excessively shaggy and hairy on his chest."[52] One of the so-called "Blue Men" (*fir ghorm*) was seen floating half out of the water in the Minch near Skye. He was described as blue, with a long face, and extremely strong: the ship's crew caught him and bound him very tightly with ropes, but he was easily able to snap them and escape.[53]

All in all, the evidence indicates that merfolk can be somewhat disproportioned and that their features have a distinct marine tone. They're often striking to look at, but perhaps not strikingly lovely. These less-complimentary descriptions of the merfolk somehow seem more convincing and authentic. Adaptations to the rigours of a marine environment might be anticipated, and the consistency of the accounts may indicate that the beautiful mermaid is rather the exception than the rule, which is for the merfolk to be blue skinned, green haired, and rather fish faced. In fact, the preference for descriptions of pale-skinned, blonde-haired lovelies may say rather more about the stereotypes perpetuated by certain folklore collectors than about the true nature of the creatures seen by their interviewees.

The Song of the Siren

Mermaids can have lovely singing voices. They even seem to assemble into choirs and perform on a regular basis—if an account from Aberdeen is to be believed, anyway. In 1688, the *Aberdeen Almanac* advised its readers to go to the mouth of the River Dee on certain dates in May or in October, when they could rely upon seeing "a pretty company of mermaids, creatures of admirable beauty, and likewise hear their charming, sweet, melodious voices." They sang various "harmonious lays," apparently, and concluded with "God Save the King." Curious as this account is, we have to be sceptical about it: the mermaids seem to be operating to some fixed schedule of performances, and their choice of finale is suspiciously patriotic—especially in the year of

---

52. Ralph of Coggeshall, *Chronicon Anglicanum*, 117–118.

53. McPherson, *Primitive Beliefs in the*, 72–73; George Eberhart, *Mysterious Creatures: A Guide to Cryptozoology* (Santa Barbara, CA: ABC-CLIO, 2002), 329; Hibbert, *Shetland Isles*, 565; *County Folk-lore* 3, 187; Ralph of Coggeshall, *Chronicon Anglicanum*, 117–118; Campbell, *Superstitions of the Highlands*, 199.

England's "Glorious Revolution," when Catholic King James II was deposed and replaced with Protestant William III.[54]

At Niarbyl Bay on the Isle of Man a mermaid would regularly sing to the fishermen on the beach, and eventually she won the heart of one and wed him. Manx people also believe in a more general sea spirit called the *cughtagh* who may be heard singing to himself in caves. This being has a voice that sounds like waves and seems to be related to the bugganes of the island (see chapter 8) as well as to the Scottish Gaelic *ciudach*, a cave-dwelling giant or monster.[55]

A mermaid's voice isn't always pleasing, nevertheless. We've already heard some mentions of their screeches, and these seem more typical. Some fishermen from Yell on Shetland caught a woman at sea once: her body was about a metre in length, and she had short arms only around twenty-three centimetres long with webbed fingers. Her eyes and nostrils were blue, she had a short neck and a pointed head that lacked a chin or ears, and her tail looked like a halibut's, supplemented by small fins at her shoulders. Her body was soft and slimy, white on the front and grey at the back. To add to her generally unappealing looks, she wailed nonstop for three hours, at the end of which the men could tolerate the sound no more and threw her back into the sea.

Like sirens, the singing of a mermaid can lure a man to disaster. A fisherman from Turnberry in Ayrshire heard an irresistible voice across the waves and set out towards the rock of Ailsa Craig, even though storm clouds were massing on the horizon. He was, of course, never seen again.[56]

Merfolk Prophecy

Mermaids can see into the future. For example, there was one who was often to be seen sitting on a rock at Careg Ina near New Quay in West Wales. One day, she got tangled in some fishing nets and was hauled in by a crew. She begged for release and, when this was granted, she warned them of an impending storm and told them to seek shelter. They did so and survived, but many other boats out that day were caught and sank. A very similar tale

---

54. Spence, *The Minor Traditions*, 50.

55. Charles Roeder, *Manx Folk-Tales*, ed. Stephen Miller (Isle of Man: Chiollagh Books, 1993), 31; Agnes Herbert, *The Isle of Man* (London: John Lane, 1909), 183.

56. Robertson, *Historical Tales and Legends*, 174–9.

comes from Pen Cemmes in Pembrokeshire, except that in this version the fisherman captor is promised "three shouts" in his time of greatest need as his reward for releasing the mermaid. What this meant was revealed some time later, rather than immediately. One calm, hot day the mermaid appeared to the man out at sea and told him to make for harbour forthwith. He did so and survived, but eighteen other men drowned in a sudden storm which blew up. Sometimes, this kind of help is given freely and without prior obligation. For example, some Manx fishermen were once in their boats off Spanish Head when the sky started to darken. A mermaid rose above the waves and called out to them "*shiaull er thalloo*" ("sail to land"). Those who did were saved; those who didn't take her advice lost their tackle or even their lives.[57]

As these last examples imply, merfolk seem especially sensitive to the weather. A man from a village near Peterhead once met a mermaid who beckoned him close and then whispered in his ear. Whatever she exactly said, he never disclosed, but he told other people of their meeting the same day it happened—and a violent storm arose later that night—whilst he himself never went to sea again. In Wales it's said that one should always "take the mermaid's advice and save thyself" and that you should "take shelter when you see the mermaid driving her flocks ashore," by which is meant that if her sheep—the white breakers—are racing up the beach, a storm is imminent.[58]

In addition, amongst fishing communities the mere appearance of the sea folk is taken at least as a sign of bad luck and frequently as a portent of storms and death; as a result, when some fishermen from Brevig on Barra saw a mermaid two miles offshore they immediately turned around and headed back to harbour—and not a moment too soon, as a terrible storm arose which nearly sank them anyway. The *fir ghorm*, the Blue Men of the Minch between Skye and the mainland, are what make the seas there restless. The channel is only calm if they are either asleep or floating on the surface and, if they are seen sporting in the water off Rudha Hunish Head, a violent

57. Davies, *Folk-lore of West*, 144–5; Rhys, *Celtic Folklore: Welsh and Manx*, vol. 1, 163; Gill, *A Manx Scrapbook*, 241.

58. Reid, *Scotland, Past and Present*, 258; *Celtic Magazine* 12 (1887): 572, correspondence from Sidney Hartland.

storm is due. On the Isle of Man, it's reported that if the mermen are heard whistling, it's a sure sign of bad weather approaching.[59]

Finally, the merfolk may have wider foreknowledge of imminent death. I mentioned earlier a mermaid seen floating in the sea at Reay in Caithness in 1809. There is a suggestion that the mermaids here performed something like the function of a *bean-nighe* or banshee (see later). They would be spotted washing bloody shirts and singing mournfully shortly before any major battle, it has been reported.[60]

Merfolk Changelings

Like the faeries on land, the sea people are known to kidnap humans. In the north of Scotland, it's believed that young women who are lost at sea have not drowned but have been abducted by mermen. There is, too, a very rare account of mermaids taking a human baby and leaving a changeling. However, in this case, in contrast to the stories of wizened and sickly faery changelings, the substitute was a healthy and very beautiful child. She grew into a lovely young woman who was seduced and abandoned by a cynical soldier. The jilted girl, Selina, pined away and died. Given her origins, she was under the mermaids' protection so that a terrible vengeance was exacted upon the soldier and those who encouraged him in his dalliance: the seducer was in turn seduced by a mermaid and a huge storm engulfed and destroyed his friend's home.[61]

Another report of child theft by mermaids comes from Fetlar in Shetland. A small boy was abducted by a sea giant called Fluker after locals had objected to the monster visiting their homes. The mother of the child was so distressed by her loss that Fluker relented and decided to restore the infant, only to find that a mermaid had stolen the child from him. Fluker was

---

59. McPherson, *Primitive Beliefs in the*, 72; John MacPherson, *Tales of Barra, Told by the Coddy* (Edinburgh: W. & A. K. Johnstone and G. W. Bacon, 1960), 186; *Yn Lioar Manninagh*, vol. 3.

60. Young, "The Reay Mermaids: in the Bay & in the Press," 26.

61. Robert Hunt, *Popular Romances of the West of England; Or, The Drolls, Traditions, and Superstitions of Old Cornwall: Collected and Edited by Robert Hunt* (London: Chatto & Windus, 1903), 155.

enraged by this; the boy was released safely, but the two sea creatures killed each other in a fight.[62]

Merfolk Magic

The merfolk can grant good fortune and even magical powers to those they favour. Some can deploy faery glamour—for instance, Cornish *bucca* can transform into a fish or a bird—but generally their magical abilities are believed to be quite limited.[63]

Mermaids can grant the traditional three wishes to humans. Sometimes they do this voluntarily, sometimes they can be forced. In one Scottish story from Port Henderson, a mermaid was grabbed by the hair by a boat builder called Roderick Mackenzie and was held firmly by him until she granted his wish that none sailing in the craft he made would ever drown. A similar story from the island of South Uist in the Hebrides has two fishermen catching a mermaid baby in their nets; the mother pleads with them to return her child, something that's only done by them in return for a promise that none of the boat's crew will ever drown.[64]

In the Cornish story of "Lutey and the Mermaid" a fisherman from Cury village, on the Lizard peninsula, was granted three wishes by a stranded mermaid whom he rescued. He chose the power to break witches' spells, the power to gain supernatural knowledge to help others find stolen goods, and a promise that these gifts would continue in his family forever. Likewise, when a man on Harris caught a mermaid she granted him three wishes if he agreed to let her go, and he chose skill as a herb doctor to cure scrofula and other incurable diseases, the power of prophecy so that he could see the future for people, especially women, and a fine singing voice (although apparently only

---

62. Jessie Saxby, *Shetland Traditional Lore* (Edinburgh: Grant & Murray, 1932), 47–9.

63. See, for example, "The Old Man of Cury" in Hunt's *Popular Romances of the West of England*; Hibbert, *Shetland Isles*, 565.

64. Mackinlay, *Folklore of Scottish Lochs*, 168; John H. Dixon, *Gairloch in North-West Ross-shire: It's Records, Traditions, Inhabitants, with a Guide to Gairloch and Loch Maree, and a Map and Illustrations* (Edinburgh: Co-operative Printing, 1886), 163; MacGregor, *The Peat-Fire Flame*, 107.

he thought that this last wish had been granted, as all his neighbours avowed that he shrieked like a mermaid).[65]

In a second Cornish story from the Lizard peninsula, concerning "The Old Man of Cury," the old man also found a stranded mermaid and returned her to the waves at Kynance Cove. She rewarded him with a magical comb, which could be used to call her to his aid. A stranded mermaid rescued from the beach and returned to the waves at Port Erin on the Isle of Man blessed her saviour's family and promised that every woman would have easy childbirths thenceforth. An identical tale is told of a mermaid found at Fleshwick in Rushen parish, except here the guarantee of safe deliveries was exacted as the price of letting a captured mermaid go.[66]

Merfolk magic is, therefore, impressive but restricted in scope. They share some, but not all, of the power of the faeries. Merfolk cannot transform themselves, but they are able to foresee and shape the future, and they can endow those they favour with new or enhanced skills.

Mermaid Wisdom

Mermaids are not usually thought of as founts of wisdom. All the same, quite a few traditional folklore stories show that the merfolk do possess curious oracular powers. Also, like oracles, it can sometimes be pretty hard to make sense of what they're saying.

Mermaids seem to have strong opinions about two matters in particular: human health and human cuisine. The latter is especially surprising seeing as mermaids aren't likely to cook anything at all and certainly not much that would be eaten by humans. This doesn't seem to stop them expressing their views. For instance, a mermaid caught in a fishing net off the Isle of Man was held captive for three weeks by the boat's crew. She refused to speak, eat, or drink until they finally relented and took her down to the beach to set her free. Other merfolk came to meet her at the sea's edge, and when she was asked what men were like, she was overheard to say:

---

65. Bottrell, *Traditions and Hearthside Stories*, vol. 1, 64–71; Campbell, *Superstitions of the Highlands*, 201–202.

66. Hunt, "Romances of Mermaids," in *Popular Romances of the*, vol. 1; *Yn Lioar Manninagh*, vol. 3; W. Gill, *A Manx Scrapbook* (London: Arrowsmith, 1929), chapter 4.

"they are so ignorant as to throw away the very water they have boiled their eggs in."[67]

There's clearly much more to tell here: A man from Skye who caught a mermaid and kept her for a year learned "much curious information" from her. Just before he let her go, he asked her what virtue or evil there was in the water in which eggs had been boiled. She replied, "If I tell you that, you will have a tale to tell," and then sank beneath the waves. Evidently, there's some magical power in boiled eggs of which most of us are wholly unaware. An indication of this is the fact that Scottish witch suspect Elspeth Reoch claimed to have acquired the second sight by means of boiling an egg on three successive Sundays and using the "sweat" that formed on the shell to wash her hands and rub on her eyes.[68]

Another mermaid, caught in nets near Fishguard in West Wales, advised the fishing boat crew:

"Skim the surface of the pottage before adding sweet milk to it; it will be whiter and sweeter and less of it will do."

This is probably very good advice, but how a mermaid would know about making soup with dairy products is anybody's guess.[69]

An incident from the Hebrides involved a captured mermaid escaping into the sea, taking with her some captive faery cows. A man called Luran tried to stop their flight and caught hold of the tail of the last cow in the herd. It was too strong for him, though, and as the fugitives disappeared into the waves, the mermaid called back to taunt him that if only he'd had porridge with milk to eat and not dry bread he would have had the strength to hold it. Once again, the mermaid's knowledge of the virtues of terrestrial food is not explained.

---

67. Joseph Train, *An Historical and Statistical Account of the Isle of Man from the Earliest Times to the Present Date*, vol. 2 (Douglas: M. A. Quiggin, 1845), chapter 18, 145; Waldron, *The History and Description*, 108.

68. Campbell, *Superstitions of the Highlands*, 201.

69. Rhys, *Celtic Folklore: Welsh and Manx*, vol. 1, 166.

In one case, the advice concerns the preparation of fish, which at least we can accept a mermaid might know about. She had been trapped on the land by the magical means of sprinkling *maistir* across her path. She spoke only once in the week she spent ashore to rather ominously warn a woman gutting fish:

> "Wash and clean well the fish, there's many a monster in the sea."

In another case a mermaid has something to say about the preparation of fish, but in this case her words don't seem to be about kitchen hygiene but instead are either a prediction or a grant of good fortune. The mermaid had been caught on a hook by some Shetland fishermen; she begged to be freed and promised to grant them anything they wished for in return. They restored her to the water and, before she sank beneath the waves, she declaimed a verse ending with the advice:

> "Muckle gude I wid you gie,
> And mair I wid ye wish,
> There's muckle evil in the sea,
> Scoom weel your fish."

> "*Much good would I give you,*
> *And more would I wish.*
> *There's great evil in the sea,*
> *So skin well your fish.*"

The captain thought this nonsense and reckoned he'd been cheated. One of the crew of the boat, however, paid attention to her words and carefully descaled the next fish he caught. He found a large and valuable pearl amongst the "skoomings."[70]

Mermaids also seem to know a good deal about human diseases and their treatment with herbal remedies. In one Scottish case, a mermaid surfaced to see the funeral of a young woman passing on the shore and called out:

---

70. Saxby, *Shetland Traditional Lore*, 139; Biot Edmonston and Jessie M. E. Saxby, *The Home of a Naturalist* (London: J. Nisbet, 1888), 228.

"If they would drink nettles in March
And eat mugwort in May,
So many braw (healthy) maidens
Would not go to the clay."[71]

A very similar story has a happier outcome because the mermaid tells a sick girl's lover about the mugwort remedy in good time; he takes her advice, makes a juice from the flower tops, and saves his beloved. There may well be some sound wisdom on herbal medicine being dispensed here, though once again quite what a sea dweller knows about weeds growing on dry land is another matter altogether.

Lastly, some of the mermaid sayings seem so cryptic it's hard to make much sense at all of them. Just before she dived out of sight beneath the waves, a mermaid who had been discovered sitting on a rock near Porth y Rhiw in South Wales said simply:

"Reaping in Pembrokeshire and weeding in Carmarthenshire."

Another, who had become stranded on the beach as the tide went out at Balladoole near Castletown on the Isle of Man called out to her rescuers, who had carried her back to the sea:

"One butt in Ballacreggan is worth all of Balladoole."

It's maybe possible to extract some sense from this, if the "butt" refers to a barrel of fish. If this is right, she may have been saying that the herring catch at the first location would always be better than that off the beach where she was found—a helpful hint for the men who saved her. It's also quite possible that she made reference to smuggling—possibly suggesting that a barrel of brandy landed at Ballacregan was worth the entire fishing village. Either way, this may be a lone example of mermaid career advice.[72]

---

71. Katherine Briggs, *A Dictionary of Fairies: Hobgoblins, Brownies, Bogies, and other Supernatural Creatures* (London: Penguin Books, 1977), 289.

72. Rhys, *Celtic Folklore: Welsh and Manx*, vol. 1, 166; Roeder, *Manx Folk Tales*, 32; *Yn Lioar Manninagh*, vol. 3.

All in all, wordplay and hidden meanings appear to be something that merfolk respected and enjoyed. I'll demonstrate this with a story from the Isle of Lewis. Some fishermen were out in their boat when a mermaid surfaced. That would normally have been interpreted as a sign of disaster, but she spoke to the captain and they exchanged some clever verses in Gaelic. It appears that his quick wit and versifying pleased her, because she sank beneath the waves again and the crew got home safely.[73]

In summary, the merfolk seem to be prepared to share their natural wisdom with us, but they don't want to make it too easily accessible for us. If you want to learn from a mermaid, you need to put a bit of effort in; you will have to puzzle out the exact meaning and relevance of what they have imparted.

Mermaid Curses

Generally, the merfolk are regarded as dangerous. This is not just because they can influence the weather; they are said, too, to pursue ships, and crews often threw barrels and the like overboard just to distract the merfolk and slow them down. The *fir ghorm* in the sea off Skye seem especially hostile to shipping and spend a great deal of their time trying to sink vessels. A boat from Peterhead in Aberdeenshire sank on the rocks below Slains Castle with the loss of all but one of her crew after a mermaid grabbed violent hold of its bowsprit. For balance, though, I should cite a report from Milford Haven in Pembrokeshire: a mermaid used to sit on the Scilly Rocks in the estuary, warning passing ships away from the dangerous reef that lay below the surface there.[74]

Merfolk can punish those who offend them or who injure those whom they protect. If you shoot a selkie, you can expect then to lose a valuable possession of your own: in the past, a cow would die or a flock of sheep might disappear. At Padstow on the north Cornish coast, the harbour silted up after a man tried shooting at the mermaid who lived there; Seaton near Looe on the south coast suffered a similar fate after a mermaid was offended. A man from Pembrey, near Llanelli in South Wales, killed a mermaid and brought a

---

73. MacPhail, "Folklore from the Hebrides—II," *Folklore* 8 (1897): 385.

74. Campbell, *Superstitions of the Highlands*, 201; Peter Buchan, *Annals of Peterhead, From Its Foundation to the Present Time [...]* (Peterhead: Buchan, 1819), 41; Blind, "New Finds," *Gentleman's Magazine*, no. 252 (January–June 1882): 480.

curse upon himself and his family for nine generations; another Welshman who caught a mermaid and imprisoned her in his home, allowing her to pine away until she died, likewise found that his house was cursed ever after. You may recall the curse placed upon Conwy in North Wales after a stranded mermaid was allowed to die of exposure. As I've said, mermaids can cause storms deliberately, but it's also said that if a selkie is shot in the sea, a storm will arise as soon as its blood mixes with the water. Manx fishermen believed that if you were to throw a stone at a mermaid—perhaps to scare her away from your nets and your catch—you would inevitably feel the pain of the blow yourself and, within an hour or so, would fall down dead.[75]

Merfolk can be vengeful too. At Knockdolion in Scotland there was a rock on the shore where a mermaid would sit at night, combing her hair and singing. A local lady who lived nearby objected to this, as it disturbed her baby in its cradle, so she instructed some men to break up the boulder. When the mermaid discovered what had been done, she cried out the following words:

> "Ye may think on your cradle, I'll think on my stane;
> And there'll never be an heir to Knockdolion again."[76]

Shortly afterwards, the cot was overturned, and the baby was killed.

Mermaids can appear lovely, but they're perilous at the same time. In the story of Lutey, who was granted his three wishes, the stranded mermaid he had carried back to the sea still tried to drag him beneath the waves with her. He drew his knife and fended her off, but she promised to see him again after nine years. True to her words, on a calm and placid night nine years later he was out fishing with a friend when the mermaid came back to claim him. Lutey knew that he could not escape his fate and was never seen again.

---

75. Hunt, *Popular Romances*, 151–2; Davies, *Folk-lore*, 144-5; Elias Owen, *Welsh Folk-lore: A Collection of the Folk-Tales and Legends of North Wales* (Oswestry and Wrexham, Woodall, Minshall, and Co., 1896), 142; Rhys, *Celtic Folklore*, vol. 1, 199; Herbert, *The Isle of Man*, 183; Hibbert, *Shetland Isles*, 260.

76. George Douglas, *Scottish Fairy and Folk Tales: Selected and Edited with an Introduction by Sir George Douglas* (London: W. Scott, 1901), 95; R. Chambers, *Popular Rhymes of Scotland* (Edinburgh: W. and R. Chambers, 1847), 331.

What's worse, it's said that a member of Lutey's family is lost at sea every nine years.[77]

A fisherman from Skye made a similar bargain to Lutey. Out fishing without success one day, a mermaid surfaced beside his boat and spoke to him. They reached an agreement: she gave him a substance that granted fertility so that his wife had three children, his dog three puppies, and his horse three foals; she also guaranteed plenty of fish in his nets, but the price for all this prosperity was high—she claimed his firstborn son.[78]

A story from Shetland contrasts the outcome of opposite attitudes to a mermaid. Two farmers went to cut some peat at Yugla. They found a mermaid there combing her hair. The first exclaimed, "Care and dole" to which she replied, "Care and dole on you." The second man greeted her politely, wishing her luck and good health, and she responded in kind. In due course, the second man's farm prospered whilst the other man's was blighted and went into decline.[79]

The overall impression you form from these accounts is that the merfolk have a vindictive nature and are inclined to reprisals—though perhaps humans are no better in this respect. A man from Sanday in the Orkneys was driving his sheep onto a small island called Holms of Ire where people pastured their flocks in the summer. In so doing, he saw a seal pup and killed it. That night all his sheep, but none of his neighbours', disappeared. This was taken to be selkie vengeance for the loss of their child.

Offerings to Merfolk

Given the temperament and the powers of merfolk, it's unsurprising that some communities would make small sacrifices to appease them. At Halloween, the people of Lewis used to attend a church ceremony that included pouring ale into the sea in the hope that "Shony" (*Seonaidh*) would guarantee a good supply of seaweed in the year ahead; so, too, on the remote isle of St. Kilda, where shells, pebbles, rags, pins, nails, and coins were thrown in

---

77. Bottrell, *Traditions and Hearthside Stories*, vol. 1, 64.

78. John Francis Campbell, *Popular Tales of the West Highlands Orally Collected with a Translation by J. F. Campbell*, vol. 1 (Edinburgh: Edmonston and Douglas, 1860), 96.

79. J. J. Haldane Burgess, "Some Shetland Folk-lore," *Scottish Review* 25, (January and April 1895): 97.

the sea. All round Scotland, in fact, meat, drink, and bread would be offered up to faery beings. On Orkney, the custom was that the first fish caught on a hook when out line fishing would be thrown back to ensure that the rest of the catch would be good. Indeed, the superstition was carried much further: people drowning were regarded as being a sacrifice to the sea spirits so that to try to rescue them would cheat the ocean of its offering and would bring bad luck on those who intervened—or even those who touched drowned bodies.[80]

A sea-sprite with closely related powers was known in Somerset. Fishermen walking from the village of Worle towards the quay at Birnbeck followed a path along a ridge. Halfway along this is a pile of stones called Picwinna's Mound, which was reputed to be a pixy site. The passing fishermen would pick up a stone as they walked and throw it onto the mound as they passed, wishing "Picwinna, Picwinna, bring me a good dinner."[81]

The Manx people used to sacrifice rum to the buggane who inhabited a cave under Kione Dhoo headland. A small amount would be poured into the sea by fishing boat crews from Port St. Mary as they passed the promontory on their way to the fishing grounds. Rum was occasionally thrown from the top of the cliff as well with the words "Take that, evil spirit (or monster)!" This dedication resembles that which accompanied the fish thrown to the merman at sea, "*Gow shen, dooinney varrey!*" ("Take that, sea people.")[82]

Orkney Finfolk

The merfolk of Orkney have a distinctive body of lore attached to them, which means they should be discussed separately from other sea-people. They are called "finfolk" by the islanders and are generally regarded as being quite separate from the selkies, although there is undoubtedly some crossover

---

80. Martin Martin, *A Description of the Western Islands of Scotland Containing a Full Account [...]* (London: A. Bell, 1716), 28; Hibbert, *Shetland Isles*, 525; John Dalyell, *The Darker Superstitions of Scotland, Illustrated from History and Practice* (Edinburgh: Waugh & Innes, 1834), 545; McPherson, *Primitive Beliefs*, 70.

81. Jon Dathen, *Somerset Faeries and Pixies: Exploring Their Hidden World* (Milverton: Capall Bann, 2010), 92; see, too, Briggs, *A Dictionary of Fairies*, "Ina Picwinna."

82. W. Gill, *A Third Manx Scrapbook* (London: Arrowsmith, 1963), part two, chapter 2, section 6.

in people's ideas about the two. On the whole, the finfolk are the more antagonistic toward humans, as well as having more significant magical powers.[83]

The finfolk live in "Finfolkaheem" (finfolk home) during the winter. This is the marine equivalent to the faeries' "Elfame" and is a wonderful undersea palace or city where they raise their own horses and cows, herd whales (for meat and for milk) and go hunting with otters. During the summer, the finfolk live on a beautiful hidden island called Hildaland. Whether this is concealed from human eyes by encircling mists or rises and sinks beneath the waves is not entirely clear.[84]

Despite their very separate and independent lives, the finfolk still come to the land. This is because they like to abduct humans, whom they take to be their domestic slaves in Finfolkaheem. People are entrapped in several ways. The finfolk may float just offshore and try to lure the curious toward them, at which point the person will be seized and dragged under the waves. Alternatively, the finmen may appear as humans in boats and try to kidnap the unwary this way.

The finfolk have their special reasons for wanting to mate with humans. Mermaids are the female children of finmen and are well known for their beauty, their pale skin, and their golden hair. However, if they marry a husband of their own kind, this beauty is said to fade over a couple of decades until they are hideous hags. To avoid this, it's said, they prefer to couple with human males, something that then permits them to discard their tails and live a mortal life. Finfolk women have two ways to ensnare human males. If their physical charms are not enough, their voices are reported to be sirenlike and hypnotic. The only hope for the man then is to have the presence of mind to repeat a rhyme that counteracts her spell:

> "God take a care of me!
> God's name, I hear the mermaid sing-

---

83. For the finfolk, see Walter Traill Dennison, "Orkney Folk-lore: Sea Myths," in *Scottish Antiquary* vol. 6 (1892): 116 and vol. 7 (1893): 18, 171.

84. "Finfolkaheem—The Ancestral Home," The Sorcerous Finfolk, OrkneyJar, accessed May 8, 2020, www.orkneyjar.com/folklore/finfolk/heem.htm.

It's bonny, it's bonny, but no so bonny
As the sound of bells ringing in heaven."[85]

Finmen, in comparison, are gloomy and violent creatures. If they feel that human fishermen have been trespassing upon their territories and taking their fish stocks, they can respond forcibly. They may merely cut the nets and the lines or sever the anchor ropes, but they may also come ashore at night and smash the boats and tackle. The best protection against this vandalism is to mark the tackle with crosses and to paint a cross in tar on the bottom of the fishing boat.

The finfolk are consistently depicted as being antipathetic to Christian religion; it's something they simply cannot abide. One story tells of a man called Arthur Deerness from Orkney who was abducted by a mermaid lover to Finfolkaheem. He might have remained there forever in his lover's arms had not a mer-cat scratched his finger in a cross pattern; this instantly broke the charm and returned him to the beach where he had been ensnared. The story of Johnny Croy describes how he managed to secure a mermaid wife by snatching her precious golden comb. To win it back, she struck a bargain with him—that she would live with him on his farm for seven years and that he would then go with her to visit her family in Finfolkaheem. During the first part of their marriage, they had seven children. When the time came to go under the waves, Johnny's mother branded her youngest grandchild on its buttock with a red-hot cross. This brutal measure prevented the mermaid from taking her baby with her—but the rest of the family disappeared forever beneath the sea. Girls travelling by boat to the annual Lammas Fair on the Orkney mainland would be marked on the chest by their mothers with a cross so as to protect them from being snatched when they were crossing the sea.[86]

Apparently, finmen also covet human silver—so much so that they may send their wives onto the land to work as healers and spinners. The women will then send their wages "back home" to their husbands. This lust for silver

---

85. Martyn Whittock, *A Brief Guide to Celtic Myths and Legends* (Philadelphia: Running Press, 2013), 236.

86. Dennison, "Orkney Folk-lore: Sea Myths," in *Scottish Antiquary* 7 (1893): 24; "Johnny Croy and His Mermaid Bride," OrkneyJar, accessed May 8, 2020, www.orkneyjar.com /folklore/jcroy.htm.

gives humans another way of protecting themselves. If you are confronted with a member of the finfolk who seems set on dragging you away, tossing silver coins in their path will usually be infallible as a way of distracting them long enough for you to make your getaway.

Many aspects of finfolk behaviour betray their faery nature. Their aversion to Christianity and its symbols is one; their desire to hoard money may be another. Thirdly, there is a story of a man who ferried a finman and a cow from the Lammas Fair back to Finfolkaheem. The finfolk took precautions to conceal the location of the island from him, but the next year he saw the same man at the fair again and greeted him. The finman immediately blinded the ferryman, reminding us of the very common story of a human midwife who accidentally penetrates faery glamour and suffers for it.

Sea-trows

The marine trows of Orkney are another type of merfolk deserving of separate treatment. Their origins are quite different to the rest of the merfolk. The story is that, after a falling out, the trows were driven from the land into the sea by the remainder of their kind, who are now called the "hill-trows." The sea-trows would love to come back onto the land, but they are scared of their cousins and so stick to the foreshore if they ever dare to come out of the water at all.

The trows are a very unappealing species, having monkey faces on oddly shaped heads, wizened bodies with scaly skin, and overlong limbs. Their feet are flat, and their fingers and toes are webbed. Their hair is matted and usually entangled with seaweed, a local word for which gives them their other name of "tangy" (although this name is also used for water beasts, too, as I'll describe later).

In their natural habitat, sea-trows are viewed as both stupid and lazy by the Orkney islanders. Their laziness is manifested in the fact that they don't catch their own food, they just steal fish from the hooks of fishing lines—although this is possibly just good sense. This filching causes a good deal of resentment on the part of the fishermen and they will try to hit the trows with their oars if ever they see them. Despite this mutual animosity, though, on the Shetland Islands the "water-trows" are given offerings; at Crawford

Muir in the 1770s a tenant was reported to have sacrificed a black lamb to the sea-trow to reinforce curses he was placing upon his enemies.[87]

Given their unwilling exile from the land, some sea-trows will submit to human society and work on farms in return for food and shelter. On the Shetland island of Copinsay, a farmer was approached by a wet, ugly creature with thick skin that glowed slightly. He was naked and had seaweed for hair and beard. All efforts to exorcise the visitor with the standard means—prayers and iron—failed so, making the best of a bad job, he was taken in as a labourer. The little man called himself Hughbo, a name derived from the Norse *haug-bui* or mound-dweller. This would normally indicate a hill-trow, but Hughbo plainly came from the sea—and presumably returned there, for the farmer's wife eventually committed the cardinal error of giving him a cloak and hood, which banished him permanently from the farm, just as gifts of clothing will drive off faeries such as brownies and hobs.

Conclusions

The merfolk are close to us in many ways: they look like us, they can talk to us, they can understand our thoughts, and they can eat our food. Even more significantly, they will share our homes, share our beds, and raise families with us. They understand our strengths and our weaknesses. The merfolk are disposed to be friendly with us. They will share their wisdom and esoteric knowledge; they will bring us the riches and resources of the sea, and they will even retrieve lost human treasures for us.

The differences between humankind and merfolk are not great—except for the major barrier that lies between us. They live under the sea, a place where humans normally cannot safely follow. It is, of course, possible now for humans to visit beneath the waves with the right equipment and training, but we should probably not seek to impose ourselves upon the merfolk's realm. They are entitled to retreat beyond the reach of people and to choose when they shall appear to us. In any event, just as it is true to say that those who go in search of faeries never find them, it is very likely that this will be true beneath the sea. There are virtually no magical means of summoning the merfolk to us (whereas several for faeries have been recorded). The most commonly reported

---

87. Hibbert, *Shetland Isles*, 525.

means of imposing our will upon them is by stealing a personal item—but this is hardly a method to foster good relations with our supernatural neighbours. The merfolk are not at our beck and call—unless they choose to be.

This physical divide between us is symbolic of the deeper, nonmaterial differences that exist: For all our similarities, we do not share their supernatural knowledge of the weather or of time to come. For all that we have in common with the mermaids, they are nearer to the faeries than they are to us.

Chapter 2

MEREMAIDS

This chapter explores a very particular form of British faery being, the fresh-water mermaid or water sprite. I have chosen to use the label "meremaid" to emphasise the difference to the merfolk. The subjects of this chapter are predominantly female and are to be found in inland lakes and pools. "Mere," meaning a body of water, is an Old English word that forms the basis of mermaid, but of course that word is now used in reference to marine beings, making some separate term necessary. Some faeries, especially the *gwragedd annwn* of Wales, live in or under lakes, such as those at Llyn Cwellyn, Llyn Corwrion, and Llyn Barfog, and it's important for us to distinguish these as well. These faery women use the lake for concealment, but they are not aquatic and do not live in the body of water itself, neither do they share the predatory nature of most of the meremaids.

The idea of the inland "meremaid" is very ancient, the very oldest of these very likely being found in the Anglo-Saxon poem *Beowulf,* in the ghastly shape of the mother of the monster Grendel, a being who is fierce and giant-like. *Beowulf* uses various terms to describe the monstrous mother, one of which is "mere-wife." Her son's name seems to be preserved in the meremaid today called the *grindylow*. Despite this pedigree, illustrations and paintings seem to prefer to suggest that these creatures are sexually alluring nymph-like beings. On the whole, it is safest to assume that the meremaids are perilous, if not outright fatal, to humankind.[88]

Meremaids will be found across Britain, although the strength of the tradition varies considerably. For example, on the Isle of Man, the name of the water sprite called the *croghan* or *crogan* is preserved but, other than knowing that she was found in wells and springs, nothing else is now recalled about her.[89]

Drownings at Midnight

In the Peak District of England is found Mermaid Pool, at the foot of a rock called the Downfall. A beautiful mermaid who lives on the other side of Kinder Scout peak is said to come to bathe there daily. However, visiting at midnight on Easter Eve in order to see the mermaid at her ablutions is extremely unwise. Although normally favourable to humans, on this night of the year she will endeavour to entice watchers into the water with her—and then drag them beneath the surface. Animals are said not to want to drink from the pool—in large measure perhaps because the waters are reputed to be inexplicably salty, but also because of the aura of menace that hangs about the place, a feature of many meremaids' haunts.

Other mere maidens include those of the ponds, pools, meres, and even wells at Fordham, Cambridgeshire, and in Suffolk at Rendlesham, and most notably at the Mermaid Pits, Fornham All Saints. The latter is allegedly the spirit of a lovesick girl who perished there, reminding us how often faery beasts are associated with ghosts. One of these East Anglian meremaids was described by a witness as "a great big thing like a fish." Local children are warned by their parents to stay away from the pools, or to always be alert if they play near them, as the creatures are always on the watch to "croom" (hook) the unwary into the depths. At Halliwell in East Yorkshire, it is said to be a boggart rather than a maiden that haunts the local spring and pool. In fact, it is reported that every sandpit in the county has its goblin, such as

---

88. Ann Radcliffe, "The Sea Nymph," in *The Mysteries of Udolpho, a Romance; Interspersed with Some Pieces of Poetry* (London: G. G. and J. Robinson), 1794; Dathen, *Somerset Faeries*, 81.

89. W. Gill, *A Second Manx Scrapbook* (London: Arrowsmith, 1932), chapter 6.

the bogie in the form of a white dog that infested the hollow at Brigham Lane End (see chapter 9).[90]

As with the meremaid of Mermaid Pool, it's normal for these beings to hunt unwary humans at night. Most are anonymous, but a few have been given names—for example Jenny Greenteeth, who has been encountered at Ellesmere in Shropshire as well as in Lancashire, Cumbria, and as far away as Somerset; Grindylow in Yorkshire; Jenny Hurn, a seallike creature with long hair in Lincolnshire; Nelly Long Arms in Cheshire; Mary Hosies in Lanarkshire; and the widespread pair Rawhead and Bloodybones. Jenny Greenteeth is especially widespread in England, being reputed to emerge at full moon to lurk near ponds, wells, rivers, or abandoned workings or to sit moaning in the trees nearby. She looks like an ugly old woman with hair like coarse grass and long claws, and she will invariably snatch and devour careless young prey who stray too near the brink—a habit which doubtless gave rise to the name of another northern water-witch called Peg wi' t' Iron Teeth.[91]

In Scotland, one encounters the *fideal*, an evil meremaid who haunts Loch na Fideil near Gairloch, in the northwest Highlands. These freshwater monsters often lurk in wait for children under lawn-like mats of pond weed and the *fideal* exemplifies this: she uses entangling bog grasses and water weeds on the loch's shore to snare her victims. By one account, a man decided to take her on and, at the end of a long struggle, both lay dead: although he had overcome the *fideal*, wrestling with her entwining weeds so sapped his strength that he succumbed and drowned anyway.[92]

In the Scottish story of Lorntie, the meremaid's vicious and bloodthirsty nature is starkly exposed. Riding by a lake, Lorntie sees a woman floundering

---

90. James Reynolds Withers, "The Pond in the Meadow," in *Poems Upon Various Subjects* (Fordham, 1864), 117; Robert Chambers, *Book of Days*, vol. 1 (Edinburgh: W. & R. Chambers, 1869), 678; Eveline Camilla Gurdon, *County Folk-lore, 37, Printed Extracts No. 2, Suffolk: Collected and Edited by The Lady Eveline Camilla Gurdon with Introduction by Edward Clodd* (London: D. Nutt, 1893), 34.

91. Simon Young, "Folklore Pamphlet: The Sources for Jenny Greenteeth and Other English Freshwater Fairies," (July 2019): 1–54.

92. Donald Mackenzie, *Scottish Folk-Lore and Folk Life: Studies in Race, Culture, and Tradition* (London: Blackie & Sons, 1935), 235-36; Edward Nicholson, *Golspie: Contributions to its Folklore [...]* (London: D. Nutt, 1897), 78–79.

and apparently drowning in the water. He dashes to save her, but fortunately his squire sees the trap and holds him back. In a rage, the maiden declares:

> "Lorntie, Lorntie, were it not for your man,
> I'd have got your heart's blood, skirling in my pan."[93]

The fatal nature of meremaids is also clear from the ballad of *Clerk Colvill*. Despite his wife's warnings, the hero decides to visit a well beneath a hawthorn tree. The hawthorn is a tree intimately associated with the faeries, so its presence here immediately alerts us to the faery nature of the spring. Clerk Colvill predictably encounters a meremaid there who is washing a silk shirt for him in the out-flowing stream. (Her laundry activities link her to the banshee, who is described in the next chapter.) The meremaid has sleeves of green (the quintessential faery colour), and Colvill immediately falls under her spell and forgets his wife. In due course, the man falls ill, blighted by her presence, at which point his faery lover loses interest in him, turns into a fish, and abandons him to struggle home to die. In another version of the song, Clerk Colvill develops a headache and cuts a strip from the silk shirt to wrap around his head—but rather than soothing his malady, it only makes matters worse.[94]

Guardians of Treasure

Most of the meremaids prey upon passing mortals. Despite this bad reputation (or possibly because of it) some were also connected to hidden hoards of precious metals or jewels in some way. A beautiful maiden with a lovely voice appeared at Child's Ercall in Shropshire and offered two men gold if they would enter the water to take it from her. As they began to wade out to her, they commented upon their luck and she instantly disappeared, surely a variation of the common idea of keeping quiet about faery favours. We must wonder, too, whether, if they had reached her, the outcome might not have been as happy as they had anticipated. Jenny Greenteeth has also been linked to treasure in one story from Newton Chapelry in Manchester.

---

93. Douglas, *Scottish Fairy and Folk Tales*, 196–197.

94. Francis James Child, ed., "42: Clerk Colvill," in *The English and Scottish Popular Ballads*, vol. 1 (New York: Houghton, Mifflin & Co., 1886), 371–389.

At Marden (Herefordshire) and Rostherne Mere (Cheshire) the meremaids are said to be guarding bells submerged beneath the pool. Attempts to retrieve the Marden bell from the River Lugg have been defeated by the meremaid's interventions. In the second case, it's also believed that a long tunnel connects the pool to the sea, which is where the meremaid actually lives (although this may just be a more recent confusion of meremaid and mermaid).[95]

Other Good Fortune

If you saw the meremaid of Mermaid Pool in Derbyshire bathing, you would become immortal. Predicting the future appears to be another part of the makeup of the many meremaids: the White Lady of Wellow in Somerset haunted St. Julian's Well there and served as a sort of banshee to the family of the lords of Hungerford.[96]

The cattle belonging to lake-dwelling spirits are often very valuable livestock. I'll mention a Welsh example later, but at Bowerhope near Yarrow in Scotland a lake cow bred with a nearby farmer's stock and produced a very fine herd. In due course, however, some neglect or offence on his part annoyed the mother cow, and she emerged from St. Mary's Loch and called all nineteen of her offspring to join her beneath the waters.[97]

Threats and Fear

Often, local people want to rid themselves of their dangerous neighbours, and almost always these enterprises fail. A very good example is the fish-tailed creature dwelling in the Black Mere at Morridge in Staffordshire. No animals will drink the water, and birds are said to avoid landing upon or flying over the lake. This is probably because, just as the meremaid is known to seize passersby at midnight and drown them, local wildlife sense it is a perilous place to be. When an attempt was made to drain the Mere, the creature emerged and threatened to engulf the whole of the nearby town of Leek in its waters. Wisely, the work was abandoned and never restarted. There are local

---

95. Westwood and Simpson, *The Lore of the Land: A Guide to England's Legends, From Spring-Heeled Jack to the Witches of Warboys* (Harmondsworth: Penguin, 2005), 326, 87.

96. Ruth Tongue, *Somerset Folklore*, ed. Kathleen Briggs (London: Folk-lore Society, 1965), 120.

97. Mackinlay, *Folklore of Scottish Lochs*, 180.

suggestions that the water sprite may be a suicide or a murdered woman, connecting us once again to the spirits of the dead.[98]

The meremaid at Wildmere Pool, Newport in Shropshire would rise to the surface of her pool to warn of impending calamities. Once, when an attempt was made to dredge the pool, she scared off the workmen with a threat to drown Newport and Meretown.[99]

From Wales comes a similar episode involving the faery woman of Llyn y Fan Fach. After a period of married life, she deserted her human husband and returned to her home with all his cattle, leaving him so distraught after her departure that he tried to drain the lake to get her back again. A monster rose from the waters and warned him to desist or see the town of Brecon drowned.[100]

There was a fearsome spirit that demanded human sacrifice infesting Lochan-nan-Deean in the Highlands near Tomintoul. The local people resolved to drain the lochan to recover the bodies of the dead, but as soon as work began, a man in a red cap emerged from the waters, very angry and roaring horrifically. The workers fled, the sprite threw all their abandoned tools into the water, and then he himself sank back into the waters of the loch, which were said to resemble boiling blood. In another version of this tale, small black creatures appeared at night and filled in the drainage channel that had been cut during the day.[101]

Something similar happened to a man who tried to drain the lochan at Kildonan in Sutherland. After a day's excavation, he was harassed all night long by a black dog barking and howling outside his cottage. The next day he gave up his attempt and filled in the channel he'd started to dig. It was said that, because of this premature abandonment of the work, he never discovered the pot of gold buried at the bottom of the pool. Another black dog guards a treasure in a pool at Dean Combe in Devon; that hoard will be safe until someone manages to drain the pool using a hazelnut shell with a hole in

98. Charles Poole, *The Customs, Superstitions and Legends of the County of Stafford* (London, Rowney & Co., 1875), 100–2.

99. Mackinlay, *Folklore of Scottish Lochs*, 160; Charlotte Sophia Burne, *Shropshire Folk-lore, A Sheaf of Gleanings* (London: Trübner & Co., 1883), 640; Davies, *Folk-lore of West*, 100.

100. Davies, *Folklore of West and Mid Wales*, 100.

101. McPherson, *Primitive Beliefs*, 69; W. Gregor, "Guardian Spirits of Wells and Lochs," *Folklore* 3 (1892): 68.

it. I'll return to discuss black dogs as a separate category of faery beast later on in this book.[102]

Given the ferocious and vengeful nature of many of the meremaids, it's unsurprising to find there is a longstanding tradition of making offerings to the sprites living in freshwater springs, doubtless to ensure that the faery, meremaid, or imp living there maintains the supply of clean and drinkable water. There is also a concomitant belief that revenge will be taken if the proper respect isn't shown and suitable dedications aren't made. For example, the "faeries" of a well in the Ochil Hills were offended by a local farmer. Soon afterwards, his dairy maid went to the well to wash the farm's butter before taking it to market. A hand snatched it away, declaring, "Your butter's awa' to feast our band in the faery ha'."[103]

Even quite small bodies of water have their guardian spirits who have to be appeased and respected. On Orkney a propitiatory ceremony was performed at the Helga Water, circling the lake three times sun-wise and then pouring water over the head. At Loch Wan in the Scottish Uplands, the local farmers offered the first lamb of the flock each year to the loch—otherwise they knew that half their sheep would drown in its waters before the season was out.[104]

Tobar-na-glas a Coille well near Corgarff in the Highlands was inhabited by a spiteful sprite called 'Duine-glas-bheg' ("the Little Grey Man"). He expected an offering to be made for every draught of water taken from the well, even if the donation was only a pin or a small coin. If a person failed to "pay," the little man would stop them drawing water from the spring ever again and would hound them until they died of thirst.[105]

White Ladies

There's a constant element in British folklore tradition, the beings called "white ladies." They can take a number of forms: they might be seen as faeries, they are very often linked to the ghosts of murdered or slighted women, but very

102. Mackinlay, *Folklore of Scottish Lochs*, 181.

103. *County Folk-lore* 7, 312; A. Fraser, "Northern Folklore: Wells and Springs," *Celtic Magazine* 3 (1878): 18, 31; see Spence, *Minor Traditions*, 34–37 for faery wells generally.

104. McPherson, *Primitive Beliefs*, 69.

105. W. Gregor, "Guardian Spirits," *Folklore* 3 (1892): 68.

many are water spirits of some description. For example, in Shropshire the sprite called the Lady of Kilsall haunts the Dark Walk by the pool there.[106]

There are many examples of this type of meremaid from around England. The White Lady of Lewtrenchard in Devon haunts wells and riverbanks, but also has a part-time job protecting local orchards from thieves. At Buckland in Surrey a white lady was sometimes seen sitting on a stone by a stream that marks the spot where a man stabbed himself to death after being rejected by a young woman. The spirit lingers there at midnight, scaring those that want to cross the brook at this point. Rather similar is the White Lady at Ragley Hall in Warwickshire, who appears at midnight and spends her time sitting on a stile, with an occasional trip to a nearby stream for a drink.

The White Lady of Longnor in the same county lives in the Black Pool by the road to Leebotwood and also comes forth at night and wanders the roads. However, according to a servant of the local vicar who met her crossing the footbridge over the brook in 1881, she's said to be "a nice young wench" and not to be feared at all. The man, being an amorous youth, decided to be forward as they passed each other on the narrow bridge and tried to give her a squeeze round the waist: he found to his alarm that there was nothing there. Luckily, he suffered no ill-consequences for his cheeky advances. The White Lady's insubstantial, supernatural nature was confirmed by another sighting, during which she joined a dance at a local public house. Lots of the men present attempted to take her hand to make her their partner, but they could never catch hold of her. That she was some sort of faery being was demonstrated by her sudden disappearance from the room at the end of the evening.[107]

The "white lass" of Thirsk haunted a small watercourse, which came to be known as White Lass Beck. Sometimes also she's seen at a stile, like her Ragley Hall cousin, but at other times she shape-shifts into a white dog and prowls the town, alarming residents with the sound of her claws on the street cobbles.

Finally, there are reports from the Isle of Man of "white ladies" who emerge from the sea at Germans and Michael and have married local men. These seem to be some sort of mermaid or selkie, rather than a sprite coming from a body of water onto the land. To add to the confusion, there are several

---

106. Tongue, *Somerset Folklore*, 120; *Choice Notes & Queries—Folklore* (1859), 26, from the Isle of Man.

107. Burne, *Shropshire Folk-lore*, 76–7.

Manx spectres in pale silk robes seen flitting around wells who also bear this label. One in white silk is often encountered near Lewaigue Bridge and may waylay passersby or enter people's homes. A man travelling from Ramsey to Laxey once met with a greyish woman accompanied by a low shaggy dog. At first, they approached each other along the road in the normal manner but, before they met and passed each other, the woman and dog suddenly vanished, leaving the man feeling weak and trembling. Lastly, it's intriguing to notice that certain standing stones on the island were whitewashed and called "white ladies" as well.[108]

Most of these "white ladies" seem harmless enough, but this was not the case with the sprite of the Maiden Well in the Ochil Hills in Scotland. This meremaid produces a mist that hangs over the well, in which you will encounter a beautiful woman. Anyone who tries to woo this lovely vision is certain to die.[109]

As may be apparent, there's definitely uncertainty as to whether these beings are ghosts or faery. Their name implies a white apparition of some description, which the association of several of the ladies with the scenes of murders or burials only reinforces, leaving them on the boundary between the classes of supernatural entity. The White Lady of Gunton Hall in Norfolk resembles a banshee (see the next chapter), for she is only heard screaming and lamenting when a death is imminent in the Suffield family. In contrast to these functions, the ladies' active attempts to catch and devour prey suggest a rather more physical nature than the spirit of a deceased person.[110]

Asrai

The last meremaid to mention is perhaps the most intriguing because of her evanescent nature. This is the asrai or ashray of Cheshire and Shropshire (no specific locations seem to be identified). This creature combines many of the features already mentioned; however, she is portrayed as far more vulnerable

---

108. Gill, *Second Manx Scrapbook*, chapter 6, section 2; Gill, *Third Manx* Scrapbook, part 2, chapter 3, section 3.

109. Fraser, "Northern Folklore: Wells and Springs," *Celtic Magazine* 3 (1878): 31.

110. "Gunton Park and House (partly destroyed by fire in 1882)—White Lady," Paranormal Database, accessed May 11, 2020, www.paranormaldatabase.com/m/detail.php ?address=7714.

than those described so far. If she is caught at night in a fisherman's nets, the asrai does not fight back like some of the creatures mentioned. Instead, she pleads for release in an incomprehensible language and, when she is not returned to the water, she curls up moaning at the bottom of her captor's boat and melts away before he returns to land at dawn. Where her hands have touched the fisherman, he's burned and marked for life. Interestingly, in Somerset it's believed that marine mermaids would likewise fade away to a bit of "brackish water and some seaweed" if they were caught.[111]

Other accounts of the asrai depict them as being more like mermaids, with green hair and either a fish tail or webbed feet. They are reputed to live for many hundreds of years, emerging from beneath the lake waters once each century to bathe in the moonlight, which helps them to grow. Very much like a marine mermaid, this version of the asrai will use promises of gold and jewels to lure men into the water, where they will be drowned or, at least, cheated of the promise of riches. The asrai is said not to be able to tolerate human coarseness and vulgarity, and this will be enough to frighten her away. (Some faeries are said to share this sensitivity to bad language.)[112]

Scottish poet Robert Williams Buchanan described the asrai evocatively, if not wholly in line with oral tradition. In his poem "*The Asrai (Prologue to the Changeling)*" he said she grew from the three elements of fire, water, and air and, not being earthly, chose to live in or by rivers, on the seashore and in damp places like caves. In his sequel poem, "*The Changeling,*" Buchanan wrote that "of the dew and the crystal air, / And the moonray mild, were the Asrai / made." Because of the risk of fading away in sunlight, the asrai were forced to retreat "far away in the darkened places, / Deep in the mountains and under the / meres."[113]

The most intriguing aspect of the asrai belief is their combination of predatory danger and vulnerability when caught. Perhaps they're a symbol (and a warning) of the dangers of travelling between elements or dimensions. Humans who visit faeryland can suffer both physically and mentally,

---

111. Briggs, *Dictionary of Fairies*, "Asrai"; Dathen, *Somerset Faeries*, 84.

112. Rosalind Kerven, English *Fairy Tales and Legends* (Swindon: National Trust, 2008), 121–3, 186–7.

113. Robert Buchanan, *Ballads of Life, Love, and Humour* (London: Chatto & Windus, 1862), 131.

and these stories demonstrate that the reverse is just as true. The supernatural stranded in the physical world loses his or her power and is prey to mortality.

Conclusions

The meremaids of inland bodies of water are very different from the marine merfolk. To begin with, they are largely solitary beings. Secondly, their interactions with us are more limited: as a rule, they appear either to try to catch us or to warn us. In this, they are typical of very many of the faery beasts to be examined in the remainder of this book.

Chapter 3

RIVER SPRITES

All bodies of water, fresh or salt, still or moving, are inhabited by faery beings and, as a result, can be perilous places to linger or to play. In the Scottish Highlands, as will be described, the conjunction of fate and liminal states is even more highly developed in the character of the banshee or washerwoman.

Sprites of River & Stream

The risk of capture that exists in the sea and around lakes and ponds exists just as strongly around rivers as well, so that it is possible to distinguish throughout Britain a species of being that we may call river sprites, so as to distinguish them from the meremaids of springs, wells, and pools as well as from the merfolk of the ocean (although, as you will see, the word "mermaid" is often applied for the sake of convenience to beings who aren't mermaids in the normal, everyday sense).

British River Sprite Types

Very typical of these freshwater sprites is "Peg Powler," found at Piercebridge on the River Tees. She will drag incautious children from the banks under the choppy waters of this river. The foam on its surface is called Peg Powler's suds, or cream, depending upon how agitated the river has become. There is, too, Peg o'Nell of the River Ribble in Lancashire—a being who lives in Peggy's Well near the river and emerges to claim a life every seven years—unless a small animal or bird has been sacrificed to her. There is a similar sprite haunting the stepping-stones at Bungerley near Clitheroe, which has been seen in several forms and which, just like Peg o'Nell, takes a life every seven years. The River Gipping in Suffolk, the Derwent in Derbyshire, and the Dart in Devon are all believed to be infested by deadly sprites; the Dart is said to claim a victim annually.

An anomalous creature that lives on the River Trent in the English Midlands deserves a mention here. Between Wildsworth and Owston the river makes a very sharp bend, a place known as "Jean Yonde" or "Jenny Hurn." Here there lives a sprite called Jenny on Boggard. He's described as a tiny man with long hair and a seal's face, who rows from shore to shore in a boat that resembles a piedish, using oars that look like teaspoons. At other times, Jenny is present but is invisible. Instead, boaters have reported feeling his craft bumping against theirs at times when the river appears to be empty. As his name demonstrates, Jenny might be regarded as a type of boggart (see chapter 9), but his close link to the waterway sets him apart from other bogies of that type. Other unnamed bogies also lurk along the Trent, beings who may be detected either by their smell or by their bite—because they appear as midges. Further to the east, in the East Anglian Fens region, another "faery" man is known called the Tiddy Mun. He, too, is closely tied to the waterways, over which he has some kind of control, and might best be thought of as a river sprite.[114]

Along the Welsh Borders, rivers are haunted by Nicky Nicky Nye who, like Jenny Greenteeth, pulls in unwary children; near Wool in Dorset, the Frome is haunted by a "water nymph" who has lured at least one small boy into the river. Many of these sprites are female, it will be observed, just like the meremaids of standing water. This is the case in Scotland too. On the River Conan, a tall woman in green with a withered, scowling face emerges from the water at certain fording places and points and beckons at passing

---

114. Young, "Folklore Pamphlet," 37; for the Tiddy Mun, see my *Faery*, chapters 3 and 11 for more information.

travellers. If they respond, they will be dragged under no matter how strong they are. There is a comparable lady in green and white who has attacked night travellers by the Lynn Burn at Lynturk.[115]

The Scottish ballad "The Mermaid of Galloway" recounts a story very similar to that of *Clerk Colvill* outlined in the last chapter. A "mermaid" sat singing on the banks of the River Nith near Cowhill Tower every new moon night. Her voice was seductive but deadly and she lured to her the young heir of Cowhill. Overwhelmed by the touch of her lips and hands, he fell asleep in her lap—upon which she bound him with her magic before pulling him below the waves of the Nith.[116]

A comparable "mermaid" was known at Dalbeattie Burn who, just like that at Cowhill, would sit on a rock combing her long hair on moonlit nights. As was the case with the marine mermaid at Knockdolion (see chapter 1), a local woman objected to the sprite's presence and had the rock removed; in revenge for which, the creature killed the woman's child. The feud continued in this case, and the bereaved mother went on to have the stream polluted with weeds and soil until the sprite was driven away. Nevertheless, she departed cursing the family to be childless.[117]

Also in Scottish rivers lives the *ceasg*, a creature of great beauty (once you have reconciled yourself to the fact that she is half woman and half salmon). Her hair is described as being "long and flossy," which I take to mean that it is very pale and silky—the name itself signifies a tuft of wool, linen, or silk.[118] There are some stories of men marrying *ceasgs*, and of the maritime skills that their offspring seemed to inherit. Regardless of her physical charms, though, she is highly dangerous—as likely to consume a person as not, although this

115. "The Water Nymph of the River Frome," Dark Dorset, accessed May 11, 2020 www
.darkdorset.co.uk/water_nymph; McPherson, *Primitive Beliefs*, chapter 4; Mackinlay,
Folklore of Scottish Lochs, 161.

116. R. Cromek, *Remains of Nithsdale and Galloway Song: With Historical and Traditional Notices Relative to the Manners and Customs of the Peasantry* (London: T. Cadell and W. Davies, 1810), 232–48.

117. Cromek, *Remains of Nithsdale Song*, 229–232.

118. Watson, "Highland Mythology," *Celtic Review* 5, 67.

maighdean na tuinne (maid of the wave) can grant you three wishes if she's been caught.[119]

From Wales come reports of the creature called the *llamhigyn y dwr*, "the water leaper." This beast is conceived as a giant toad with wings and it lives primarily on sheep that have slipped from the banks. However, it will also break fishing lines and then shriek fearfully, paralysing fishermen with terror so that they can be dragged under the water without a struggle. There is also brief reference to a so-called "torrent spectre" that controls the Welsh mountain streams; this seems to be some form of the *cyhyraeth*, who'll be discussed later. She (or possibly he—the sources differ on gender) is said to collect large rocks as ballast for when she flies above storms; when she returns to the mountain cave where she lives, she drops these boulders and they form the bed of mountain torrents. It has also been claimed that at least one "mermaid" (*morforwyn*) has been seen in the River Conwy at Trefriw, some miles inland from the sea. Whether she's a true mermaid gone astray or a freshwater sprite is unclear.[120]

On the Isle of Man there is a pool along the Ballacoan stream, which is inhabited by a *nyker*, a water faery. A beautiful cow girl was once abducted into the river by this sprite. People heard her calling her cows near the pool, but then a mist descended, a voice was heard replying to her calls—and she was never seen again. Another *nyker*, in the form of a horse or pony, or sometimes a handsome young man, is known to haunt the pond called Nikkesen's Pool in Lonan Parish. In male form, the *nikkesen* sings a beautiful but mournful song in an unknown tongue, with which he tries to tempt girls into the water with him. If a girl enters his pool, her body is never found again; instead, on moonlit nights, he may be seen near the pool dancing in a circle with his victims. As a last remark, it's interesting to note that the word "*nyker*" is a good Old English term for a water faery, which, regrettably, has been entirely

---

119. Watson, "Highland Mythology," *Celtic Review* 5, 67; Mackenzie, *Scottish Folk-lore*, 251; Briggs, *Dictionary of Fairies*, 69.

120. Owen, *Welsh Folk-lore*, 141; Choice Notes—Folklore, 32; Rhys, *Celtic Folklore: Welsh and Manx*, vol. 1, 36.

lost in the modern language—yet it has been preserved on the Celtic island of Man and, I suspect, in Wales, in the form of "Nicky Nicky Nye."[121]

Interactions with Sprites

It was said that a sure way of detecting the presence of river sprites was to look for rings and bubbles on the water surface. Extreme caution would be needed if these telltale signs were seen, for then the risk was great that attempts would be made to snatch women and children away to act as the creatures' servants. Another trick tried from time to time by the sprites was to take on the appearance of domestic implements in the hope that a passerby would pick the item up and so be trapped. In one case, the sprite was disguised as a wooden beetle (a mallet), to which a woman of Teviotdale took a fancy and carried home. During the night, her window sprang open and a voice started to call her name. Fortunately for her, she instinctively blessed herself when she heard the ghostly voice—at which the beetle became animated and flew out of the window. Had she pronounced the blessing over the item when she first picked it up, we are assured by the storyteller that all would have been well.[122]

Given the perilous nature of many river sprites, it's unsurprising to learn that, across Britain, people for centuries have made offerings to appease them. They can dispense great fertility and prosperity upon a neighbourhood and, accordingly, salt was offered to the River Tweed to ensure a good catch of fish each year. On the Scottish island of Unst, people would go to the head of the Yelaburn and throw down three stones to guarantee good health.[123]

If a person drowned in the River Dee in Scotland, the body could be recovered by casting an item of the drowned person's clothing on the water; the next day, the corpse would be found, wrapped in the item offered. On the River Don at Inverurie dropping biscuits on the water was practiced in the same way: wherever the biscuit sank, there the body lay.[124]

121. Morrison, *Manx Fairy Tales*, 83; Gill, *A Manx Scrapbook*, chapter 4; Mona Douglas, *"Restoring to Use our Almost-Forgotten Dances": Writings on the Collection and Revival of Manx Folk Dance and Song* (Isle of Man: Chiollagh Books, 2004), 18.

122. *Folk-lore and Legends: Scotland* (W. W. Gibbings, 1889), 171.

123. Hibbert, *Shetland Isles*, 525.

124. McPherson, *Primitive Beliefs*, 64.

Loireag

The Scottish water sprite called the *loireag* is a strange amalgam of traits. Despite her riverine origin, she is especially known as "patron" of cloth making and is insistent upon the strict maintenance of traditional practices in the craft—a very human and domestic interest. In the past, when all cloth was homemade, women would appease the *loireag* with offerings of milk—in default of which she would suck the goats, sheep, and cows dry—and in this she behaves very much like hobs and similar more domestic faeries whenever they are aggrieved. Generally, the *loireag* is described as small, plaintive, cunning, and stubborn.[125]

The *loireag* shares certain characteristics with other Highland beings, such as the *glaistig* and the *urisk* who will be discussed in chapter 8. They all have connections to human domestic affairs, as well as a taste for milk and cream, which might have justified dealing with them all together later under the heading of "Hobs." At the same time, they all have links to running water, which might have made it appropriate to deal with them all here. As a rule, too, these creatures are female, which might have justified treating them all with the hags. The truth is that, for many of these faery beings, boundary crossing identities are the norm. Exactly the same could be said of the "banshees" that I'm about to describe. They could have been included with the hags, too, but their special association with flowing freshwater persuaded me to deal with them in this chapter.

Washerwomen

Most people have heard of the banshee, the sprite who predicts death within a family by her wailing. There is a special form of this faery being called the *bean-nighe* who's inextricably linked with rivers and fords—so much so, in fact, that it's said in the Hebrides that her feet can look like a duck's, being red and webbed.

---

125. Alexander Carmichael, *Carmina Gadelica: Hymns and Incantations [...]*, vol. 2 (Edinburgh: Oliver and Boyd, 1900), 320.

Bean-nighe

The *bean-nighe*, the washer of death shrouds, is found on the Hebridean Islands. She can be seen after dusk at eerie river pools or fords and sometimes at remote lochs, and she is regarded as a warning to all of some imminent mortality. She will be sighted, at night or early in the morning, washing linen or folding it and beating it on underwater stones. Her washing predicts death, but unlike the banshee, her knowledge of the future is not limited to just one family or clan but to the whole of the community.

The *bean-nighe* can become very absorbed in her work, washing the "death clothes" and singing her dirge, making it possible for daring humans to sneak up upon her. Opinion is divided on her response to humans approaching her in this manner. In some parts of the Scottish Highlands she is regarded as friendly and not inevitably linked to death; others say that hurt always follows the *bean-nighe*, although it may not be her doing, and that merely seeing her may bring illness or prove fatal. The *bean-nighe* can often get agitated if she is seen; in one case, a boy who got too close was violently dipped in the river for his presumption.

In Perthshire it's said that, if you see the *bean-nighe*, you should try to creep up behind her and ask who she's washing for—indeed, to fail to do so might prove fatal. She won't be able to escape until she has answered your questions and, if you get between her and the river, as the price of her release she may grant you three wishes (although it's said that any wealth acquired this way will seldom benefit the recipient). The possibility that the *bean-nighe* can be surprised and made to bestow favours led to the Highland saying that a successful man "has got the better of the *nigheag*." Despite her apparent reluctance to disclose information in many cases, there is an account of her actively pursuing and stopping a young man of Houghgeary, near Uist, so that she might announce his fate to him—which was drowning at half tide at Sgeir Rois before the year was out. Just as she herself can't be avoided, once the events are predicted, the victim will not be able to escape them.[126]

Although the *bean-nighe* is easily recognised by the fact that she's washing, there are other identifying features. Some observers say that she has one

126. Watson, "Highland Mythology," *Celtic Review* 5, 49; MacGregor, *The Peat-Fire Flame*, 297; Campbell, *Superstitions*, 43.

nostril, one large tooth, and a single webbed foot, but she can also shape-shift and appear as a raven or crow. In Perthshire, the *bean-nighe* is described as "small and rotund," dressed in the telltale emerald green of faery, whilst one seen on Eriskay was dressed oddly, if rather prosaically, in a topcoat with a large brooch.[127]

On Skye, the washerwoman is squat like a shrunken, miserable child; if she's met, she'll tell you your fate as long as you answer her questions truthfully. If this *bean-nighe* sees you first, though, she'll render you powerless. On the islands of Mull and Tiree, the *bean* has exaggeratedly pendant breasts, which she throws over her shoulders when she is busy with her washing. If you're able to approach her silently and place one of her nipples in your mouth, you may claim her as your foster-mother, to which she'll reply that you are in need of such assistance and will then be bound to answer any question you might ask her. If the clothes of a foe are being washed, and the enquirer doesn't intervene, that person will be sure to die; if the clothes are those of the witness or a friend's, the *bean-nighe* can be told to stop her work, and this will save the wearer. In Inverness-shire only those "under the shadow of death" are able to see the washerwoman. She is said to be the ghost of a woman who died young in childbirth, leaving behind unwashed clothes. Because of this, she will continue to wash until the date of her natural death has passed.[128]

One encounter with the *bean-nighe* intriguingly created a second portent of death. A man called Hugh, the day before a battle, spotted the *bean* at her washing, crept up and placed her nipple in his mouth, requesting foreknowledge of his fate. He was told what he asked, but in a roundabout way. The *bean* told him that, if his wife served butter with his breakfast the next day, there would be victory. The man's spouse did not do so—as Hugh had anticipated would be the case—and he went into battle prepared for death. His head was severed during the fighting, but this did not kill him: instead, he remounted his horse and has, ever since, acted as a premonition of death for the Maclaine family of Lochbuie.

127. Campbell and Hall, *Strange Things*, 283; MacGregor, *The Peat-Fire Flame*, 297.

128. MacGregor, *The Peat-Fire Flame*, 297; Campbell, *Superstitions of the Highlands*, 43.

There is one story in which a man attempted to escape the fate predicted for him by a *bean-nighe*. A ghillie of the MacDonalds on the Isle of Skye saw the *bean* washing a shroud at Benbecula. He crept up and seized her, demanding his three wishes, which were to know whom she washed for, to marry his heart's desire, and always to have the loch near his home full of seaweed. She told him that the clan chief was doomed to die and that this would mean he would leave Skye forever. Displeased with the answer, the ghillie threw the shroud into the water and stormed off to deliver the bad news to his laird. The MacDonald chief was dismayed, but in response he acted quickly: he killed a calf, made a coracle with its hide, and then left the island forever, paddling out to sea alone. The life of the cow and the flight may have been intended to break the faery's spell, or it may be that the chief simply chose to die on his own terms and alone.[129]

Caointeach

On the islands of Skye, Jura, Tiree, and Islay, and in Argyllshire, the equivalent being to the *bean* is called the *caoineacheag* or *caointeach*—the (little) weeper or "keener." Views as to her role are rather mixed. Some believe that she exclusively forebodes violent death, such as in fighting, whilst others say that she has much more of a role as a banshee for a clan than marking deaths in a wider community. For example, on Kintyre a keener locally called the *cannachan* is the special spirit of the MacMillan family and her appearance will mark a death within that clan. The keener may foretell events generally and is not necessarily indicative of misfortune. She can't be approached and forced to divulge information or to grant wishes, though, unlike the *bean-nighe*.[130]

The keener has been described variously as a small woman in green and wearing a cap, only so big as a child, or a "'little white thing' … white and as soft as wool" who seems to lack a physical body. One woman who touched the *caointeach's* head, under the impression that she was a child in tears, found it to be very soft. Another, who once picked her up, found her to be very light and soft, just like a tuft of wool. The keener tends to emerge at night, meaning that people tend to hear her rather than actually meet her.

129. MacCulloch, *The Misty Isle of Skye*, 243.

130. D. Mackenzie, *Scottish Folk-lore and Folk Life*, 239–40; Watson, "Highland Mythology," *Celtic Review* 5, 50.

Her voice has been described as a mournful wailing, weeping, screams, or even as sounding like falling or flowing water. These last descriptions underline their close association with rivers and pools as well as their role in marking or foretelling tragedy.[131]

She will haunt the vicinity of houses, circling them clockwise, but, just like the *bean-nighe*, she will also be encountered at fords and rivers, beating clothes on a stone. Some think of the *caointeach* as kind and friendly, whilst others believe that they're irritable creatures—for they've even been seen fighting together. This view is supported by the evidence that the keener does not like to be disturbed in her labours and will strike trespassers on their legs with the shroud she's busy washing—a blow that can sever their legs. Another man who accidentally stepped on the stone in the river on which she did her washing had his neck twisted in revenge; he had to beg the *caointeach* to put it right and had then to promise not to repeat his trespass again. In another case, a slap from her caused paralysis.[132]

Just like any other faery associated with human dwellings, the offer of clothing can repel the *caointeach*. In one case, she was bewailing a death outside a house where a wake was being held; one of the mourners took pity on her, sitting outside in the cold and wet, and well-meaningly suggested that she should move to the sheltered side of the house and put on a proffered plaid. The *caointeach* left and was never seen again by the family.[133]

Gwrach y Rhybin

The Welsh form of this sprite is the *gwrach y rhybin*, who is regarded as a portent of disaster and death. The Welsh name itself isn't fully translatable, although the first element means a witch. She is hideous to see, with a long nose curving down to her chin and just two or three long, sharp black teeth, unkempt red hair, a very pale face, long, thin arms, and leathery wings. The *gwrach y rhybin* comes at night, flapping outside windows and calling out the name of the person destined to die. She may also be seen in the mist on

---

131. R. C. MacLagan, "'The Keener' in the Scottish Highlands and Islands," *Folklore* 25, 84.

132. Lewis Spence, *The Fairy Tradition in Britain* (London: Rider & Co., 1948), 54; MacLagan, "'The Keener' in the Scottish," *Folklore* 25, 86.

133. MacDougall, *Folk Tales and Fairy Lore,* 215.

mountains, at crossroads, or by a lake or watercourse, splashing her hands. Any person who sees her in these circumstances is fated.[134]

The *gwrach y rhybin* is normally a woman, calling for her husband or child, but she can sometimes appear in male form mourning the imminent death of a wife. If the sound she makes is inarticulate, it will signify that the hearer is the one fated to die. Lastly, Welsh folklore also identified *yr hen wrach*, "the old hag," who seems to have been the spirit of the sickness ague.[135]

Manx Washerwomen

The Manx islanders identified their own faery washerwomen too. These beings were conceived as a kind of *liannan-shee* (a vampiric faery lover) who would be seen washing clothes in streams, always dressed in red. She would beat the clothes with a stick or on the river rocks, sometimes using one hand only whilst in the other she held a candle; on other occasions, the candle might be seen stuck into the earth of the riverbank. The appearance of the little red washerwoman was a sign of things to come but, unlike the other examples so far examined, in this case she presaged no more than very bad weather.[136]

Conclusions

Some river spirits are actively antagonistic to humankind; others may foresee their deaths but will not actually precipitate them. Seeing the *bean-nighe* can be advantageous for you if you have the courage to seize the opportunity and approach her, but the risk is that you may learn things you did not want to hear.

---

134. Rhys, *Celtic Folklore: Welsh and Manx*, vol. 2, 453.
135. Wirt Sikes, *British Goblins* (London: Sampson Low, Marston, Searle, & Rivington, 1880), 216–218; Rhys, *Celtic Folklore: Welsh and Manx*, vol. 2, 452.
136. Gill, *A Third Manx Scrapbook*, chapter 2.

Chapter 4

KELPIES

Kelpies are Scottish faery beasts of the freshwater. They live in deep pools in rivers and streams—but not in the still water of lochs or pools or in the sea like the water horses described in the next two chapters. Despite this clear distinction, there is sometimes confusion between the different classes of faery beast in some of the sources, and the term "kelpie" may be loosely applied to all such water horses. Check the source you're reading: if it doesn't live in flowing water, it isn't a kelpie.

Kelpie Characteristics

Kelpies are humanlike, but they often appear in equine form so that they can carry the unwitting to their deaths. In this, again, they contrast with water horses and bulls, which are, in their natural state, four-legged but which can adopt human form for the purposes of finding prey.[137]

Kelpies can assume a range of other guises so as to entrap unwary humans. They can appear as large mastiffs, baying in a horrifying manner reminiscent

---

137. Walter Gregor, *Notes on the Folk-lore of the North-East of Scotland* (London: Folk-lore Society, 1881), chapter 12; "A Sketch of Scottish Diablerie in General," *Fraser's Magazine* 25 (1842): 326.

of human laughter. The one inhabiting the river at Rumbling Bridge in Perth-shire produced light and noise so as to lure people towards the water; at Leur-bost in the Hebrides, the kelpie looked like a huge eel—one day in March 1856 it emerged from the loch and ate a blanket that had been left lying on the shore.[138]

Often there is something about a kelpie-horse that will betray its nature. Many a traveller would have been spared death if they had paused to wonder why they had found such a fine horse wandering stray or if they had exam-ined it closely—sparks often issue from kelpies' nostrils or they may have snakes for a mane.[139]

Kelpies will often be heard laughing, yelling, and calling at night in re-mote Highland glens. Sometimes they will beat the surface of the water with their tails, producing a sound that has been likened to thunder. Alarming as a kelpie's cries may be, their songs are far more distressing.

When a kelpie sings, it means one of two things: either that it is hunt-ing humans or, worse still, that it has caught one. It will sing to celebrate the moment when a person has mounted it and is already doomed and unable to escape. One song had these words:

> "And ride weil, Davie
> And by this night at ten o'clock,
> Ye'll be in Pot Cravie."

Another, recorded at Cairney in 1884, went as follows:

> "Sit well, Janety, or ride well Davie
> For this time morn, ye'll be in Pot Cravie."[140]

Pot Cravie is the anglicised version of the Gaelic Poll na Craobhan, a deep pool on the River Spey. The song celebrates that the victim will be plunged

---

138. Nicholson, *Golspie: Contributions to Its*, 22; Constance F. Gordon Cumming, *In the Heb-rides* (London: Chatto and Windus, Piccadilly, 1883), 172.

139. Cyril H. Dieckhoff, "Mythological Beings in Gaelic Folklore," *Transactions of the Gaelic Society of Inverness* 29 (1918): 241; McPherson, *Primitive Beliefs*, 63.

140. Gordon Cumming, *In the Hebrides*, 172; MacDougall, *Folk Tales and Fairy Lore*, 309.

into the kelpie's lair and won't be returning. The beautiful black horse who lingered here was notorious for the way it entrapped its prey. It would first be seen grazing in a silver harness in a meadow with other horses. Anyone who approached, thinking to ride the horse, would be frozen on the spot by a glance from the kelpie's fearsome eyes; the dangerous power of the faery stare has long been known. Then, however, the horse would approach, mildly and placidly, allaying any fears and allowing the prospective rider to mount.[141]

The Kelpie's Nature

It seems that kelpies have an innately malevolent and bloodthirsty nature. They are said to be "always malignant," taking delight in raising floods that overwhelm unwary travellers; their least dangerous exploits are annoying millers by stopping mills' water wheels turning.

Besides the deaths they can cause, kelpies can compound the losses they inflict by cruelly misleading potential rescuers. The kelpie of Waterstone, for instance, would deliberately call from the wrong direction to lead people away from the site of a drowning. Their least malign habit was the stealing of oatcakes from cottagers' hearths, but even these pranks could get so wearisome that people would move home to escape them.[142]

These water beasts aren't invariably evil, though. Kelpies will reward a person who has done them some sort of favour or kindness. A kelpie in human form wanted to cross the River Dee at Inchbare one stormy night. The boatman agreed to take him across—and charged no fee for this. As his passenger departed, a song was heard:

"The Dee shall be quiet and merciful ever
While you and your sons have a boat on the river."[143]

141. MacDougall, *Folk Tales and Fairy Lore*, 309.

142. John Milne, *Myths and Superstitions of the Buchan District* (R. Jack, 1891), 19.

143. McPherson, *Primitive Beliefs*, chapter 4; "Fairies in the Highlands," *Celtic Magazine* 4 (1879): 13.

There is also another Highland story in which a man's wife is abducted "under the hill" by some faeries. Other faeries show him how to recover her, and a kelpie carries him to the distant faery palace where she is held captive.[144]

The Kelpie's Lair

Kelpies are widespread in the north of Scotland, and stones which bear their hoof marks are quite common; at Morphie in Kincardineshire a famous stone carries the fingerprints of the notorious kelpie. They are freshwater beasts, and they will haunt fords and riverbanks, awaiting human prey.[145]

Plainly, bathing in any river is potentially perilous, especially in any deep pools along its course. In fact, any activity that involves being too close to the water's edge can be dangerous—as with two anglers who vanished from the shores of Loch Borrolan, leaving behind only their gear and some large hoof-prints in the sand. Fording rivers, not least those in flood, is a particularly risky matter.

The kelpie's commonest trick is to await solitary travellers in the form of an attractive horse. A person travelling on foot late in the day or at night would arrive at the impassable crossing but see a horse fortuitously grazing nearby, already saddled. The need to continue the journey would be so great that they would succumb and mount the strange animal, which would then carry them as far as the midpoint of the ford and tip them in to drown at the deepest place.

Most kelpies assume the form of a pretty pony (as at Loch Venachar) or of a striking black horse with staring eyes, and in these guises, they will try to tempt children in particular into mounting them. It's important to appreciate that kelpies can only take those who interfere with them or who allow them to do so, hence the subterfuges used to woo and to catch the unwary. A golden horse came out of the Waters of Fleet, near Golspie, and tried to lure a woman away by getting her to follow and drive it. Luckily, she realised what she was dealing with and escaped certain death.[146]

---

144. "Fairies in the Highlands," *Celtic Magazine* 4 (1879): 13.

145. Archibald Watt, *Highways and Byways Round Kincardine* (Aberdeen, 1985), 462–4.

146. Donald Mackenzie, *Tales from the Moors and the Mountains* (London: Blackie and Son, 1931), 117; William Grant Stewart, 'Part IV,' in *The Popular Superstitions and Festive Amusements of the Highlanders of Scotland* (London: Aylott and Jones, 1823), 99–107.

To touch a kelpie in horse form with your hand is fatal. It will stick to the creature's hide and you will then be unable to dismount before it plunges into the water. Frequently in the stories all that attests to the fate of the luckless rider is the heart, lungs, and *sgamhan* (entrails) which will float ashore a little later.[147]

River crossings should always be approached with caution, and it's wise, too, not to accept offers of help from strangers. The bridge was down over the River Don at a crossing called the Bridge of Luib. A farmer needed to cross and, as he stood there, he was approached by a tall man who offered to carry him. The farmer agreed reluctantly, but his need was great, and he climbed on the other's shoulders. Halfway across, the stranger turned into a kelpie and a fierce struggle took place. The farmer escaped with his life, but a boulder was hurled after him which is still known as the Kelpie's Stone and can be seen at Corgarff.[148]

So notorious were certain kelpies that traditions arose about the rivers they infested. The Dee, for example, was said to demand three lives a year; the River Spey was said to take one. The drownings in the Spey were ascribed to the white horse that lived beneath its ripples. This kelpie would surface on stormy nights, whinnying, and would walk patiently beside benighted travellers until they mounted it—and were then carried at high speed into the river's depths.[149]

Kelpie Prophecy

Kelpies have some power of foreseeing the future, as is suggested by the story of the old man sewing beside the Burn of Strichen. A man seeking to traverse the Burn of Strichen heard a voice and saw an old man sitting nearby, mending a pair of trousers. This seemed like an innocent scene, but the traveller obviously suspected a trap and eavesdropped on the old man. As he sewed, he muttered to himself, "This one will die here and this one will die there." The traveller realised what he was confronted by and with a cry of "And this one will die here!" he struck the old tailor, who vanished. In an instant, a kelpie

---

147. Sutherland, *Folk-lore Gleanings,* 98.

148. McPherson, *Primitive Beliefs,* chapter 4.

149. MacGregor, *The Peat-Fire Flame,* 68.

appeared, neighing fiercely, in a deep pool in the stream—thereby proving the traveller's instincts to have been correct.[150]

Another example comes from the River Conan where, one harvest, some men engaged in cutting the grain saw a kelpie rise up at a "false ford" in the river (a place which looked safe to cross but was surrounded by deep pools) and cry out "The hour but not the man has come." The creature then disappeared "like a drake" and, before the reapers had much time to contemplate the meaning, a rider in great haste came galloping down the lane towards the ford. The men in the field tried to persuade him to wait until "the hour" had passed, but he was in a hurry; eventually, they confined him against his will in the nearby church. When, after a suitable length of time had passed, the harvesters went to free the rider, they found he had collapsed and drowned in the water trough inside the church, so that the kelpie had taken its prey in spite of their best efforts.[151]

Kelpies in Human Form

Kelpies might take male form and try to seduce girls, but there is always something to give their monstrous identity away, whether it is grey hair on their chests, hooved feet, or sand or rushes in their hair. When in the form of a man the kelpie is said often to be ugly, unkempt, cross, and ill-tempered, delighting in trouble.[152]

In one story, the kelpie takes little trouble to disguise the carnal nature of his designs upon the female but is outwitted. A woman travelling alone found herself lost at night and had to make do with a deserted building as shelter. Soon after she had stopped, a dog appeared and settled down with her. Then a kelpie arrived and told her to make up a bed, as he would lie with her that night. The dog told her how to respond, and she replied that she had no bedding. The kelpie disappeared but soon came back with a load of straw to lie upon—and repeated his intention. This second time the dog advised the woman to ask for a drink of water, and she gave the kelpie a cracked dish, which he took to the nearest stream. Unable to fill it, he returned, and she

---

150. MacPherson, *Primitive Beliefs,* chapter 4.

151. Douglas, *Scottish Fairy and Folk Tales,* 182.

152. McPherson, *Primitive Beliefs,* 63

advised him to try sealing the break with moss. This still wasn't sufficient, and the water all seeped away before he reached the door. The kelpie went backwards and forwards all night, until eventually dawn came and the woman knew she was safe. As with all faery beings, kelpies are most dangerous at night.[153]

The kelpies of Selkirkshire in Scotland seem to prefer to appear as human males, we are told. They would stand on the edge of a cliff over the water and try to attract a person to them. Once the victim was near enough, they would be seized, and the pair would plunge together into the water below. The kelpie's other habit was to leap on the backs of humans and to ride them like horses until they died of exhaustion. This is a complete reversal of the habit of taking horse form and allowing victims to mount them, but it is not entirely isolated. For instance, it is reported that the Isle of Man faeries would also ride human victims at night.[154]

Sometimes it appears that the kelpie may assume human form just for pleasure and to test his strength against another human. In the story of "The Two Shepherds," which is set near Lochaber, it is known that the river between their two farms is dangerous at night. One shepherd visits his neighbour during the evening and stays until after dark, when he is escorted home by his friend's son. Returning to his own cottage, the son feels his bonnet being snatched from his head as he crosses the river. When he turns to retrieve it, he finds a huge man holding the hat. They fight and the boy soon finds himself being dragged towards a nearby loch. He grabs an oak tree as they pass and clings tight to this; even so, the kelpie's strength is so great that the tree roots start to rip from the earth. It is only with the arrival of the dawn that the young man is safe. Perhaps because he was bested and cheated of his prize, this kelpie was never seen again.[155]

The main reason for kelpies appearing as men is to seduce women and, unlikely as it may sound, there is even a tradition of marriages with kelpies.

---

153. Alexander Stewart, 'Twixt Ben Nevis and Glencoe: The Natural History, Legends, and Folklore of the West Highlands (Edinburgh: W. Paterson, 1885), 39; Walter Gregor, "Kelpie stories from the North of Scotland," Folk-Lore Journal 1 (1883): 294.

154. Blind, "New Finds in Shetlandic," Gentleman's Magazine, no. 252 (January–June 1882): 371; on faeries riding humans, see my Faery, 78.

155. Douglas, Scottish Fairy and Folk Tales, 200.

One branch of the Munroe clan was reputed to have married the kelpie of Beann na Caltuin and, for several generations thereafter, the descendants of the union had manes and tails. According to another account, the kelpie father refused to help the mother look after their part-human son, but he did agree to provide her with a daily supply of trout. The boy grew up to be called *Dubh Sith*, the faery man, or *Sitheach*, the dwarf. Despite his diminutive size, he was famed as a great warrior.[156]

Taming Kelpies

I mentioned earlier that kelpies will often appear to hapless travellers, saddled and bridled and ready to be ridden. The harness is used by the kelpie to look more inviting to the weary walker—it appears to be a tamed horse that has been lost or has strayed, but evidently, it's one that's safe to ride. Even though this bridle is worn to trap victims, it can also be the kelpie's downfall, as it makes it vulnerable to being tamed by humans. Using either the kelpie's bridle, or one specially prepared, it is possible for the brave and enterprising to catch and subdue these ferocious beasts.

Using the Kelpie's Bridle

The black kelpie of Poll na Craobhan on the Spey was tamed by a man nicknamed Little John one Beltane's eve. He crept up on it disguised under an ox skin. He snatched away the horse's bridle and grabbed the beast by its forelock, forcing it to obey his every command. John hid the kelpie's bridle and only harnessed it with his own equipment. The kelpie proved to be a valuable horse: it worked very hard whilst consuming very little food, and it made Little John rich. Unfortunately, one day his daughter Sheena decided to go out riding the horse. She found the kelpie's original bridle hidden in the stable and unwittingly put it on the beast, thereby restoring its kelpie power. The result was that it plunged headlong into the river with Sheena on its back and neither was ever seen again.[157]

---

156. J. F. Campbell, *Popular Tales of the West Highlands: Orally Collected with a Translation by the late J. F. Campbell,* vol. 2 (Paisley and London, Alexander Gardner), 205; "The Fairy Man, or The Clan Donald's Last Struggle," *Celtic Monthly* 10 (1885): 211.
157. MacDougall, *Folk Tales and Fairy Lore,* 309.

Now and then, a kelpie may lose its bridle, a misadventure that leaves it in a weak and vulnerable position. A story is told of a Highland farmer who found a harness on his land and hung it in his stable. The next day a fine horse was waiting outside his farm and, as it seemed to be stray, he decided to use it until someone came along to claim ownership. The animal was hitched to a plough and proved very strong and fast in its work. The man was so pleased with his find that he decided the next day to ride the horse to market. He saddled it up, using the bridle he had found, and then set off. He was, of course, never seen again: once the kelpie had its own bridle back, the man was in its power.[158]

Using a Blessed Bridle

Kelpies in their animal form can be caught, tamed, and made to work in a plough like any farm horse provided that a blessed bridle is used—that is, one with crosses cut into the cheek pieces. If you are able to get the bridle on in the first place, you can keep and work the kelpie as long as you wish thenceforth.

A man saw a large black horse grazing the banks of the River Ugie near Peterhead. He managed to bridle it and then employed the beast in hauling the stones to build a bridge at Inverugie. When the kelpie was at last released, it sang out in complaint at its sore back and bones. This protest may not be so surprising, as the very same kelpie seems to also have been caught and put to farm work at Ugie, and the farmer had worked it until it was lean and weak. When he was away one day, his wife decided to remove the bridle so that the horse could graze more easily in a field. Forthwith it galloped off crying:

> "Harrow, harrow wi' fa [with what] ye like,
> Ye's harrow ne mair with me ye tyke [dog, boor]."[159]

There are similar accounts of kelpies being forced to work in the construction of water mills at Magie on the River Deveron, at Berryleys, and at Fintray, and it is reported that the bridge over the Esk at Shielhall was

---

158. Mackenzie, *Tales from the Moors and the Mountains*, 118.
159. McPherson, *Primitive Beliefs*, 66.

constructed with similar forced labour. Forcing a kelpie to work is not without its dangers, nevertheless. One of the Grahams of Morphie caught and bridled one that lived in a pool in the North Esk River near Forfar and used it to draw the stones for his new castle. However, one day someone took pity on the hard-worked steed and made the mistake of taking the bridle off before feeding it. The creature promptly escaped through the wall of the stable (although no mark was left behind), but not before it had pronounced a curse on the castle, to last as long as the water horse lived. The misfortune wished on the place came about and it was, in time, deserted and demolished.[160]

Submissive Kelpies

Kelpies can be forced to work for humans, but they very occasionally might choose for some reason to assist a person. At Corgarff a man had taken his grain to be ground at the local mill of Garchorry. When this was done and the meal was in sacks and ready to be carried home, he found that his horse had slipped free of its tether and bolted whilst he was inside the mill. He cursed and wished to himself that he had a replacement horse, even if it was a kelpie. Suddenly, a horse appeared wearing a halter. He gratefully loaded the sacks on its back and led it home. He tied the strange horse to a harrow whilst he carried the flour into his granary, but when he went outside again, he found both horse—and harrow—had disappeared. Just then, he heard a great splash from a nearby pool on the River Don. He ought not to have been surprised by any of this. The faeries are renowned for listening in to our idle talk and for answering our wishes and, when he was so fortuitously approached by a horse in his hour of need, he should have been suspicious. It appears that, in this case, the kelpie was prepared to tolerate being hitched and driven, just for the hope that it might then be able to cause some nuisance, or even carry off a victim.[161]

---

160. Nicholson, *Golspie*, 22; McPherson, *Primitive Beliefs*, 66; Chambers, *Popular Rhymes of Scotland*, 334; see generally Gregor, *Notes on the Folk-lore*, chapter 12; Grant Stewart, *The Popular Superstitions*, part 4.

161. McPherson, *Primitive Beliefs*, 65.

Beating Kelpies

Kelpies have various weaknesses. The first is that they cannot attack a human unless they are first approached or interfered with by that person. This is why they have to lure prospective victims into petting or mounting them. Secondly, as I've described, their bridle is the source of their power so that possession of it gives possession of the beast. In its human form, the kelpie may wear a cap which has the same properties. Thirdly, they are neither invulnerable nor indestructible. They are mortal, and they can be killed. Moreover, despite being magical beings, they can be subdued by other supernatural powers: for example, the story is told of a farmer from Glen Fillan who unwittingly hired a giant boy to work on his farm. Given his nature, he had an appetite to match and began to eat the farmer out of house and home. Various plans were hatched to get rid of the giant, one of which was asking him to catch and harness the local kelpie. There was a struggle, but such was the young giant's strength that he subdued the kelpie and set it to work.[162]

A kelpie can be killed with hot iron. The creatures have a habit of frequenting certain farms and alarming the inhabitants and, in one such case, the farmer resolved to take steps to stop his family being terrorised. He heated two spits and waited until the kelpie appeared and then plunged both into the beast's side. It died instantly and dissolved into a heap of powder.[163]

Kelpies can, surprisingly, also be drowned. There was one at Braemar who took a fancy to a human woman and wooed her by various means, including keeping her well supplied with oatmeal. He used to get this by stealing it from the mill of Quoich. One day the miller spotted the kelpie carrying off a sack of meal, and he hurled at him a stone object called a "faery whorl" which was used to stop the mill wheel turning at night, and so prevent the faeries using it. The whorl broke the kelpie's leg, and he fell into the mill leet and drowned. Other equally prosaic fates include two kelpies mauled to death by dogs and one driven off by a hail of well-aimed stones. A miller who was plagued by a kelpie entering his mill after dark and upsetting the grain and meal left his boar-pig in the mill one night; the boar fought and beat the kelpie, which

---

162. Mackenzie, *Tales from the Moors*, 117–124.

163. Gregor, *Notes on the Folk-lore*, 66.

never troubled the miller again. For such a fearsome monster, they seem surprisingly straightforward and easy to defeat.[164]

Conclusions

It is tempting for some people to "explain" kelpies and the similar water horses and water bulls as nothing but the personification of the dangers of bodies of water and riverbanks. This is neat, but it is too facile. If all these stories were was warnings to children about the dangers of weedy pools and to late night travellers about the perils of stumbling home drunk from the tavern, they would limit themselves to such incidents, and the kelpies would clearly be the "nursery demons" to which some bogies have been reduced (see chapter 9).

There is more to kelpies than this, though. They spend most of their time out of the water, on dry land working and plotting to trick or seduce human beings. They are not bare symbols of danger; there is intelligence. Kelpies are clever and calculating, which is why those interested in exploring faery mysteries need to be on their guard for them.

---

164. McPherson, *Primitive Beliefs*, 63; Dempster, "The Folklore of Sutherland-shire," 223, 224, 229; Gregor, "Kelpie Stories," 293.

Chapter 5

WATER HORSES AND BULLS

Whilst kelpies are humanlike beings who may adopt horse form, water horses and bulls are almost always to be seen as beasts. Secondly, whereas kelpies live in the running freshwater of rivers and streams, water horses and bulls inhabit the still water of lochs and pools or the sea.

As I shall describe, there are various signs by which they may be distinguished from normal livestock; it's also important to point out the difference between these "water beasts" and other faery cattle. The faeries (and the merfolk) keep their own herds of cattle, presumably for their dairy produce. Although they may have distinctive markings, such as a white hide and red ears, and be unusually fertile or productive, faery cattle are otherwise largely undistinguishable, in either looks or manner, from the normal cattle on human farms. This faery livestock can blend with a herd and not be noticed. Water bulls and water horses, in contrast, can be solitary and very violent beasts.

How to Spot a Water Beast

The faery water beasts can be distinguished from normal livestock by the fact that they are generally noticeably larger, fatter, and sleeker. They have fiercer tempers, and they are stronger and livelier than normal livestock. Their neighs and bellows are extremely loud. Like cattle from the faery herds, water horses, cows, and bulls are known to crossbreed with ordinary herds and produce very good stock for the lucky farmer. The resulting crossbred foals show the marks of their faery parent, being known, for example, for their hanging ears, flashing eyes, red nostrils, fiery spirits, and spread black hooves. Hybrids with water bulls are identified by their cropped or slit ears and are called *corky fyre* by the inhabitants of the Scottish Western Isles.[165]

These creatures live in lonely freshwater lakes and tarns and in sea lochs. Their presence may be detected by waves on the surface of the water on a still and windless day. At Loch na Beiste near Gairloch an attempt was made to drain the loch so as to rid it of its evil inhabitant; the water level was lowered sufficiently to uncover something looking like the upturned keel of a boat, at which point the workmen abandoned their efforts. A very similar creature called Mourie was seen in nearby Loch Maree—to which bulls were sacrificed on August 25 each year. Another unusual sighting involved a mysterious grey horse spotted by a herder amongst his horses pasturing by a remote loch. He didn't recognise the animal and, when he looked at it more closely, he saw instead an old man with long grey hair and beard. At that instant, the herder's horse took fright, bolted, and galloped for miles. Quite often, in fact, it is the reaction of other horses that betrays the real nature of a water horse. For example, a man on Eriskay in about 1892 was out one night to look after one of his mares that had just given birth to a foal. He saw a horse in the distance which he thought might be his, but a terrible scream and the bolting of two of his neighbours' horses, which had been grazing nearby, persuaded him to give up on his errand and run all the way home.[166]

---

165. Stewart, *'Twixt Ben Nevis*, 39; Martin, *Western Islands of Scotland*, 157.

166. Mackinlay, *Folklore of Scottish Lochs*, 171–72; Dixon, *Gairloch in North-West Ross-shire*, 162; Gregor, *Notes on the Folk-lore*, 67; Campbell and Hall, *Strange Things*, 300.

Water Bulls

The water bull, *an tarbh uisge* in Scottish Gaelic, is a mild beast and friendly to humans. It looks very much like a normal bull but dwells in lakes and, out of the water, can be identified by the volume of its call. Particularly famous bulls live in Loch Awe and Loch Rannoch; Loch Leethie is known for its bull, which roars thunderously at night—especially during frosty weather.[167]

Temperament & Habits

The *tarbh uisge* is not normally seen as dangerous (especially when compared to its equine equivalent) and is seen as being a benefit to a farm. It lives in lonely tarns and only appears at night, when it might be seen grazing with the herds of cattle. Normal bulls predictably object to these trespassers amongst their cows, but the *tarbh uisge* is powerful and determined and will always see off its rival in such contests, then enjoying the herd alone. Water bulls have no (or very short) ears, and when they mate with conventional cows, their offspring are also distinctively short-eared, the ears looking as though they have been cut off with a knife. The calves are also notable for their highly spirited tempers. Living in Loch Garten in the Highlands there was reportedly a cross between a horse and a black bull that was of immense strength. The water bulls themselves are variously described as being small and ugly with deep black curly hair or else the size of a stirk (a year-old bullock), with rough, blue-grey fur. Their hides are soft and slippery to the touch, and their lowing is said to sound like a cock crowing.[168]

Despite their generally solitary and retiring nature, water bulls will sometimes defend humans against those who intend to harm them—which can include water horses, as will be examined later in this chapter. In a story from Argyll, for instance, a rejected suitor tried to abduct a young woman and rape her, but a *tarbh uisge* appeared, crushed the man to death, and then carried the woman safely back to her home.[169]

---

167. Sutherland, *Folk-lore Gleanings*, 98.
168. MacGregor, *The Peat-Fire Flame*, 79, 81; Sutherland, *Folk-lore Gleanings*, 98; Campbell, *Superstitions*, 216; Campbell, *Popular Tales*, vol. 4, 300.
169. G. Henderson, *Survivals of Belief Amongst the Celts* (London: Macmillan, 1861), 139; Campbell, *Superstitions of the Highlands*, vol. 4, 304.

Powers

Given their faery nature, it is hardly surprising to discover that the *tarbh uisge* may have supernatural powers of hearing and that it can appear at will. For example, some men were sheltering from a storm one night in a hut near Borerary on the island of St. Kilda. They were cold and hungry, and one wished he had a fat ox. Instantly, they heard a huge bull outside, but were too scared to look out. The next morning, there were numerous tracks of its hooves around the hut. Stormy weather is closely linked to the raging of these creatures: at Great Chart in Kent a bull appeared inside the church during a thunderstorm during the 1600s. It stampeded up and down, killing and injuring members of the congregation, before escaping through a wall, which it partly demolished.[170]

Manx Bulls

The water bull is best known in Scotland, but there are other examples around the British Isles. There seem to be few instances of faery bulls in Wales, other than a fire-breathing specimen that lived in the waters of Llyn Cowlyd in Snowdonia; on the Isle of Man, however, this being is very widely found, there being called the *tarroo ushtey*.[171]

One example of the *tarroo* was spotted as recently as 1859, in the vicinity of Ballure Glen—people travelled from all over the island to be able to see it. This *tarroo* was said to be small and dark, but not very different in appearance from a normal bull. One witness has compared it to a bear; others say that whilst it is normally black, the *tarroo* can change its colour to blend in with a herd in a field. As a species, the *tarroo* lives in river pools and bogs, primarily, although one was seen on a pebble bank on the beach at Port Cornaa, and they tend to avoid humans as much as possible.[172]

---

170. *The Wonders of this Windie Winter. By Terrible Stormes and Tempests, [...]* (London: G. Eld, 1613), C2v.

171. See for example, Ian, "Llyn Cowlyd," Mysterious Britain & Ireland: Mysteries, Legends & The Paranormal, November 7, 2012, http://www.mysteriousbritain.co.uk/folklore /llyn-cowlyd/.

172. Henry Irwin Jenkinson, *Jenkinson's Practical Guide to the Isle of Man* (London: Edward Stanford, 1874), 151–2; Moore, *The Folk-lore of the,* chapter 4; Gill, *A Third Manx Scrapbook,* chapter 3, section 6; Douglas, "*Restoring to Use,*" 19.

On Man, it's believed that the water bulls were dangerous to other cat-tle—not deliberately by devouring livestock but because of their interest in the cows. Especially around May Day, they are prone to get in amongst the farmers' herds and will lure cows away to the lochs (and, occasionally, unac-companied children are also vulnerable to taking). Alternatively, the water bulls will mate with the cows, and the results of the *tarroo* interbreeding with regular cattle are undesirable (unlike in Scotland) as the cows will either abort or will give birth to calves that are misshapen monsters, comprising skin and flesh without bones. Admittedly, the *tarroo* will sometimes mutilate or kill bullocks in herds when competing over mates, but they are too quick and nimble for farmers to ever catch them and prevent the depredations.[173]

The best protection for herds from the attentions of the *tarroo* is to make crosses of rowan and tie them to the cattle's tails. In one Manx story, a farmer found a *tarroo* amongst his herd and unwisely struck it with his stick, caus-ing the bull to bolt and plunge wildly into the sea. This brought a blight on the man's grain crops, but he did not learn his lesson. When he found the bull grazing with his herd a second time, he tried to catch it, but the *tar-roo* escaped. A blight fell on his potatoes. Although he was advised to show greater respect for supernatural livestock, the man was not to be lectured, and the next time he was ready: using a rowan stick, he drove the bull into a shed and penned it. On the next market day, the bull was driven into town with the rowan stick, but most people realised what it was and made no offers of purchase. Late in the day a man expressed interest, but only if the farmer rode the beast, as he boasted he easily could—because it was so doc-ile and obedient. The foolhardy farmer climbed onto its back and, at first, all went well—until the rowan wand fell from his grasp—at which point the *tarroo* galloped off into the sea with the farmer clinging on. He survived this ordeal—but was much chastened.[174]

The Manx bulls are often heard bellowing at night, so loudly that the ground will tremble and people living nearby will be disturbed from their sleep. Certain locations are avoided during the hours of darkness as a result, because the bulls will emerge from their rivers and play in meadows. At

---

173. Leney, *Shadowland in Ellan Vannin* (London: E. Stock, 1880), 139; Train, *Isle of Man,* vol. 2, chapter 18.

174. Briggs, *Dictionary of Fairies,* "Tarroo-Ushtey."

Granane in the parish of Lonan a *tarroo ushtey* was once in the habit of coming out of the river and roaring around a house there, apparently trying to get
in. The inhabitants had to bar the doors and were awoken every night by the
noise and by their own fear. They eventually were driven away from the place.
In another example of the fear the bulls could instill, two boys who'd been out
stealing apples at Cronk Leannag were on their way home when they came
face-to-face with a huge bull with blazing eyes the size of cups. It charged
them and they fled, after which it plunged into a swamp and was gone. Drainage on the islands has diminished the number of water bulls that are sighted
today, as many of the marshes they once infested have disappeared.[175]

Remedies

As we've just seen, people would often rather move house away from a nuisance water bull than try to take measures against it. Nevertheless, they can
sometimes become such a menace that something drastic has to be done.
The problem, then, is that they're fairly indestructible.

The Scottish water bulls are said to be invulnerable, except to silver shot.
A report is given of one Highland farmer who had lost some sheep to a bull
and was determined to get revenge. The bull had been seen on the local loch,
going up and down and "as big as a house." The man had first tried to catch
it with a hook baited with a dog, but the bull had broken free—although the
loch had been seen to be filled with blood afterwards. Water bulls have also
sometimes been caught with sheep tied to oak trunks, but they can break
free of these too. In this case, the farmer then loaded his shotgun with sixpences and lay in wait—as did his sons, armed only with dung forks.[176]

Despite the general difficulties of killing bulls, there is a report from the
island of St. Kilda of a man who slew one with a bow and arrow. The Manx
form of the beast seems just as strong and insuperable. At Granane, just mentioned, the residents tried to solve the problem of the *tarroo* by bringing their
own large bull onto the farm. It fought the water bull and was gored to death.

---

175. *Yn Lioar Manninagh*, vol. IV (1901-1905), I; John Rhys, *Manx Folklore and Superstitions*,
ed. Stephen Miller (Isle of Man: Chiollagh Books, 1994), part 1; Gill, *A Second Manx
Scrapbook*, chapter 6.

176. John MacCulloch, *The Highlands and Western Isles of Scotland [...]*, vol. 4 (London: Longman, Hurst, Rees, Orme, Brown, and Green, 1824), 330.

Another report suggested that, whilst sticks and pitchforks were no match for the water bull, a shotgun or rifle would be effective. Such extreme force didn't always seem to be needed, though. There was once a *tarroo ushtey* that lived in a pool where the promenade at Ramsey now runs; it threatened a local man, and he raised his stick as if to strike it, but then pulled his blow. This was found to render the beast powerless.[177]

Water Horses

Water horses, also called in Gaelic *each uisge*, are Scottish faery beasts that live in freshwater lakes or in the sea (but not in flowing water, which is the home of the kelpie). There's even a well, the *Fuaran na Lair Bann*, "The White Mare's Well," at Balmore near Inverness, that has a resident *each uisge*.[178]

Although water horses are reported at numerous lochs and lochans, including Loch Arkaig, Loch Sunart, and Loch Ness, it is said that there is never more than one *each uisge* in existence at any one time. Most freshwater lakes reported having a water horse at one point or another.

Water horses are, by and large, extremely dangerous, being predatory upon humans. Because they are so large, unearthly, and grim looking, simply seeing one can be so terrifying as to make a strong, healthy man physically ill for days. Most of the folklore concerning these beasts therefore relates to our efforts to escape or defeat them. Rarely, though, they can be subdued and made use of by people.[179]

Water Horse Nature

Water horses in their natural form are described differently across the Highlands. On Skye, it's said that they have a bill; everywhere else they look more conventionally horse-like with a long, slippery brown snout. They may be grey, black, or brown in colour and are far wilder than normal horses. A horse seen at close quarters on Loch Evort in November 1856 was described as having neither mane nor hair of any kind, but rather a "slimy black skin

---

177. Dalyell, *The Darker Superstitions*, 545; MacGregor, *The Peat-Fire Flame*, 80; Gill, *A Second Manx Scrapbook*, chapter 6; Waldron, *The History and Description*, 43; Roeder, *Manx Folk-Tales*, part one.

178. Fraser, "Northern Folklore: Wells & Springs," *Celtic Magazine* 3 (1878): 20.

179. "A remarkable case of fantasy," *The Times*, November 22, 1856, 12.

like that of a porpoise."[180] It sank below the water only to reemerge shortly afterwards in the form of a huge naked man with the same shiny dark skin. The *each uisge* of Loch Venachar in Perthshire was one of many that was able to speak; it only emerged from the waters to graze the banks at the hottest times of day. Those seen on the road, waiting for an incautious rider to mount them, may be identified by the water weed wrapped around their hooves.[181]

Water horses predominantly appear in four-legged form, but they can sometimes disguise themselves as humans in order to allay the fears of victims, approaching them in the shape of a comely young man or woman or as an old woman looking for help. They might even appear as inanimate objects—a ring or a tuft of wool. Sometimes a bright light may be seen moving on the water at night—a sign of the beasts swimming up and down.[182]

Most water horses seem to be male and to prey upon female humans, but this isn't exclusively the case. A piper attending a dance at Golspie was admiring an attractive woman until he glimpsed that she had horse's hooves beneath her skirt. He wanted to go outside the house where the dance was being held to relieve himself, but she refused to let him go unless she kept a firm grip on one end of his plaid. He decided to abandon the garment, throwing it off and taking to his heels. The horse-woman followed, but he was luckily a swift runner and escaped. The following day the man was out riding when he saw a colt on the road ahead of him. It always kept the same distance until, after some miles, it veered off the road and disappeared into a cave. Shortly afterwards a woman emerged from the cavern and started to dance, confirming for the man the identity between horse and girl.[183]

Water Horse Abductions

The consistent trait of water horses is the carrying off of unsuspecting riders. This is something the *each uisge* shares with the kelpie, and the two types of beast often get mixed up, with all of them being termed "kelpies." To be sure

---

180. "A remarkable case of fantasy," *The Times*, 12.

181. Campbell, *Superstitions of the Highlands*, 204; Leyden, *A Journal of a Tour*, 13–14 and footnote; "A remarkable case of fantasy," *The Times*, 12.

182. Campbell, *Superstitions of the Highlands*, 205.

183. Nicholson, *Golspie*, 15.

exactly what you're dealing with, try to discover where the horse came from: still water (or the sea) means an *each uisge*, flowing water means a kelpie.

Abductions can arise in various ways. A frequent story told involves a group of children that find a beautiful horse and get on its back. Whether it's half a dozen or a dozen that want a ride, the beast's back is always long enough to accommodate. Once the group is mounted, the animal will career off into the loch, perhaps into an underwater cavern, and devour them. All that remains to show what has happened to the abductees will be the heart and lungs, livers, hair, and entrails (or perhaps the shredded caps and clothes) of the victims, floating on the surface of the loch. A survivor lives to tell the tale, of course. At Lagan-nan-Gillean (the Boys' Lake) in western Argyll, a lame boy was unable to stay on the horse when it bolted for its lair; at Loch Lindie and Lochan a'Ghille one of the boys poked the horse with his finger, found that it got stuck, and then had to cut off the digit with his pocketknife to free himself.[184]

Luckily for some potential victims, a telltale sign will alert them to the real nature of what they are dealing with before it's too late. Sometimes the water horse will speak to a child hesitating to climb on its back; in its human form the *each uisge* may be betrayed by its odd, snuffling voice. On Barra, a cow girl was approached by a very handsome man who asked her to comb his hair. She readily agreed, and he laid his head in her lap. As she combed, she found reeds tangled with the locks, and realised that this was an *each uisge* in human form. He started to doze, and she slipped out of her skirt and ran away.[185]

When he awoke and found his prey was gone, the water horse was so enraged that he stamped stones into dust with his hooves. Fortunately, after this reverse, he was seen no more in that neighbourhood. In another version of this incident, the girl's brother fought and killed the horse the following day. In yet another version, from the Isle of Eigg, the water horse fell asleep clutching a tress of the girl's hair. She had to hack it off with a sharp stone before gently raising his head from her lap and slipping away. Despite the

---

184. Sutherland, *Folk-lore Gleanings and Character*, 98; Katherine Whyte Grant, *Myth, Tradition and Story from Western Argyll* (Oban Argyll Scotland, The Oban Times, 1925), 2; Nicholson, *Golspie*, 17, 21; MacGregor, *The Peat Fire Flame*, 72, 77.

185. MacPherson, *Tales of Barra*, 190.

frequent tales of attempted seduction, an *each uisge* in human form is not always good looking; one who appeared to a girl alone at a shieling on Islay was very tall and large, being rough and hairy with no skin on his face and large round eyes. She threw a ladleful of boiling water on him, a simple and effective way of driving him off. Even so, there seemed to be a herd of water horses in the vicinity, so the girl ran to the byre, turned out a cow, and lay down to sleep there, protected by a magic circle drawn around her. She was safe and sound the next morning, but the cow had been killed.[186]

A very fascinating variant on this theme comes from the island of Islay. A servant girl was herding her master's cattle when, as is usual, a young man approached her and asked that she comb and arrange his hair. She was happy to oblige for such a handsome youth but then was shocked to find seaweed amongst his locks. He fell asleep, and she managed to slip away from him. Despite her head start, as she neared the farm, she looked back and saw that he was gaining on her, now in the form of a horse. At that moment, an old wise woman who lived on the farm saw what was happening and released the farm's bull from its byre. This bull had been sired by a water bull and had been very well treated over the years. It dashed to the girl's aid, and a terrible fight began between the two faery beasts. The struggle took them both into the sea where they disappeared. The next day, the bull's mangled corpse was recovered but, equally, the water horse was never seen again either.[187]

The *each uisge* has the power to appear in a number of forms, so as to lull potential victims. At Shawbost on Lewis, two cousins were at a remote cottage tending their cattle when an old woman unknown to them approached, seeking shelter for the night. She seemed to know the area well, so they let her stay. In the morning, one of the cousins awoke and found her relative dead and bleeding beside her. The old woman was no longer in the bed but, looking outside, the surviving girl saw a horse trotting off—clear proof that their visitor had been an *each uisge* in disguise. A similar tale comes from Trotternish on Skye, but in this case one of the younger women awoke in

---

186. MacPhail, "Folklore from the Hebrides—II," section 1, *Folklore* 8 (1897): 400; Campbell, *Popular Tales*, vol. 2, 206; Campbell, *Superstitions of the Highlands*, 204, 208.

187. Campbell, *Popular Tales of the West Highlands Orally Collected with a Translation by the Late J. F. Campbell*, vol. 4 (Paisley: Alexander Gardner, 1893), 304; Grant, *Myth, Tradition and Story*, 2.

the middle of the night to discover their old visitor sinking her teeth into the arm of another of the sleepers. The first girl leapt up and fled, but the old woman assumed her horse form and made chase. A little way from Bracadale church, the girl jumped over a stream and, at the same time, the cocks crowed. The *each uisge* could not cross the stream and the fugitive was safe. In a third story from Lewis, the water horse takes on the form of a young woman asking to stop and rest for a while at a shieling; her true identity is betrayed in due course by the sand, gravel, and seaweed in her hair. As mentioned before, any sort of vegetation, such as rushes or goosegrass, entangled in the hair is a regular clue of a stranger's supernatural nature.[188]

If a water horse singles you out as its prey, it appears that it's impossible to escape your fate. A young woman was courted by a handsome youth—until she found rushes in his hair, at which point she ran home with the *each* in hot pursuit. She managed to get into her cottage and slam the door in his face, but he warned, "In a year and a day, I'll come seeking my dear." The girl avoided the place where they'd met and got engaged to a local boy, but on their wedding day a year later, a large black horse galloped up, seized the bride, and carried her off. She was never seen again—although a low voice has sometimes been heard singing near the loch. A similar story from the island of Mingulay tells of a girl who agreed to wed a mysterious man after a year and a day. Awaiting the happy day, she began to sicken and pine away. Her family realised that she was betrothed to a water horse and resolved to prevent the marriage. However, on the appointed day of the wedding the man returned and there was nothing that anyone could do to stop him carrying her off. He led her to a nearby well, into which they vanished together. The only traces of her that were found afterwards were bits of her clothes and some blood, which filled the spring. Water horses, in short, seem to be of a naturally violent and unpleasant disposition. There is even a story from Loch Cateran of one that devoured an entire funeral procession.[189]

Although death by being drowned or devoured is the usual fate of maidens abducted by water horses, this isn't always the outcome, and some weddings with *each uisge* don't prove fatal. There are several accounts of young

---

188. MacGregor, *The Peat Fire Flame*, 67, 74–75.

189. George Henderson, *Survivals in Belief Among the Celts* (Glasgow, Macmillan, 1861), 163–164; MacCulloch, *The Highlands and Western*, vol. 4, 331.

women who are carried off to the beast's hall under the loch to become the horse's bride. A baby is born, but after the typical magical period of a year and a day the girl is often able to escape, leaving her husband and infant bereft.[190]

Water Horses Tamed

Just as with the kelpie, it is said to be fatal to place a hand on a water horse's hide, as it will adhere, and you'll then be dragged into the lake. Touching them in human form is just as deadly. Nonetheless, if you can grasp hold of a water horse's bridle, it will be in your power and you will enjoy good luck—you may even acquire the second sight and be able to see the Good Folk and look into the future. Alternatively, if you can harness one of the beasts with your own bridle, or place a cap over its head, it will have to work for you so long as the shackle or cap remain in place. Sometimes these beasts will even voluntarily submit to subjection. Normally, though, it is impossible to saddle these horses—they will rip the gear to pieces with their teeth and pulp it with their hooves.[191]

TAMING WITH THE EACH UISGE'S BRIDLE

As with kelpies, the bridle is the key element in many of the stories about the *each uisge*, being the feature in which the water horse's supernatural powers reside. The horse's bridle is part of its deception of unwary riders. Appearing like a fully broken and rideable horse, people are more likely to climb on its back and to surrender themselves into its power.

A man called MacGrigor managed to subdue the famous water horse that lurked around Loch Ness. It would appear to unsuspecting walkers, bridled with fine trappings and ready to ride, and as soon as they had succumbed to temptation and mounted, it would carry them into the lake and devour them. MacGrigor was able to cut off this enchanted bridle, thereby rendering the *each* powerless. This being done, for a while man and beast bargained together over the return of the harness, but they couldn't agree. The water horse said he'd never be able to take it into his house and blocked his way, but

---

190. Watson, "Highland Mythology," *Celtic Review* 5, 52.

191. Sutherland, *Folk-lore Gleanings and Character*, 98; MacCulloch, *The Highlands and Western,* vol. 4, 331; Mackinlay, *Folklore of Scottish Lochs*, 171.

MacGrigor was able to throw the bridle to his wife through the window. As the house was protected by a rowan cross over the door, the water horse had to admit defeat and give up. As for MacGrigor, perhaps we can infer his fate from another story. A drover of Nether Lochaber, walking home one night, found a discarded bridle in the road. He picked it up but found that it was red hot to the touch. He consulted an old wise woman who advised that it must have been lost by a water horse and, if he hung it on a crook made of rowan wood, it would bring his household good fortune.[192]

The magical properties that are inherent in a water horse's bridle are further revealed by the details of the career of Gregor Wilcox, the so-called "warlock of Strathavon." Gregor had two famous charms in his possession, which enabled him to perform his magic. One was the bridle of a water horse, taken (it was said) using luck, cunning, and a sword, from the black Loch Ness water horse, or from that of Loch Spioradan. This alone was a powerful weapon, but the warlock employed it in combination with a mermaid's "stone." This item was a crystal ball that had been acquired from a stranded mermaid by Wilcox's grandfather. He had found her, carried her home, and only consented to return her to the sea if she surrendered the stone. Using the two items together, and subject to the right ceremony, Gregor Wilcox could break witches' spells, expose thieves, find lost property, and help barren women.[193]

Taming with Your Own Bridle

Placing your own bridle upon an *each uisge* brings it within your control and enables you to use it for whatever purpose you choose for as long as the harness remains in place.

Whilst it's possible to bridle and employ a water horse, these episodes can end badly. A man called John MacInnes of Glenelg was struggling with his farm work. One day a stranger approached him and said that he could have a horse to assist him on certain conditions. MacInnes consented to these and soon afterwards found a horse grazing in one of his fields. He used it for ploughing and hauling and managed his workload much better with its

---

192. Mackinlay, *Folklore of Scottish Lochs*, 174–5.
193. McPherson, *Primitive Beliefs*, 260.

help. At nights, when it was stabled, he was required to speak a blessing and sprinkle earth from a molehill over the animal. After a while, with all going so well, and because he had become so familiar with the horse, he forgot the ritual one night. The horse promptly seized him in its teeth and carried him off into the local loch (in another version of this incident, MacInnes's error was to neglect the blessing and then to mount the horse to carry him home after a long day of ploughing).[194]

Even if harnessing and using a water horse doesn't prove fatal, it may still turn out to be ruinous to a farmer. A farmer may find a strange horse grazing on his land over winter. In the spring it's found to be docile and sleek and, when bridled, will work better than any of his other horses, so much so that, in due course, it is harnessed as the lead horse in a team for ploughing. This will be the point at which the *each uisge* reveals its faery nature and gallops off into the nearest loch, taking the rest of the man's horses with it. Sometimes, too, he's dragged along with them.[195]

WATER HORSE HELP

Very occasionally, a water horse might choose for some reason to assist humans. At Dirlot Castle in Sutherland in the north of Scotland, an *each uisge* guarded treasure that had been buried under a lake near the fortress. Anyone who tried to dive for it would never resurface, and the only evidence of their fate would be a heart and lungs seen floating on the water some time later. At Carishader, near Uig on Lewis, the local *each* was on such friendly terms with the local people that it used to visit them in their homes. In a fascinating instance from Vaterstein on the Isle of Skye, an *each uisge* comforted a widowed woman after the death of her daughter. It appeared in her cottage in the form of a man and sat up with her all night, keeping the fire alight by magical means before vanishing in the morning.[196]

---

194. Mackinlay, *Folklore of Scottish Lochs*, 176–7; MacGregor, *The Peat-Fire Flame*, 78; Ross, *Scottish Notes & Queries* (1893), 134.

195. Campbell, *Superstitions of the Highlands*, 204; Henderson, *Survivals in Belief*, 138.

196. Sutherland, *Folk-lore Gleanings and Character*, 98; MacPhail, "Folklore from the Hebrides—II," *Folklore* 8 (1897): 383.

Banishing Water Horses

Given their generally violent nature, it is understandable that people have often tried to devise strategies to get rid of water horses in their neighbourhoods. Fortunately, they can be killed, or measures may be taken to defend ourselves against them.

The horses can be destroyed by various means. If a person is brave enough, they may get close and stab an *each uisge* to death with a knife or similar blade. This suggests that, like many of faery kind, they are susceptible to iron. However, other sources allege that water horses are only vulnerable to silver bullets. There is an account of a farmer at Loch Rannoch who used to hunt for the local *each uisge* using guns loaded with sixpences.[197]

Other strategies have been tried. West of North Uist lie the Monach Islands on which was a small lake called the Lake of Virtues, which was inhabited by a water horse. It was such a nuisance that the islanders had even considered abandoning their homes to escape it. A woman called MacLeod proposed destroying it by bringing a very large bull onto her farm. This was agreed on by the community, and the bull was put to graze in a meadow by the loch. Before too long, the *each uisge* emerged, covered in mud and weeds, and a tremendous fight ensued. The water horse cunningly gave ground until it was in the water, although it had until then appeared to be getting the worst of the fight. In contact with its element, its strength increased and both animals disappeared beneath the waves. The next day some lungs floated ashore; it wasn't possible to determine whether they were the bull's or the horse's, but it seems most likely that the bull was overcome. A nuisance *each uisge* at Erista was killed by an expert archer who specialised in this type of pest control—although even he needed three arrows to kill the beast. Fascinatingly, in another case it appeared that a water horse that had killed a man was subsequently itself killed by other horses in the same loch, possibly because it smelled of the human it had just consumed.[198]

If you meet an *each uisge* and you doubt your ability to fight and kill it, what can you do to protect yourself? There are several options available to

---

197. J. G. Campbell, *Superstitions*, 214; Mackinlay, *Folklore*, 178.
198. J. G. Campbell, *Superstitions*, 205, 214; "Faery Tales," *Celtic Review* 5, 166; MacGregor, *Peat Fire Flame*, 75; Campbell, *More West Highland Tales*, 206.

you. A good preventative (as with all fae beings) is to carry a Bible or leaves from scripture with you. Other techniques that are effective against faeries are also efficacious against an *each uisge*. If you can get across any watercourse, you will be safe; wearing rowan sprigs will protect you, and they can also safeguard your home. Thirdly, as with all faery kind, the symbols of Christian religion seem effective. A young woman on the Isle of Skye discovered that her handsome boyfriend was actually an *each uisge* when he fell asleep in her lap and she found sand and mud in his hair. She cut off her skirt and made a dash for it. A little way down the road, though, she paused, took out her crucifix and rubbed it across the route he would have to follow to catch her. This invisible mark formed an insuperable barrier against him. Simple magic will also work against an *each*. Another Skye woman, trapped alone at an isolated shieling by a horse rampaging up and down outside, drew a circle on the ground, scribed a cross within that, and then stood inside the mark. This was an absolute protection against the beast.[199]

Lastly, quick thinking and boldness may be sufficient. Earlier I described a horse driven off by scalding water; here's a similar incident. A woman of the Buchanan family on Skye was in her cottage making porridge when a stranger entered and asked her name. The household had tamed and harnessed another *each uisge*, which they were using for their ploughing, and probably because of this she identified the true nature of her visitor. She knew it was unsafe to tell him her name and thereby put herself in his power, so she replied that she was "myself." Then she splashed him with the boiling hot porridge. Howling, he ran out and the woman heard the "tame" water horse enquire who had hurt him. When he replied "myself," any possibility of taking revenge was averted.[200]

Conclusions

Water horses and water bulls are not just "faery cattle." They may mix with our herds and behave like our livestock when it suits them, but they are far cleverer and far, far more malign. They conceal themselves within herds to hide from us and to allay any fears we may have, but they are not herd animals; they

---

199. MacCulloch, "Folklore of the Isle of Skye," *Folklore* 33 (1922): 308; MacGregor, *The Peat-Fire Flame*, 67, 74.

200. MacCulloch, "Folklore of the Isle of Skye," *Folklore* 33 (1922): 308.

have motivations and plans that are entirely their own. Humans must always be alert to their presence, especially when they have assumed other forms, and be aware of the steps that can be taken to protect themselves.

To repeat a point made earlier, the improved perception of merfolk is a relatively recent amelioration. The earlier, much more dangerous nature of these water beasts is still to be found in the Scottish accounts of water horses, bulls, and kelpies. The exact details of these characteristics are fascinating, however. Water bulls, while they can be alarming because of their size and the volume of their bellows, are not dangerous to humans—unlike their earthly equivalents. In contrast, water horses (unlike mundane steeds) are positively and actively harmful.

More curious still, the water horse is often at its most insidious and malign when it takes on human form. It's salutary to appreciate that the *each uisge* has realised that one of the best ways of achieving its destructive impulses is to disguise itself as one of us; then it can deviously insinuate itself, getting very close to a potential victim whilst allaying all apprehension on the other's part and using human nature against itself.

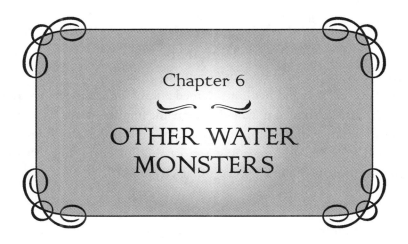

Chapter 6

OTHER WATER MONSTERS

An astonishing variety of other faery water beasts have been identified around the British Isles. This chapter groups together these obscure monsters.

Shoopiltee

On Shetland there is a species of water horse called the *shoopiltee*. One authority on the folklore of the islands has described the creature as a water deity in special charge of the sea and streams. It can appear in a number of forms, such as a sea monster to fishermen or, on land, in the form of a Shetland pony (or shelty).[201]

This water beast lives in burns near to water mills and is generally retiring in nature, vanishing into the streams or in a flash of fire. Local people once sacrificed ale or pins and coins to it to ensure good catches at sea. Its tail is said to be something like a waterwheel or propeller. In its equine form, the *shoopiltee* will carry riders away, careering over cliffs and into the sea. Sometimes, too, it appears as the "*njugl*" (see next page), making it clear that there

---

201. Hibbert, *Shetland Isles*, 525, 565.

is a great deal of overlap between the different monsters—in the minds of Shetland islanders at least.[202]

Tacharan

This is a tiny kelpie or water sprite found in the Scottish Highlands and Islands. Several fords and pools are named after it, indicating its usual habitat, and it's also celebrated in ballads. The name implies "dwarf" and emphasises its diminutive dimensions; interestingly, the word is also found in the compound *tacharan-sithe*, meaning a faery child or changeling. This usage emphasises the supernatural aspects of the creatures.[203]

Njugls

Occupying a midway point between kelpies and water horses is the Shetland *njugl* (or *niggle*, *neogle*, *nygel*, or *noggle*). It has a horse's body and a human head—although some accounts describe it as a trow-like kelpie in the shape of a grey-coloured pony with large glaring eyes and terrible teeth. Rather like the *shoopiltee*, its tail is sometimes said to resemble a waterwheel or a propeller, although this telltale feature is kept hidden between the hind legs most of the time.[204]

The *njugl* frequents lochs, burns, meadows, and marshy ground. It will appear to travellers as a docile and tame pony, tempting them to ride it by its quiet and attractive nature. However, once they have mounted it, it dashes for the water. When the *njugl* reaches or enters the water, it vanishes and is replaced by a blue flame. Unlike mainland specimens, it seems that riders can escape the horse before it's too late, either by simply leaping off, by invoking a holy name, or by plunging a knife into the beast's back.[205]

The *njugl* also appears near water mills and will stop the wheel turning so as to force the miller to come outside, at which point he finds a saddled grey pony quietly grazing. Once again, if he is foolish enough to mount it, the

202. J. Haldane Burgess, "Some Shetland Folk-lore," *Scottish Review* 25, 92.

203. Carmichael, *Carmina Gadelica*, vol. 2, 367.

204. *County Folk-lore* 3, 189; James Nicolson, *Shetland* (Newton Abbot: David & Charles, 1984), 55–59.

205. Blind, "New Finds in Shetlandic," *Gentleman's Magazine*, no. 252 (January–June 1882): 369.

miller will get a ducking, being carried out to sea in a flash of fire. The *njugl's* less malign habit is to surface suddenly and scare passing children. Only a silver bullet can kill the beast, but it can be scared off by throwing either a knife or a lighted brand or torch at it. Even a few sparks falling on the water seem sufficient to drive the *njugl* out to sea. Another proven remedy is to recite passages of scripture to the monster should you encounter one.[206]

Nuckelavee

This sea monster from Orkney was part horse and part terrifying man. The *nuckelavee* has been described as having a huge head like a man's but with a pig's snout and a very wide maw, from which came breath like steam. There is only one eye, and that is as red as fire. The body is like a horse's but with fins as well as legs. In the middle of the back there sprouts what seems to be a rider, except that he has no legs but rather grows directly from the horse. Overall, the creature has no skin, just raw flesh with black blood visible flowing in yellow veins.[207]

The *nuckelavee's* breath is venomous, and it is able to wreak destruction on the land, blighting crops and livestock and devouring anyone it meets, but at the same time, it seems oddly vulnerable. The monster doesn't like fresh or running water, so it never appears in the rain, and it can't cross flowing streams—a fact which of course gives those unlucky enough to meet it some hope of escape.[208]

The development of the kelp burning industry on the islands is believed to have driven the *nuckelavee* away with the noxious smell produced, although it took revenge by inflicting a cattle plague on the inhabitants.[209]

In the rest of northern Scotland, the role of the *nuckelavee* is performed by the *uilebheist*, a sea monster with several heads.

---

206. Marwick, *The Folklore of Orkney*, 23; Saxby, *Shetland Traditional Lore*, 140; J. Haldane Burgess, "Some Shetland Folk-lore," *Scottish Review* 25, 92.

207. Dennison, "Orkney Folk-lore: Sea Myths," in *Scottish Antiquary* 5, 131.

208. Douglas, *Scottish Faery and Folk Tales*, 197.

209. Marwick, *The Folklore of Orkney*, 23.

Shellycoat

On Loch Lomond, just where the River Ettrick flows into the lake, there lives a foal covered in seaweed and seashells, which is called Shellycoat. It is a benign beast and merely plays tricks on local people and, in any event, its approach is always announced by the rattling of its shells. For example, two men travelling at night heard a voice crying "Lost! Lost!" They followed it but were led up the river for miles until they realised that they were being "led" by the horse. Shellycoat then galloped off ahead, laughing at their predicament.[210]

Shellycoat is also known around the east coast of Lowland Scotland. Here, it's reputed to have a touchy temper, so that those who offend it might expect to be thrashed and the sound of its shell coat rattling will instil fear. As a result, the creature has had various local names along the lines of "smiter" or "beater." One man at Leith on the shore of the Firth of Forth so annoyed the Shellycoat there that it picked him up with its teeth and tossed him to and fro until he was dead. Rather like a selkie, the source of Shellycoat's power is said to be that shell-covered coat, which could be removed and hidden under a rock on the shore.[211]

The Boobrie

The boobrie is a mysterious being of the Scottish Highlands that often appears as a bird but which can also take the form of either a water horse or a water bull (in which cases it's called the *tarbh boibhre*). Its call sounds like a bull bellowing, although it is said to prefer horse shape. As a bird, the boobrie has a long neck and bill and webbed feet with large claws. It inhabits inland lochs and will consume calves, sheep, and otters.[212]

Biasd na Srogaig

This creature is unique to the Isle of Skye and seems to be some sort of horse. The name means "the beast of the horn," and it is evidently a sort of unicorn,

---

210. Dalyell, *The Darker Superstitions of*, 543; *Folk-lore and Legends*, 184; Stephen Oliver, the Younger [pseud.], *Rambles in Northumberland, and on the Scottish Border [...]* (London: Chapman and Hall: 1835), 97; Douglas, *Scottish Faery and Folk Tales*, 181; Briggs, *Dictionary of Fairies*, "Shellycoat."

211. Spence, *Minor Traditions*, 17–18.

212. Henderson, *Survivals in Belief*, 145; Campbell, *Popular Tales*, vol. 4, 307.

which has a single horn on its forehead as well as very long and very clumsy and ungainly legs. It lives in lochs and is mainly used as a "bogey" to scare children now.

A related creature is the "big beast of Lochawe," which was reputed to have twelve legs and to look like a horse—or sometimes an eel. It would be heard in the winter, breaking the ice on the surface of the loch.[213]

Manx Horses

On the Isle of Man, there are two horselike faery beasts, the *cabbyl ushtey* (water horse) and the *glashtyn, glashtin,* or *glashan.* The horse lives both in rivers and in the sea. It poses a constant threat to the islanders' livestock, as it will emerge from watercourses and rip cattle to pieces. Sometimes it even carries off children. The *cabbyl* is white or brown in colour, and there are said to be several in rivers and marshy spots across the island. In the parish of Lonan, a *cabbyl ushtey* or *cabbyl vooir* (big horse) has frequently been seen at twilight on the seashore or on the tracks leading up the cliffs. It is said to be white or dun coloured, and it can travel as easily in the sea as upon the land. It might carry off unwary riders who mount it, but unlike the Scottish examples, these victims do not drown but find that they can breathe underwater. The *cabbyl* might, too, consent to be haltered and used by farmers; it's very strong and easily hauls up loads of seaweed from the beaches to fertilise the fields.[214]

The hob-like *glashtyn,* who undertakes heavy labour on farms, is also, curiously, known to appear in the guise of a water horse. This dark grey colt is found in several locations across the island, haunting boggy fields and pools and emerging at night onto meadows and lake banks. Sometimes it is seen mixing with herds of mountain ponies. The *glashtyn* in horse form seemed to be quite small, and there are no mentions of it posing a threat to either livestock or humans; in the shape of a one-year old lamb it would get amongst the flocks in the fold and cause mischief but no harm. The *glashtyn* has been known to give people a fright by galloping off if they are foolhardy enough to mount it. Luckily, it's possible to jump clear of these Manx beasts,

---

213. Campbell, *Superstitions of the Highlands,* 217–8.
214. Gill, *A Manx Scrapbook,* 226; Douglas, *"Restoring to Use Our,"* 19.

something that's not possible with the Scottish equivalents. If you ever come across a solitary horse on the Isle of Man, examine it carefully before getting too close. If it has human ears, you're dealing with a *glashtyn*.[215]

It's interesting to note that the *glashtyn*, with its horse and human forms, is closely mirrored by the *glaistig* of the Scottish Highlands. This being, which I'll describe in detail in part 2 later, may appear as either a woman or as a pony, in which form it may help people across rivers in a flood. It may also take equine form merely to play tricks on people, such as nibbling at the thatch of their cottages at night.[216]

There's also a second fae horse on the Isle of Man called the *cabbyl oie* or "night horse," who appears to be of largely benign disposition and may just be another manifestation of the *cabbyl ushtey*. He roams the roads of the island at night and will willingly carry travellers who are out late home to their doors. However, if the horse takes a dislike to the person it's carrying, it may toss them off or even carry them away into a river or the sea (unless they've protected themselves with a blessing). There is also a possible third type of faery horse, called by some the "spirit horse." Galloping hooves have frequently been heard across the island without there being any horses in the vicinity who might have produced the sound. Other witnesses have seen a white horse, often high on the mountains, and some strange hooved tracks have also been found.[217]

Ceffyl y Dwr

The Welsh *ceffyl y dwr* (water horse) closely resembles Scottish equivalents. Its appearance heralds drownings, and it may even cause these itself, carrying off unwary riders into lakes—or into the sky. However, a clergyman is

---

215. Roeder, *Manx Folk-Tales*, 25; Moore, *Folklore of the Isle of Man*, chapter 4; C. Roeder, ed., *Manx Notes & Queries, With an Account of [...]* (Douglas: S. K. Broadbent & Co. Ltd., 1904), 98; Gill, A *Manx Scrapbook*, chapter 4; Gill, A *Third Manx Scrapbook*, chapter 3, section 6; Campbell, *Popular Tales*, vol. 1, xlvi; Douglas, "*Restoring to Use Our,*" 18.

216. Campbell, *Superstitions of the Highlands*, 180, 183.

217. Gill, A *Manx Scrapbook*, chapter 4; Moore, *The Folk-lore of the*, chapter 4; Roeder, *Manx Folk-Tales*, 22; Train, *Isle of Man*, vol. 2, chapter 18; *Gill, A Third Manx Scrapbook*, chapter 2.

able to ride one of the *ceffyl* without danger, just so long as he remains silent for the duration of his journey.[218]

There is also an isolated report of the Welsh sea-horse. These are very shy and extremely seldom seen, but they will occasionally come ashore, both in the day as well as at night, and graze in fields. The slightest noise will spook them, though, at which they will flee to the sea or vanish into the clouds.[219]

Tangie

On Orkney and Shetland, *tangy* can be another name for the sea-trow (chapter 1), but there was also a sea-horse called the *tangie* that rides on the waves, stirring them up. He is said to try to catch mortal girls as wives by suddenly rushing up the shore on the surf. *Tangie* is very distinctive, being cream coloured with a white mane and blue eyes. Sometimes the *tangie* gets mixed up with the kelpie and the *each uisge*, so that there are also reports of *tangies* appearing as black horses that will gallop away with unsuspecting riders over cliffs, turning into blue flames as they plunge into the waves.[220]

Water Fuathan

The *fuathan* are a large group of vicious beings, many of which are water sprites living in salt- and freshwater, particularly around river crossings and waterfalls. The name has been glossed as meaning "the spirit of panic" or as "evil spirit." It derives from a verb meaning "to hate" and may most simply be translated as spectre or phantom.[221]

Amongst the *fuathan* are numbered many creatures that might also be called *urisks* (see part 2 for "land *fuathan*") as well as the *fideal* and the *cuachag*, which were mentioned earlier. Because the term applies to such a wide range of supernatural beasts, it's not safe to generalise about their temperaments. Some can be friendly and harmless, but probably the majority are dangerous monsters and are so called in Gaelic—*athach*. The *fideal* lived in Loch na Fideil near Gairloch and lured men into the water, perhaps by

218. Owen, *Welsh Folk-lore*, 138.

219. Blind, "New Finds," *Gentleman's Magazine*, no. 252 (January–June 1882), 478.

220. Saxby, *Shetland Traditional Lore*, 140; George Stewart, *Shetland Fireside Tales; Or, The Hermit of Trosswickness* (Lerwick: T & J Manson, 1892), 136.

221. Campbell and Hall, *Strange Things*, 249.

challenging them to fight, where she hugged them until they drowned. The *fuath* known as the *cuachag* inhabited the river in Glen Cuaich and was similarly perilous, causing floods and being appeased with offerings.[222]

Some *fuathan* seem to have a sort of communal moral function, policing the usage of bodies of water and their resources, over and above their pure nastiness. In the Hebrides it was regarded as wrongful to kill fish during the spawning season—for understandable reasons. If you did, you would be cursed and a *fuath* would pursue you. Several stories are told to illustrate how this social crime was punished. A man called Alexander, of Buaile Mor on South Uist, was fishing in a stream one night when he saw a figure approaching downstream. He called to the stranger to step away from the water so as not to frighten the fish; the man complied but then Alexander realised something like a mill wheel was rolling towards him. Hurriedly, he gathered up his catch and gear and made off. The fish he'd caught he hid under a rock and then headed for the nearest house. Crossing the moor, however, he was repeatedly thrown down. The next morning, returning to collect his catch, Alexander found that all had gone save for one he had ripped the head off by standing on it during his hurried departure the night before. A second man called Ronald, who lived at Bornish, was fishing with a net at spawning time. When he tried to haul in his net, he realised a gigantic man held the other end. Ronald fled but was pursued all the way home by the *fuath*. Alasdair Mor of Skye was another who was fishing during the night at spawning time when he was joined by an unknown figure. In this case, when dawn came, his companion disappeared in a flash of flame and all the fish they had landed together turned out to have disappeared. Lastly, three men who went fishing at Hornary found a man unknown to them standing on the stepping stone in the stream they meant to net. He held out his hand and helped two across; to the third he said, "Your hour is not yet come." The other two fell ill and soon died.[223]

Conclusions

Very little is known about many of the water beasts described in this last chapter of part 1. Many do not conform to the clearer boundaries that

---

222. Mackenzie, *Scottish Folk-Lore and Folk Life*, 235–36; Nicholson, *Golspie*, 78–79.
223. A. Goodrich-Freer, "The Powers of Evil in the Outer Hebrides," *Folklore* 10 (1899): 273–4.

applied to many of the beasts I described earlier. Whilst it was often possible to separate out freshwater and marine dwellers, several of these last creatures may be found in both environments.

Differences aside, the basic lesson in all cases is to be extremely cautious. Be careful when you are alone near any body of water and be extremely wary of any person or animal you meet there. Other than merfolk (and they're not to be trusted 100 percent), water beasts are malevolent and deadly. Although a few lucky and well-prepared individuals have managed to get the better of them, most humans who have had close encounters have done well to have a lucky escape. Fascinating as the water beasts may be, they should be avoided, or at the very least approached with the utmost care.

Part 2
LAND BEASTS

This second part of the book examines the faery beasts that live almost exclusively on land. As in the last part, as the chapters progress there will be a transition away from beings that have some resemblance to humans (and to conventional faeries) towards supernatural creatures that are very clearly "beasts." Even so, the humanlike beings I describe are sufficiently wild and animalistic to make it most appropriate to discuss them as faery beasts. Many often seem more like monsters or ghosts than the traditional denizens of faery. Some have no fixed shape at all, making it clear that we are in a strange and dangerous world.

Chapter 7

HAGS

I turn now to consideration of a range of largely malevolent female sprites that might be termed "hags." Before we examine the various types of supernatural females who might be grouped together under this heading, we need to think about terms.

What Is a Hag?

The distinction between some of the more dangerous female faeries and hags is difficult to locate. In large degree, it is a matter of personal preference, depending upon such factors as dress, appearance, behaviour, and where the being lives. Today, with the popular view of faery kind inclined to more cuddly and kindly conceptions, the category allocated to "faery" is likely to be quite restricted; traditional views of the species were more accommodating and treated many creatures as faery that would now be regarded as "hags." Let's not forget, though, that for all her morbid and mournful character, the banshee is nothing but a "faery woman," a *bean sith* in Scottish Gaelic.

As an example of the problems of definition, Hugh Miller described the belief in the north of Scotland in a green woman with a "goblin child" who would go from cottage to cottage at night, bathing her infant in the blood of the youngest human child. Another "green lady" used to go house to house spreading smallpox. The colour green is, of course, typically faery, but how we should classify these females—as faes or as "goblins" (whatever they may be precisely)—is hard to determine. Miller may have used the word goblin to denote a trow, but then, what is a trow if it isn't just an ugly and ill-tempered faery of the Northern Isles?[224]

There's a strong correlation between hags and giant dimensions. A woman of monstrous size and strength could well be classed as a hag; what probably distinguishes hags from giantesses is that the former combine some sort of supernatural power with their unnatural size and strength. Hand in hand with monstrous size in the popular imagination goes hideous appearance, and this is true of hags. Of course, ugly, malevolent women are also conventionally classed as witches and, yet again, there is considerable overlap. However, whilst hags and witches may well share magical powers, the latter are almost always regarded as being human, whereas there seems little dispute that hags have a wholly supernatural origin.

Types of Hags

In Scottish tradition there are many unnamed hags (or *cailleachs*) that haunt various spots and pose a threat to travellers. Given their predisposition to violence, they react badly towards people who defy or disparage them, but they can be repelled by iron (both of which are true of faeries as well). The story is told of a young man from Islay who toasted the local *cailleach* in mocking terms when he was at the inn one night. Walking home, she ambushed him, and so began a vendetta between the two. The youth had a knife specially made to defend himself, but one day during harvest he put it down in a field whilst he was working. The *cailleach* spotted her chance, got between him and his blade, and then squeezed him to death.[225]

Another common tale of a malevolent hag will describe a woman whose sole interest seems to be to murder strangers. Even if there's no violence, there will be an atmosphere of menace in any encounter with her because of the

224. Hugh Miller, *Scenes and Legends of the North of Scotland; Or, The Traditional History of Cromarty* (Edinburgh: Johnstone and Hunter 1835), 70.

225. John Gregorson Campbell, *Witchcraft and Second Sight in the Highlands and Islands of Scotland: Tales and Traditions Orally Collected by the Late John Gregorson Campbell,* (Glasgow: James MacLehose & Sons, 1902), 189.

woman's size and looks. Typically, a huntsman will be alone in a hut one night when an old woman comes to the door seeking shelter. She's admitted but is extremely wary of his dogs and asks the man to tie them, giving him one of her hairs as a leash. He pretends to secure them as bidden but wisely doesn't make use of the proffered hair. As the crone sits by the fire she starts to swell in size and then attacks the man, calling out to her hair to strangle the dogs. Of course, they're not restrained, and they help the man defeat his assailant. In some versions, the hag is torn to pieces by the hounds, but then starts to reassemble before his eyes—at which point, it's clearly time to escape.[226]

There are also some named hags or groups of hags who have particular characteristics and habits and who should be examined individually. Here I examine the banshees, *cyhyraeth*, *cailleach bheur*, mist women, *baobhan sith*, and several others. Arguably, for their characters, the *bean-nighe* and the *caointeach* described in part 1 could be included in this chapter as well, but because of their very strong affinity to flowing water, I dealt with them as river sprites. Conversely, as will be seen, the *cailleach bheur* has intimate links with rivers and lakes, meaning that she might have been discussed in part 1.

Banshees

A banshee is an ancestral spirit or faery woman (*bean sith*) who is attached to a particular family or clan. A very well-known example is that of the Macleod family of Skye. The clan has a legend of a beautiful woman who came to their castle just after a son was born and chanted verses over him, foretelling his future and acting as a protective charm upon the boy.[227]

Over and above being able to foresee the future, it appears, too, that banshees can actively shape events that are yet to come: for this reason, for instance, there are two hills in Aberdeenshire where travellers will leave barley-meal cakes for the local banshees, believing that failure to do this would lead either to a death or some other terrible misfortune.[228]

---

226. Stories about such monstrous women are told of Ben Breck in the Highlands, Appin Hill in Argyll, and Beinn a' Ghlo mountain in Perthshire. See, for example, Campbell, *Superstitions of the Highlands*, 123.

227. Walter Y. Evans-Wentz, *The Fairy-Faith in Celtic Countries* (Oxford: Oxford University Press, 1911), 99.

228. Evans-Wentz, *The Fairy-Faith in Celtic*, 437–8.

Although the primary function of the Scottish banshee is prognostica-tion, it isn't all they do. The McCrimmon family were pipers, but none had any outstanding skill, until one day the banshee of the castle approached the youngest son, known as the Black Lad, whilst he was playing. She asked him if he wanted skill without success or success without skill, the usual terms offered in cases where faeries bestow some mastery. He chose the former and the banshee wrapped one of her hairs around the chanter of his pipes and then told him to play any tune he liked, whilst she held her fingers over his as he did so. By this means, she transmitted wonderful musical ability to him.[229]

The appearance of the banshee is generally unappealing, if distinctive. That of Loch Migdal has been spotted sitting on a rock in a green silk dress; she has long hair, yellow like ripe corn, but no nose. Another sighted in the same locality had webbed feet so that (although they are not seen washing shrouds for the dead like the *bean-nighe*) banshees are generally regarded as water spirits of some kind; curiously, some can become restless if they have to cross water. Sometimes they have manes and tails so that they are much closer to water horses or kelpies; others resemble old crones, perhaps with large, round eyes. Others can be hairy with large eyes.[230]

Cyhyraeth

The Welsh equivalent of the banshee is the *cyhyraeth*—the groaning spirit (the name is related to the word for "sinews" and denotes her corpse-like or skele-tal appearance). She makes a "doleful, dreadful noise in the night," disturbing people's sleep and sounding like the groans of the dying. The cry would pres-age a funeral or an epidemic or would precede bad weather on the coast. The unpleasant groaning is heard three times, each time getting nearer but at the same time quieter and less shrill. At its loudest it has been said that it sounds like a person suffering from the stitch. The groaning sound also apparently intensifies if the *cyhyraeth* finds its way obstructed for any reason. Those vis-iting someone mortally ill will hear the *cyhyraeth* on their way to the bedside and will then find that the sick person's voice sounds exactly the same.[231]

---

229. MacDougall, *Folk Tales and Fairy Lore,* 175.

230. Campbell, *Popular Tales,* vol. 2, 205.

231. Sikes, *British Goblins,* 220.

The *cyhyraeth* can be heard several months before the death it marks, or it can replicate the circumstances of the death, for example by following the future route of the funeral cortege, by coming to rest at the point where a grave will be dug, or by moving along the shoreline with lights showing before a shipwreck occurs. Some say it only precedes the deaths of those who have been ill for a long time or of those who have been mentally ill. In other places, the *cyhyraeth* seems to be a more physical spirit, passing through the streets and lanes of a neighbourhood and rattling on the windows and doors of every house in addition to its awful groans.[232]

Other "Banshee" Types

Most—but not all—the "banshees" are female, yet a few male sprites are found who share the function to predict death or misfortune. In the Scottish Highlands people may encounter several of these.

The Rothmurchans have the *bodach an dun*, the "ghost of the hill," Gartnibeg House is haunted by the *Bodach Gartin*, and the *bodach glas*, the grey man, will make an appearance to foretell a death in the clan McIvor. The MacLachlan family of Killichoan Castle were served by a brownie, but this being, described as a small grey-haired man, would also behave like a banshee when any member of the clan was heading off to war; then he would cry and wail at a nearby waterfall as well as insisting that all the preparations for the farewell meal be carried out exactly and in full. At Gilsland in Cumbria resided the "Cauld Lad" who was supposed to have been a boy who died of cold but then remained with the household. When a person was about to fall ill, he came to the bedside with his teeth loudly chattering; if they were facing death, he laid his icy hands on the part of the body that would be the cause of their last sickness.[233]

Finally, across England there was belief in a being called the "grim" or "church grim." This faery is described in the 1628 chapbook *Robin Goodfellow— His Mad Prankes and Merry Jests*. The grim appears at night "when candles

---

232. Sikes, *British Goblins*, 219–222.

233. William P. Nimmo, *Omens and Superstitions: Curious Facts and Illustrative Sketches* (Edinburgh: William P. Nimmo, 1868), 9; Archibald Campbell, *Records of Argyll: Legends, Traditions, and Recollections of Argyllshire Highlanders, Collected Chiefly from the Gaelic* (Edinburgh: William Blackwood and Sons, 1885), 187.

burne both blue and dim" and can take several forms. It "walks with the owl" and loudly imitates that bird's calls at the windows of those lying sick, causing them to despair of recovery. It can appear as a black dog or similar terrifying shape, haunting churchyards in stormy weather or, more trivially, scaring off revellers from parties and stealing their food and drink.[234]

It is interesting to discover that banshees are a type of faery still quite regularly encountered today. Perhaps because the name is so well known, people seem to be more ready to identify and name their experiences. Banshees have continued to be reported since the beginning of the twentieth century. Three quarters of these cases were from Ireland, doubtless reflecting the significance of the faery woman in national tradition there. Three quarters, too, were regarded by the witnesses as foretelling a death, although not necessarily that of a family member. Another case was linked to a serious assault which the victim survived, and a couple of others lacked any "cause" as such. What was common to all was, naturally, the wailing, howling voice that was heard. Witnesses repeatedly emphasised that this sound was not the cry of any animal but that it was a unique combination of shriek, moan, and song, often covering a huge range on the musical scale and often having no fixed or certain source. It could be both in the head and heard externally, a very real and quite often shared experience.[235]

Cailleach Bheur

The *cailleach bheur* is a wild, giant hag with a blue face and a vicious temper; she's also called the "winter hag" or the "hag of the ridges," but her name literally means the sharp or shrill old wife, denoting the cutting blasts of icy winds. She lives on high mountains in Scotland such as Ben Nevis, where she has imprisoned Bride, the spirit of summer, and she embodies the coldest time of

234. Briggs, *Dictionary of Fairies*, "Church grim" and "Grim"; James Orchard Halliwell-Phillipps, "The Tricks of the Fairy Called Grim," in *Illustrations of the Fairy Mythology of A Midsummer Night's Dream* (London: Shakespeare Society, 1845), chapter 6; Elizabeth Mary Wright, *Rustic Speech and Folk-lore* (London, H. Milford, 1913), 194.

235. Marjorie Johnson, *Seeing Fairies: From the Lost Archives of the Fairy Investigation Society, Authentic Reports of Fairies in Modern Times* (San Antonio: Anomalist Books, 2014), 145-147; Simon Young, ed., The Fairy Investigation Society, *Fairy Census* 2014–2017 (n.p., 2018), 141, 156, 274, 302, www.fairyist.com/wp-content/uploads/2014/10/The-Fairy-Census-2014-2017-1.pdf.

the year, most particularly the wintry weather of early April, when she carries a wand, or hammer, in her hand with which she hardens the frosty ground and suppresses grass and other vegetation and delays the arrival of spring and good weather for men and beasts. The hag sends terrible tempests, called "*cailleach* weather" or "wolf-storms." When, finally, the sun defeats her, she will fly off in a terrible rage for another year. Just before she does this, though, she will cast away her wand in disgust, and it will fall under a gorse or holly bush—explaining why grass never grows beneath these. After spring wins out, the *cailleach* turns into a cold, damp boulder throughout the summer, but in some versions of her story she is transformed into a beautiful woman who brings luck and plenty. At the end of the good weather, the *cailleach* ushers in the cold again by washing her plaid in the whirlpool at Corryvreckan; it comes out snowy white and thereby signifies the start of winter. Another tradition states that, when the foam spouts highest from the maelstrom, the *cailleach* has "put on her kerchief" and is at her most deadly.[236]

The *cailleach bheur* is also called *cailleach-uisge*, the water woman, and she may be encountered in wild places, cleaning fish by a stream. She also acts as a guardian to wild animals, most particularly deer, herding and milking them on the mountains. Normally, it is considered bad luck for a hunter to see her but occasionally she may allow her deer to be hunted by favoured individuals.[237]

The *cailleach* is so closely linked to bad weather and with water that she's said to be responsible for drowning fertile valleys. She created Loch Eck, whilst Loch Awe is the result of an accident: she forgot one night to cover the well on top of Ben Cruachan where her cattle drank and it overflowed, flooding the glen beneath. The *cailleach* in this case is said to have been so horrified by the accident that she turned to stone. Related ideas make her the shaper of the Scottish landscape, linking her to many natural features and processes.[238]

The *cailleach* can take a multiplicity of forms. The *cailleach bheur* is a blue-black hag with one eye, matted hair, red teeth, and grey clothes. She is very long lived and has had hundreds of children. She can swell in size and

236. Carmichael, *Carmina Gadelica*, vol. 2, 236; Dalyell, *The Darker Superstitions of*, 542; K. Grant, *Myth, Tradition and Story*, chapter 2; Mackenzie, chapter 7.

237. Mackenzie, *Scottish Folk-lore and Folk Life*, 152.

238. Leslie, *The Early Races of Scotland*, vol. 1, 142.

she can turn into a range of animals such as deer, cats, and ravens.[239] This *cailleach* also keeps flocks of deer, cattle, and pigs. On the winter nights she can sometimes be seen driving her deer down onto beaches where they can feed on the seaweed whilst other vegetation is sparse.[240]

Given her watery associations, it's to be expected that the hag has a form found in the sea or water courses. The *cailleach muileartach*, the hag of the sea, is bald with a dark blue face and a single eye and a single tooth; she lurks in swollen rivers and fords, where she attempts to drown travellers, or she calls up storms along the Scottish coast. Despite her fearsome role as the "mother of the sea of darkness," she can also heal the sick and raise the dead with a touch of her finger. A male counterpart of the *muileartach* is the "brounger" of the Scottish eastern coast. If this spirit was thought to be present when a fishing boat was out at sea, it had to circle three times to dispel his enchantment.[241]

The *cailleach bheur* has various close relatives across Britain. The Manx *caillagh y grommagh*, "the old woman of the gloom," appears on the island on the morning of February 12 each year, trying to gather firewood to warm herself. If she can find enough dry sticks, the following spring will prove to be wet. If, however, the morning is damp and she can't gather enough wood suitable for a fire, the spring will prove to be dry.[242]

There's a headland in Malew parish on Man that's named after her—Gob ny Callee. Here, the old woman stumbled whilst trying to step between two mountain peaks and it's said that the land bears the impression of her heel and her bottom. The *caillagh* is also called *faihtag*, a name which reflects her prophetic abilities.[243]

Mist Women

The Welsh *gwrach y rhybin* (described in part 1) is sometimes called the "hag of the mist" because she may sometimes appear to an ill-fated individual in the fog on a mountainside. Another Welsh sprite is even more deserving of

---

239. Mackenzie, *Scottish Folk-lore and Folk Life*, 125–132.

240. Campbell, *Superstitions of the Highlands*, 22-29, 122, 133; Mackenzie, *Scottish Folk-lore and Folk Life*, 152.

241. Mackenzie, *Scottish Folk-lore and Folk Life*, chapter 8.

242. *Yn Lioar Manninagh*, vol. 1 (1890–92), 223.

243. Gill, *A Manx Scrapbook*, chapter 4.

the title, though: this is the Old Woman of the Mountain, a faery being who was found all over the country.[244]

The Old Woman (as she appeared in Monmouthshire) was described in detail by the Reverend Edmund Jones in the late eighteenth century. She was seen as a poor elderly female, dressed in grey and carrying an empty milk pail. At night, or on misty days, she would come up behind travellers and cry out in distress. The result of an encounter would, unavoidably, be that the person would get lost, however well they knew the route they were following—either the road would be made to look different or they would find themselves heading in the opposite direction to that they intended.[245]

The Old Woman's voice might be heard very near and then, immediately, very far off. If people were already lost in the mist, they might see the Old Woman ahead and try to catch up with her to ask for directions. As is common with faeries—especially Welsh ones—this chase would prove fruitless as the faster the traveller went, the further behind she or he would seem to fall. The Old Woman can never be caught and she never looks behind her. Pursuit would only result in the traveller getting even more hopelessly led astray and not infrequently they would end up stumbling into a bog, at which point the Old Woman's mocking laugh would be heard. If you do find yourself led astray like this, putting your hand on iron such as a knife will dispel the Old Woman's enchantment. During the nineteenth century, interestingly enough, the Old Woman was seen less on the highways and more underground, in "coal pits and holes of the earth," according to the Reverend Edmund Jones. He may have been seeking to imply that she is a demon emerging from subterranean places, but the faeries have always been conceived as dwelling below ground.[246]

In Somerset there are references to a "Woman of Mist" who lived on Bicknoller Hill in the western Quantock Hills. She herded deer on the hillside, something for which the *cailleach*, *glaistigs*, and various other Scottish faery females are known too.[247]

---

244. Owen, *Welsh Folk-lore*, 142.

245. Edmund Jones, *A Relation of Apparitions of Spirits in the County of Monmouth, and the Principality of Wales [...]* (Newport: E. Lewis Etheridge, and Tibbins, 1813), 35.

246. Sikes, *British Goblins*, 49–53; Jones, *A Relation of Apparitions*, 37.

247. Tongue, *Somerset Folklore*, 120.

Other Hags

As I've already described, the difference between "hags," banshees, and other types of faery women can be vague. For example, the people of Tiree identified certain streams and pools of water at which *cailleacha sith*, "faery hags," might habitually be seen, perhaps at their washing. In truth, the Highlands of Scotland seem to abound in various monstrous female creatures; every hamlet used to have its own named hag. For example, there is the *muireartach*, a hideous and violent being with just one, blue-coloured eye, whilst Glenmoriston is inhabited by the *Cailleach a' Chraich*. In the past, this creature was known to waylay lone travellers and kill them in a very curious way: she would snatch their bonnets and dance on them until a hole was worn through—at which point the owner promptly expired. A dog can protect its master from this fate, but usually it is nearly flayed alive in the process.[248]

The *baobhan sith* is a particularly fierce and dreadful female of the Highlands who may appear as a crow or raven or as a lovely girl in a long green dress. The gown conceals the fact that she has deer hooves instead of feet, a clear indication of her inhuman nature. The *baobhan sith* is known for seducing and then consuming unwary men—slitting their throats, ripping out their hearts, and drinking their blood.[249]

In the Scottish Highlands, a number of faery women are concerned with or oversee women's domestic tasks such as spinning and weaving. In part 1, I mentioned the *loireag*, who is a Highland faery specifically responsible for overseeing the making of cloth through all its stages, from loom to fulling. She demands observance of all the traditional methods and customs such as the singing of the various songs that accompany each different part of the process, and, if there is any neglect, she will undo any work she's dissatisfied with. Offerings of milk were made to the *loireag*, in part to propitiate her and in part to stop her sucking milk from the livestock in the fields. The *loireag* will bewitch the livestock to stop them getting away from her. She was

---

248. Campbell, *Superstitions of the Highland*, 105; Mackenzie, *Scottish Folk-lore and Folk Life*, 156; Alexander Macdonald, "Scraps of Unpublished Poetry and Folklore from Glenmoriston," *Transactions of the Gaelic Society of Inverness*, vol. 21 (1896), 34.

249. "Fairy Tales," in *Celtic Review* 5, 164.

described as a small woman but very scary; uttering a holy name could drive her off, nonetheless.[250]

Another Scottish spirit, the *gyre-carlin*, was also linked to cloth-making. It was said that if unspun flax was not removed from the distaff at the end of the year she would steal it all. Conversely, if asked by a woman for the endowment of skill in spinning, she would enable the recipient to do three to four times as much work as other spinners. Despite these domestic aspects, the *gyre-carlin* had a more fearsome side to her character. She was the Lowland equivalent of the *cailleach*, armed with an iron club and sustained by a diet of human flesh. Perhaps for this reason, she was also called *Nicnevin*, which seems to mean something like "daughter of bones."[251]

The *cailleach* has some function in protecting wildlife and is often seen herding deer—or even appearing as a deer—and there are several comparable beings across Scotland. In Dumfriesshire the *doonie* performs the same role. She's reported to have saved a boy who fell from a cliff when he was out collecting young rock doves, but she warned him to never trouble the birds again—for she might not be there a second time to catch him.[252]

The *Brown Man of the Muirs*, although male, acts as a guardian to wild beasts on the Scottish Borders. He was spotted in 1744, a solid, angry looking dwarflike figure dressed in bracken red clothes and with glowing eyes like a bull's. He scolded a young man out hunting game, saying that it was a trespass on his land and an interference with the beasts under his care. The dwarf claimed to live on berries, apples, and nuts alone—and invited the youth back to his home to see. The hunter was about to leap across a burn to join the dwarf when his companion called to him. The dwarf vanished, and the two concluded that it would have been fatal to have gone with him. Nevertheless, they scorned his warning and shot some more game before returning to their homes. This was believed to have led to the sickness and death within a year of the man who had spoken to the Brown Man.[253]

---

250. Watson, "Highland Mythology," *Celtic Review* 5, 54.

251. *County Folk-lore* 7, 34; Mackenzie, *Scottish Folk-Lore and Folk Life*, 149–50.

252. Aitken, *Forgotten Heritage*, 37.

253. William Henderson, *Notes on the Folk-lore of the Northern Counties of England and the Borders* (London: Folklore Society, 1879), 251.

In the Firth of Cromarty, the weather is under the control of *Gentle Annie* or *Annis*, a hag with a blue-black face. She is renowned for her treachery, as days may start fine and calm, encouraging fishing boats to put out to sea, but then violent gales might sweep in from the northeast. Both in her name and her responsibility for storms, this hag forms a bridge between the Scottish *cailleach* and more southerly relatives.[254]

In England, there are far fewer traces of any terrible supernatural hags. In Leicestershire is preserved a fairly limited recollection of *Black Annis*, a savage woman with a blue face, long teeth, and iron nails who lived in a cave on the Dane Hills and dragged people inside to devour them. She was also reputed to prowl the countryside, howling horribly and snatching people from their homes through the windows. That's about as far as the tradition extends now, although it is suggestive of much more detailed and widespread knowledge that has been lost.[255]

Conclusions

It can be hard to draw any dividing line between the *cailleach* and characters such as the *loireag* and *gyre-carlin*, although the sense is that there is a definite difference here between "faery women" and monstrous females. Involvement with domestic activities seems to be an important defining feature, as must be violent or aggressive character. Faery women, like all faes, can sometimes be unpredictable and vindictive, whereas a constantly bloodthirsty and enraged nature is central to the hag. On this interpretation, characters concerned with spinning like Habetrot are definitely faeries—to be approached with caution but not terror—whereas the *cailleach* is unquestionably a monstrous crone.

---

254. Mackenzie, *Folk-Lore and Folk Life*, 159.
255. *County Folk-lore* 1, 4.

Chapter 8

HOBS AND GOBLINS

Hobs are generally envisaged as large and normally hairy beings with bandy legs, akin in habits to the domestic brownies of northern Britain but more uncouth and much stronger: a hob can free a loaded cart's trapped wheel, it has been said, either by pushing or lifting the vehicle, whilst in one story from Derbyshire a hob was able to scythe through pieces of iron as easily as weeds. One hob living at Millom in Cumberland was described as "a Body aw over rough," in other words, covered in coarse hair.[256]

Lobs, Hobs & Puck

The essence of the hobgoblin, in fact, is its semi-feral, hirsute nature. Poet John Milton, in *L'Allegro*, bequeathed us a classic description of the type, portraying a "drudging Goblin" who undertakes the work of ten farm labourers and who is content to receive in return just a dish of cream and shelter

---

256. Sidney Oldall Addy, *Household Tales with Other Traditional Remains Collected in the Counties of York, Lincoln, Derby, and Nottingham* (London: Nutt, 1895), 39; John C. Atkinson, *Forty Years in a Moorland Parish: Reminiscences and Researches in Danby in Cleveland* (London, Macmillan & Co., 1891), 65; John Pagen White, *Lays and Legends of the English Lake Country, With Copious Notes* (London: John Russell Smith, 1873), 160.

at night. This "lubber fiend" lies down at night and "basks at fire his hairy strength." The physical might and the animal pelt are the hallmarks of this species.[257]

Milton's vocabulary tells us more, in fact. His hob is "lubber," which means clumsy, awkward, or stupid. A "lob" is a dolt or blockhead (from the Welsh *llob*), and it is notable that in *A Midsummer Night's Dream* Shakespeare has a fairy call Puck "thou lob of spirits" and that in the play *The Knight of the Burning Pestle* "Lob lie by the Fire" is the offspring of a giant and a witch, uniting ungainly size with malignity. In another contemporary play, the sprite declares his intention to leave the town and go "To frolic amongst country lobs" where he will plainly feel at home.[258]

Puck, Hobgoblin, and "Robin Goodfellow" are all identical in English folktales. Folklorist Joseph Ritson was told by an informant that Robin Goodfellow does all the farm chores and then lies before the fire, looking like a "great rough hurgin bear;" "hurgin" means "urchin," a hedgehog, and vividly conjures up the bristling nature of Robin's hairiness.[259] The sprite is often celebrated as a great shape-shifter, and according to Shakespeare, his guises include "a headless bear." Ben Jonson once nicknamed him "Puck-hairy."[260] Fascinatingly, in Michael Drayton's epic poem, *Nymphidia*, Puck, or Hob, is met with "walking like a ragged colt;" as we shall see later, the faery beast called the tatterfoal looks exactly the same. The comparisons of hobs to wild beasts have been constant over centuries.[261]

Twentieth-century poet Edward Thomas added a final layer of meaning to the name. In his poem "Lob" he described an old countryman he met one day in Wiltshire. He did not learn the man's name, but he identified him with literary Lob. "He has been in England as long as dove and daw / Calling the

257. John Milton, *L'Allegro*, lines 105-114.

258. Shakespeare, *A Midsummer Night's Dream*, II, 1; John Fletcher and Francis Beaumont, *The Knight of the Burning Pestle*, 1607, III, 4, http://www.luminarium.org/renascence-editions/bf1.html; William Haughton, *Grim the Collier of Croydon*, 1605, IV, 1 (vol. 102, *Tudor Facsimile Texts*, University of Illinois, 1912).

259. Anthony Munday, *Fidele & Fortunio*, 1584, line 566; *The Two Lancashire Lovers*, 1640, 222; Ritson, "Dissertation II on Fairies," 10.

260. Ben Jonson, *Love Restored—A Masque*, 1612 and see, too, *The Sad Shepherd*, 1637, III, 1.

261. Drayton, *Nymphidia*, 1627, line 283. Note, too, that the Irish "leprechaun" derives from the adjective "lubberkin" and that "urchin" was another Tudor word for a fairy.

wild cherry tree the merry tree."[262] Hobs and lobs are an ancient part of the British countryside, personifications of its cheerful, simple spirit; they're a part of its natural fauna and deeply in tune with it, for all their lumbering coarseness. Puck in Rudyard Kipling's *Puck of Pook's Hill* is a similar spirit of the ancient land, and we'll also see this identity, or harmony, with the landscape later in this chapter in the Manx *fynoderee*.[263]

Given his bulk and his brawn, it's hard to class Puck with the conventional faeries. Ben Jonson highlighted this in a masque of 1612, in which Robin Goodfellow declares that he's "none of those subtle ones that can creep through at a key-hole, or the cracked pane of a window. I must come in at a door." This is the simple, solid, and down-to-earth hob.[264]

The Yorkshire hobs are still described, by those who have glimpsed them, as small, brown, active, and naked, albeit covered in black hair. With their hirsute bodies, simple needs, dim wits, and brute strength, hobs are much closer to farm livestock than to either ourselves or to sharp and scheming faeries. For all these reasons, they are classed here as faery beasts.

There are many variants upon the hob's name including hobgoblin, hobthrush, and hobthrust; the latter two derive their second element from the Anglo-Saxon word *thyrs*, meaning giant, again making their outsized origin plain. Puck had a similar multiplicity of names, being known too as Pug, Pug-Robin, and Hodge-Poke (in which the first element is a nickname for Rodger, just as Hob and Robin are both nicknames for Robert, and all were used to mean "country yokel").[265]

The goblin element of the hob name can, on its own, imply a less friendly sprite. Goblins can be just as solitary as hobs, but they are much more malicious and bad tempered, as I shall describe at the end of this chapter. Finally, a strange member of the clan from Somerset is unlike any of the foregoing.

---

262. Edward Thomas, *Collected Poems* (London: Faber and Faber, 2004), 39.

263. *Tarlton's News out of Purgatory*, 1588, 55, 222; Rudyard Kipling, "Weland's Sword," in *Puck of Pook's Hill* (London: n.p., 1906).

264. Ben Jonson, *Love Restored*, 1612, http://www.luminarium.org/editions/loverestored.htm.

265. Jonson, *The Devil Is an Ass*, 1616, I, 1; T. Churchyard, *A Handful of Gladsome Verses*, 1592; and see Robert Nares, *A Glossary or Collection of Words, Phrases and Names* (Stralsund: n.p., 1825), 628.

The "blue burches" appear as wisps of smoke in houses and play pranks in kitchens.[266]

Hard Work & Other Hob Habits

Hobs are generally found in the north of England: for example, there are numerous places associated with them and named after them in Yorkshire alone. They prefer to live in holes and caves in hills and cliffs and are seldom seen in the daytime. It is possible sometimes to lure them out, although they may emerge suddenly and give the visitor a fright—as used to be the case with the denizen of Hob's Cave in Mulgrave Woods, near Whitby. If you called out to him, he was sure to reply:

> "Ah's tying mah left fuit shoe;
> An' Ah'll be with thee—noo!"
> (I'm tying my left foot shoe and I'll be with you—now!)

At which point, he presumably leapt from his hiding place and gave the visitor a fright. This hob seems tolerant of human company, teasing them with games of peek-a-boo, as if it were only threatening a delicious shock rather than any serious harm.[267]

At night, hobs will emerge and undertake menial tasks such as threshing, winnowing, and leading the stock for neighbouring farms, performing prodigious labours equivalent to the work of ten men but seeking no remuneration except a little food. They don't seem to be attached to any one farm or family but will come and go as they choose. On the downside, they may occasionally indulge in mischief, such as stopping the butter churning, drinking all the ale from the barrels, or undoing all the household chores. One time, the hob of Manor Farm, East Halton in Lincolnshire, decided it would be funny to put the wagon on the roof of the barn; the same hob also objected to the site chosen for the new church in the centre of the village and removed the stones nightly until the builders submitted to his will. The res-

---

266. Tongue, *Somerset Folklore*, 121.

267. John C. Atkinson, *A Glossary of the Cleveland Dialect: Explanatory, Derivative, and Critical* (London: John Russell Smith, 1868), 263.

idents of the farm were said to leave a candle lit in a window every night "to keep the Hob quiet."[268]

In addition to their good-natured devotion to the most laborious tasks around farms, hobs take on other guises. One hobthrush from Dore in Derbyshire was a cobbler. A shoemaker was worried that he was unable to make enough money from his trade to support his family. One morning, though, he came down to his workshop to find that some leather he had cut out the night before had been made up into a fine pair of shoes. He sold these for a good price the same day and with the money earned was able to buy enough leather for two new pairs of shoes. These were expertly made up the next morning—and so it went on, with his income and his stock of shoes growing rapidly. Naturally he was curious to know who was helping him, so the cobbler stayed up one night to spy in his workshop. He watched the hob complete a pair of shoes, and the shoemaker immediately put them away in a cupboard. The hob repeated the process, working so quickly and so tirelessly that the shop quickly filled with shoes, and the cobbler had to start throwing them out of the window as soon as they were completed, he had so many. Like all faery beings, hobs demand respect for their privacy and insist that any good turns that they do are not made public.[269]

Another common faery habit has also been imputed (once at least) to hobs. At Ipstones in Staffordshire a changeling left in exchange for a human baby, who had been put down to sleep in a hayfield during harvest, turned out to be a "hopthrust," as they were termed locally. Although it never grew and never spoke, the human mother cared for it well, in spite of her tragic loss and in the hope that the hobs might restore her own child to her in recognition of her kindness. For the duration of the changeling's life, whenever she wished for them, she would find small gifts of money concealed about her home in drawers and corners.[270]

---

268. Ingrid Barton, *North Yorkshire Folk Tales* (Stroud: The History Press, 2014), chapter 5; Kai Roberts, *Folklore of Yorkshire* (Stroud: The History Press, 2013), 96; Leland L. Duncan, "The following extract from a letter," *Folklore* 8, (1897): 69.

269. Addy, *Household Tales*, 38.

270. Elijah Cope, "Some Local Fairies," in *Memorials of Old Staffordshire*, ed. Rev. W. Beresford (London: George, Allen & Unwin, 1909), 89.

Benevolent hobs have also been associated with healing. The best-known example of this comes from the North Yorkshire coast. A hob inhabited a cave at Runswick Bay and would cure children afflicted with whooping cough if invoked with this verse:

"Hob-hole Hob! Mah bairn's getten t' kin'-cough:
Tak' 't off! Tak' 't off!"[271]

Puck, in his guise as a hob or lob, is one of these hardworking and helpful sprites. In *A Midsummer Night's Dream* a fairy observes that "Those that Hobgoblin call you, and sweet Puck, / You do their work, and they shall have good luck."[272] Puck will voluntarily undertake the full range of chores and regular tasks that must be performed in houses and on farms; he is "excellent in everything" and can do in six hours what it would take human workers twice as long to complete.[273] Specifically, in the farmyard Puck threshes grain and chops up firewood. In the dairy he churns butter. In the house he will grind malt, meal, and mustard; he sieves flour; he can mend linen, break hemp, dress flax, and spin thread; and he sweeps the kitchen and washes dishes at night. Conversely, Puck will punish lazy householders and their staff. Puck was so closely identified with farmwork, in fact, that he was often imagined in Tudor times carrying a flail for threshing, or else with a broom and candles.[274]

---

271. Atkinson, *A Glossary*, 262.

272. *A Midsummer Night's Dream*, II, 1.

273. *The Life of Robin Goodfellow, His Mad Pranks and Merry Jests*, 1628, in Halliwell, *Illustrations of the Fairy Mythology*, chapter 6, 120: Second Part, "How Robin Good-fellow Helped a Maid to Work."

274. *The Cobbler of Canterbury*, 1608, "Robin Goodfellow's Epistle," in F. Ouvry and H. Neville Davies (eds), *Library of English Literature*, vol. 2, (D. S. Brewer, 1976); Robert Burton, *The Anatomy of Melancholy* (London: Henry Cripps, 1621), 124; Ritson, "Dissertation II on Fairies," 10; Samuel Rowlands, "Of Ghosts and Goblins," *More Knaves Yet? The Knaves of Spades and Diamonds,* 1612; Ben Jonson, *Love Restored*, 1612, http://www.luminarium.org/editions/loverestored.htm); Reginald Scot, *The Discoverie of Witchcraft*, Brinsley Nicholson, ed. (London: Elliott Stock, 1886), book 4, chapter 10; Mary Howitt, "The Carolina Parrot," in *Mary Howitt's Poems*, (London: Nelson & Sons, 1872), 150; Halliwell, "The Pranks of Puck," in *Illustrations of the Fairy Mythology*, 165; Haughton, *Grim the Collier of Croydon*, IV, 1.

Ill-Humoured Hobs

Hobs are handy beings to have around a farm or smallholding. They will undertake endless amounts of arduous labour for very little expense, and they never seem to need a rest. However, this comes at the expense of a touchy temperament and a propensity for rather wearing practical jokes. The Yorkshire hobs have been described as "cheery creatures with little malice—unless they are unappreciated."[275]

For all their brutish stolidity, hobs are sensitive to criticism. Any questioning (real or perceived) of a hob's abilities or judgment will be met with bad temper. In East Yorkshire the hobthrusts are said to let beer run to waste, break crockery, throw pans, spill milk, and rattle things together if offended. A Lake District farmer with fields full of ripened grain ready for reaping wished to himself that his crop might be harvested and in the barn before the good weather had changed. The farm hobthrush heard his wish and laboured all night to get the harvest in. The next day it turned out to be sunny after all, and the farmer wished to himself that his crops had got another day's ripening in the field and that the overenthusiastic hobthrush was in the mill-pond. He was overheard, of course, and his grain was dumped in the pond instead.[276]

Like domestic brownies, hobs do not require cash payment for their work, but they do expect recognition in kind—that is, by the provision of food and drink. If this is neglected, the hob's ire will be roused. At Farnsdale in North Yorkshire, a son and his new wife inherited a farm from his father. With it came the resident hob who did many of the chores around the holding. The wife, being unused to the etiquette of faery helpers, begrudged him his nightly jug of cream and left whey instead. The indignant hob duly departed, taking the farm's prosperity with it. A similar case on a farm near Whitby in 1828 provoked the hob into making noise, pulling off bed covers at night, and killing poultry.[277]

---

275. Ingrid Barton, *North Yorkshire Folk Tales*, 83.

276. John Nicholson, *Folklore of East Yorkshire* (London: Simpkin, Marshall, Hamilton, Kent & Co., 1890), 80; Briggs, *A Dictionary of Faeries*, 224.

277. Roberts, *Folklore of Yorkshire*, 99.

The last statements notwithstanding, any suggestion of payment can seriously alienate a hob. Whilst leaving out food can be accepted as sharing, providing them with clothes to wear will cause serious affront. For example, at Upleatham near Redcar the hob attached to the Oughtred family was outraged over a workman's jacket mistakenly left hanging overnight on a winnowing machine. This was simply a misunderstanding, so when the garments are deliberately made or donated, albeit always with the best intentions, the offence is that much greater, and the hob will generally abandon its former home. This happened at Millom in Cumberland, Elsdon Moat in Durham, Close House at Skipton in Craven, and at Sturfit Hall near Reeth. At Overthwaite in Westmorland in about 1650 insult was added to injury because, after the hob called the Tawney Boy had only been helping out at the farm for barely six months, the family decided that his hair should be clipped at the same time as giving him a suit of clothes. In Yorkshire at Hart Hall in Glaisdale, the offence was not the act of presenting clothes, but their quality: the hob objected to them being coarse hemp, and this precipitated his departure. In like fashion, the hob at East Halton in Lincolnshire was driven away by hemp when he had expected linen.[278] In this respect, Puck behaves like any other hob. He expects his bowl of cream in recognition of his unstinting labours, but the provision of clothes is guaranteed to provoke great offence.[279]

Amongst the household spirits like hobs, mischief often manifests itself by the disgruntled being *undoing* work that's already been done: Robin Round Cap of Spaldington Hall near Selby in Yorkshire undertook plenty of useful chores, assisting the threshers and the milkmaids, but he also displayed a mischievous streak and delighted in mixing chaff into the winnowed wheat, putting out the fire, or upsetting the milk pail.[280]

278. Richard Blakeborough, *Wit, Character, Folklore & Customs of the North Riding of Yorkshire: With a Glossary of over 4,000 Words and Idioms Now in Use* (London: Henry Frowde, 1898), 203; White, *Lays and Legends*, 160; William Hutton, *The Beetham Repository*, 1770, ed. John Rawlinson Ford (Kendal: T. Wilson, 1906), 172; Atkinson, *A Glossary*, 243; Roberts, *Folklore of Yorkshire*, 96–8.

279. *The Cobbler of Canterbury*, 1608, 'Robin Goodfellow's Epistle'; Ritson, "Dissertation II on Fairies," 10; R. Scot, *The Discoverie of Witchcraft*, 1612, book 4, chapter 10.

280. Roberts, *Folklore of Yorkshire*, 98.

Given such a propensity for pranks, it could be very valuable to have a hob on your side in a dispute. One account from Mulgrave in North Yorkshire dates from about 1760 and concerns the faery denizen of a small hill called Hob Garth. A misunderstanding arose between two local farmers and one of them escalated it into a feud by breaking his neighbour's hedges and setting his sheep free. Mysteriously, though, the damage was repaired, the sheep were returned, and much worse damage was inflicted on the guilty party. This happened a second time and locals realised that the local hobman had sided with one of the pair. Soon after, the favoured farmer met a little old man, bent double over a walking stick, and with very long hair and very large feet, hands, eyes, and mouth, who assured him that in years to come he would always do well at lambing time. In subsequent years this happened, whilst the malicious neighbour lost many sheep.[281]

In one case, a hob sympathised with local people who objected to the re-siting of the church at Marske-by-the-Sea in North Yorkshire. The old one had been demolished and the stones transported to the new location, but overnight the hob would rebuild the church on its original site until the builders bowed to the inevitable. Related to this story of religious observance was the belief in Cumberland that, if you didn't eat your fill of food on Shrove Tuesday at the start of Lent, Hob Thruss would cram you full of barley chaff.[282]

Horrible Hobs

Hobs who have been permanently alienated by the household in which they have been living may desert it and go to live on their own—as did the hobs at Breedon Hill in Leicestershire and at Over Silton in Yorkshire—the latter because someone neglected one night to leave out the bread and butter that he expected daily as his reward for churning the cream. Probably worse, though, the creatures may choose instead to stay, but only in order to cause a nuisance. It's sometimes said that a hob scorned becomes a boggart (see next chapter).[283]

---

281. Blakeborough, *Wit, Character, Folklore & Customs*, 207.

282. Blakeborough, *Wit, Character, Folklore & Customs*, 205; White, *Lays and Legends*, 161.

283. William Grainge, *The Vale of Mowbray: A Historical and Topographical Account of Thirsk and Its Neighbourhood* (London: Simpkin, Marshall & Co., 1859), 325–6.

Where a hob has become an unbearable housemate, one solution to the problem may be to try to move away from it. However, in a series of stories with a theme that is also found linked to both boggarts and brownies, getting away generally turns out to be impossible. At Farndale in North Yorkshire a family resolved to escape from the annoyance caused by the household hob and had packed up the carts with all their belongings. As they left their former home, a neighbour enquired if they were "flitting" or not. The hob's voice came from the milk-churn—"Aye, we're flitting"—and the family promptly resigned itself to its fate and turned around and went back. Identical incidents are recorded at East Halton in Lincolnshire and at Hob Hill and Obtrush Rock, both in Yorkshire.[284]

Exorcising Hobs

Hobs can be laid, or exorcised, just like ghosts and boggarts (see later). As has already been mentioned, this can be achieved quite unwittingly just by presenting the unwelcome hob with clothes, but specific ceremonies also exist. Laying may involve as little as pronouncing a blessing or similar: for example, at Dalswinton in South West Scotland a farmer and the local minister agreed that the farm hob should be baptised. He was taken by surprise and holy water was thrown in his face, a well-intentioned act that had the effect of driving him away forever. Sometimes, though, much more complex rituals will have to be followed if you want to be certain of having expelled a particular sprite. The hob called Robin Red Cap at Spaldington Hall outside Selby in North Yorkshire eventually became too much of a nuisance with his pranks- despite the help he gave to the farm workers—and he was laid by means of the simultaneous prayers of three churchmen, by this means being confined to the farm's well—and that only for a limited period of time. The Somerset blue burches was laid by a blessing and, in response, fled to a

---

284. John Phillips, *The Rivers, Mountains, and Sea-Coast of Yorkshire* (London: J Murray, 1853), 201–11; Bruce Dickins, "Yorkshire Hobs," *Transactions of the Yorkshire Dialect Society* 7, part 13 (1942): 18–22; Atkinson, *Glossary*, 262.

nearby pond in horse form, taking us right back to some of the earlier faery beasts that were examined.[285]

A sprite called Hob the Headless was found haunting a stretch of the road from Hurworth to Neasham near Darlington. Luckily, the fear he caused was limited by the fact that he could not cross the River Kent, which flowed under the road at Neasham. Eventually Hob was laid under a stone by the roadside for ninety-nine years and a day. Despite this exorcism, the road was not rendered wholly safe, because anyone sitting on the stone became glued to it. Another hob was found at Hob's Hole, a deep pool on the River Tees at Coniscliffe, where he apparently took the occasional person by drowning.[286]

Most layings proceed on the basis that the hob will be inimical to the Christian religion. This needn't be the key factor, though. From Galdenoch Mill in Galloway comes the story of how the miller and his wife got rid of the nuisance brownie (or hob) who lived there with them. This hob was in most respects like his kin—he did chores at night but was not averse to the occasional trick. The miller's wife found him deeply annoying, and the two finally had a blazing row one day. The sprite responded violently, more like a boggart than a hob, holding her over the fire until her clothes started to burn and then plunging her in the well until she was almost drowned. After this brutal treatment, he left the mill in peace for a time. However, the hob returned after a while, and his mischief was greater than ever, so the local minister was called in to lay the unwelcome presence. A long ceremony of singing hymns and psalms followed. The religious aspect of it didn't seem to trouble the hob at all: he just sang along, mocking and interrupting the preacher. What finally drove this creature away was the noise; he agreed to leave just to get away from the reverend gentleman's bawling.[287]

---

285. Tony Bonning, *Dumfries & Galloway Folk Tales* (Stroud: The History Press, 2016), 57; *Roberts Folklore of Yorkshire*, 100; Sutherland, *Folk-lore Gleanings and Character*, 93; Tongue, *Somerset Folklore*, 121.

286. William Hylton Longstaffe, *The History and Antiquities of the Parish of Darlington, In the Bishoprick* (London: J. Henry Parker, 1854), 15.

287. Trotter and Trotter, *Galloway Gossip*, 46.

Highland Hobs

Over and above the English brownie and Lowland Scottish broonie, domestic faeries who live with farmers and help out around the farms, there's a host of other Highland Scottish beings with particular farming connections who more closely resemble the potentially intimidating hob than the milder (and physically smaller) brownie. Many of these are female and seem to have some traits of the "hag" and of the water sprite about them as well.

Gruagach

The *gruagach* lives in local caves and looks after the cattle of a farm or a village, for which duties she receives a daily bowl of whey or a regular offering of milk that should be poured out over a holed stone or special slab of rock called the *cloch na gruagach* (the *gruagach's* stone) whilst asking the sprite to protect the herds from death and disease. As long as this bargain is maintained, the cattle will be safe from all pests and predators.

APPEARANCE

The *gruagach* takes various forms. She has been spotted in a tall hat with long golden hair, dressed in green, but another writer captured the creature's looks as being like "a seedy brownie,... with long hair on his head; an old wrinkled face and his body covered with hair."[288] On Skye the *gruagach* often appears as a tall young man, dressed in black like a church minister, wearing a hat and carrying a wand, although at Troda on the island the creature was referred to as "The Old Man with the Grey Beard," and at Scorrybreck a female *gruagach* with long hair used to be seen, lying on the roof of a cattle byre. She would sing to the farm's cattle and kept them safe from all disease or accident.[289]

---

288. Campbell, *Popular Tales*, vol. 2, 401.

289. MacDougall, *Folk Tales and Fairy Lore,* 217; Samuel Johnson, "Ostig in Skye," in *A Journey to the Western Islands of Scotland* (London, 1775); Campbell, *Superstitions of the Highlands*, 18-22, 155, 183; MacCulloch, "Folk-Lore of the Isle of Skye," *Folklore* vol. 33, 207.

HABITS

The Scorrybreck *gruagach* was typical of her kind. She was very strong and could surpass even young men in endurance, although in another account a *gruagach* killed itself through overwork, trying to thrash an entire barn full of corn in one night.[290]

Like many of her kind, if the creature is offered clothes, she'll desert a farm, and if her regular helping of milk is forgotten, or is not served exactly as she likes it, she'll wreak havoc, turning the cows into the crops and such like. In cases of this kind, it's noticeable that cattle don't panic as they normally might if they got loose at night, suggesting that the *gruagach* will stay with them as a calming presence, for all her devilment. A few *gruagachs* will indulge in such mischief purely for a love of annoying people with their pranks.[291]

The *gruagach* is very strong and can underestimate its own strength: for instance, in one case from Scorrybreck on Skye, a *gruagach* had been teasing a woman by thwarting her attempts to drive her cattle into a byre; when she realised what was happening, she lost her temper and cursed him; he, in turn, gave her a slap which killed her. He was so remorseful that he sat up all night with the person who watched over the corpse, feeding the fire to keep her warm.[292]

Gruagachs (like brownies) can become very proprietorial about the houses in which they choose to live: they will supervise and spy upon the servants and punish those who are lazy, thievish, or rude. Generally, though, they can be protective towards humans.[293]

Glaistig

Glaistigs are often portrayed as violent hags, but their more benign aspect is as dairy maids and cowherds, seldom being seen but using their physical

---

290. See Briggs, *Dictionary of Fairies*, "Grogan or Grogach" or Spence, *The Fairy Tradition in Britain*, 101.

291. MacDougall, *Folk Tales and Fairy Lore*, 217; Campbell, *Popular Tales*, vol. 2, 401; Johnson, "Ostig in Skye," *A Journey to the Western Islands of Scotland*; Carmichael, *Carmina Gadelica*, vol. 2, 306.

292. Campbell, *Superstitions of the Highlands*, 185.

293. MacDougall, *Folk Tales and Fairy Lore*, 223; *Celtic Monthly* 5 (1892): 125.

strength and powerful voice to keep the cattle in check. When the family are eating or the herdsman has fallen asleep, the *glaistig* will be watchful, keeping the cattle out of the crops or away from cliffs. The *glaistig* of Glen Duror was once a dairy maid before she was abducted from her child bed by the *sith* folk and, in her *bean-sith* form, she took great care over all aspects of the management and care of the cattle.[294]

NATURE & APPEARANCE

As in the Glen Duror case, *glaistigs* are said to be human women who've been placed under a faery enchantment and thereby have acquired a faery nature. For this reason, the *glaistig* can sometimes transform into a dog to better herd and protect the livestock; nonetheless, she's said to be more human than faery, being more solid and substantial than a *sith* woman. Proof of this semi-human nature may be the fact that the *glaistig* attending the Lamonts of Ardnadrochaid died of sorrow and shame after she failed to protect the household's cattle against rustlers. Another *glaistig* was stabbed to death by an outraged laird of the MacMillans after she crept up behind him and grabbed and held him.[295]

The *glaistig* is heard much more than she's seen, and she apparently spends a good deal of her time invisible, which may account for the varied descriptions we have. Some have described a tall woman; others say she's small, stout, and very strong. Her face has been said to be wan and grey and to look like a stone covered with lichen, but other witnesses have recalled her more favourably—as a little woman with yellow hair, as a young woman with long hair or as a "lump of a lassie" with white hair like flax. She may appear dressed in green with a wand, and she moves with a supernatural gliding gait. The *glaistig* is unique amongst the hobs in that she is also a shape-shifter, being able to assume the bodies of dogs, as mentioned, but also goats, mares, foals, and sheep.[296]

---

294. MacDougall, *Folk Tales and Fairy Lore,* 267.

295. Campbell, *Superstitions of the Highlands,* 172; Campbell, *Superstitions of the Highlands,* 157, 161.

296. Mackenzie, *Scottish Folk-Lore and Folk Life,* chapter IX, 177; Campbell, *Superstitions of the Highlands,* 166.

Habits

The *glaistig* lives near to farms but is a solitary being, normally keeping to a convenient ravine nearby. She is a half-water, half-land sprite and is probably never far from some body of water; one derivation of the name is "water imp," and her diet includes a lot of fish and eels. In addition, the *glaistig* expects a pail of milk nightly and will react angrily if this is withheld or forgotten—the calves may be found amongst the cows in the morning, depriving the household of milk at breakfast, the cream may not rise, or a cow may die. In some places, milk is also offered at other important points in the farming year, such as when the cattle are first left out overnight each year and when they are brought inside for winter. The *glaistig* of Ault-na-Creige on Mull was driven away when a boy played a prank and left out boiling milk; another at Morven was outraged by a well-meant cup of tea. The *glaistig* of Glen Duror seemed particularly sensitive to signs of human activity. She not only lived away from houses amongst the rocks in the glen but, it was reported, quit the area entirely once steamers appeared on Loch Linnhe and blasting started in the new quartz quarry.[297]

As a rule, *glaistigs* are harmless and pleasant: they will play with children and take especial care of lonely elderly people or those with mental disabilities. Less endearingly, they make sure other farm servants do their work properly. Milkmaids will be punished if they do not clean the cows well before milking them, and the *glaistig* will also check the udders after milking to check that a proper job has been done. Servants who are lazy or who don't show the *glaistig* sufficient respect will be made to suffer, perhaps with a couple of hefty clouts. Some *glaistigs* are even more brownie-like, washing clothes or tidying up houses at night, in which role they are called the *maighdean sheombair* (chambermaid), but they could become nuisances, too, in houses by making noise and playing pranks, such as upsetting furniture, putting dust in the food or pulling off bed linen. They would also interfere with tools and spinning wheels left out overnight. Even so, they would not live on the premises, but might be seen arriving for the "night-shift" from their wilderness abodes. The attachment to a house or family might even become so

---

297. MacDougall, *Folk Tales and Fairy Lore*, 267; Campbell, *Superstitions of the Highlands*, 159; Watson, "Highland Mythology," *Celtic Review* 5 (1892): 63.

close that the *glaistig* took on a banshee-like role, seeing future events (such as the arrival of visitors, which would provoke her to greater efforts around the house) and crying out if joy or misfortune are imminent. This was, for example, the case with the so-called "elle-maid" (elf-girl) of Dunstaffnage Castle in Argyll.

FORCED LABOURS

Glaistigs can be captured and forced to undertake tasks for humans, building barns or castles in a single night, for example. However, when they're compelled by duress or taken captive, they will often exact a revenge by cursing the captor. One man was granted herds of cattle, but was told that his children would grow like rushes—shooting up tall and straight—but then wither away like ferns; the clan would be as impermanent as the mist. *Glaistigs* can voluntarily bestow skills (in one case, as a thief) and they might voluntarily undertake good deeds other than their farm work too, for example appearing as a foal and carrying a person over a dangerous stream at Erray on Mull.[298]

NASTY GLAISTIGS

For all her devotion to a family and to its dairy herds, the farm *glaistig* could be irritable, whilst the *glaistig* in her wild state is a nuisance, if not a downright menace. These have been regarded as the enemies of men: one *glaistig* on Arran lived in a cave that people called "Uamh na Beiste," the "Cave of the Monster." Many stories from the Highlands describe how the wild *glaistigs* will tease and annoy, often with a view to abducting and killing a human if the opportunity presents itself. Some delight in waylaying and attacking travellers. The *glaistig* of the ford of the River Meig would ask those trying to cross what weapons they had about them. Whatever you made the mistake of naming, you would be unable to wield against her.[299]

Those dealing with such creatures should always be on their guard, ideally taking the precaution of having a naked blade about themselves at all times. Two brothers from Onich were pestered by a *glaistig* whenever they went out hunting on *Monadh Dhubh* and stayed in a shieling. Eventually, they fell out

---

298. Campbell, *Superstitions of the Highlands*, 159–183; Fionn, "A Loohaber Hag: The Glaistig of Llanachan," *Celtic Monthly* 9 (1901): 189.

299. Mackenzie, Scottish *Folk-Lore*, 241, 181.

and the *glaistig* promised the brothers vengeance; the next time she appeared, they took no risks and set their dogs on her. The two hounds got the better of the hag, but one returned with only a few tufts of hair left on its body, and the other came back looking like a plucked chicken. In the worst example of this fatal tendency, four men staying in a bothy overnight wished that their girlfriends were with them. Unexpectedly, the young women appeared soon afterwards. Only one of the men was suspicious about this, and he kept his sweetheart at a distance all night with the help of his dirk. His caution was wise, for the women were actually four *glaistigs*, and the other three had drained their unsuspecting partners of all their blood. In another version of this story, set at a place called Creag a' Bhais, "The Rock of Death," one of the men spots that the women have deer's hooves, and he fends them off all night by playing his (metal) Jew's harp. At dawn, they turn into eagles and fly off.[300]

In fact, robust, even violent, treatment of a *glaistig* can actually pay dividends. The gift received from her might be an immediate advantage, such as the man who was allowed to kill a white hind amongst the deer herded by a *glaistig* after he called off his hound from savaging her. Sometimes, much longer-term benefits may be granted. A man called MacLachlan, living at Glenahurich, discovered that a *glaistig* was killing his newborn foal each year. After the third was born, he caught the hag in the act of trying to drown the young horse and violently seized her. Faced with certain death, she bargained for her life by granting prosperity to him and to his descendants, as well as endowing him with the second sight. Similar good fortune was bestowed upon the blacksmith of Strontian in the Highlands (it's notable, by the way, that the Gaelic name of this place is *Sron an t-Sithein*, meaning the "Peak of the Faeries"). This blacksmith always liked to leave his forge tidy at the end of the day, but he kept finding it in disarray every morning. He decided to wait one night to see what was happening, hiding behind the door with one of his largest hammers. Sure enough, a *glaistig* entered and began to create chaos, whereupon he smashed his hammer down upon her head. To avoid a second blow, she begged for mercy and granted to all of his descendants perfect skills in the smith's craft.[301]

---

300. MacDougall, *Folk Tales and Fairy Lore,* 243, 259; *Celtic Monthly* 3 (1894): 176.

301. MacDougall, *Folk Tales and Fairy Lore,* 237, 251, 263; Campbell, *Superstitions of the Highlands,* 177; Spence, *The Fairy Tradition in Britain,* 41.

Urisks

The *urisk* (or *uruisg*) is said to be a "large lubberly supernatural," a half-human and half-fae (or even half-goat) spirit that is often very like a domestic brownie.[302] They are the offspring of a relationship between a man and a *leannan sith*, having very long hair, long teeth, and long claws. During the summer, the *urisk* lives alone in caves in wild places. In winter, they shelter in barns and outbuildings and, in return for being allowed to lie before the fire and to receive a bowl of cream, they will undertake farm chores such as herding and threshing. They are very strong and clever but can be savage if provoked. They will desert a farm if neglected or insulted, although it's not clear whether or not presenting clothes is a welcome act or an affront. One farmer even gelded his *urisk* in an effort to tame it, an act which he seems to have got away with scot-free.[303]

Apparently the solitary *urisk* can crave human company and may tag along with lone travellers at night. This can prove a disturbing experience for the human, either because the *urisk* is a silent companion dogging his or her heels or because it engages in conversation, on which occasions it has hair-raising stories to tell from heaven, hell, and the otherworld.[304]

The *urisk* can also make a nuisance of itself with taunts and jeering and, rather like the *glaistig*, it may from time to time do this solely to provoke a human's ire so that there's an excuse to fight and kill it. In some forms, such as the *peallaidh*, the *urisk* haunts rivers, falls, lochs, and the seashore and is more dangerous. This creature's name means "the shaggy one," and he is described as a hostile sprite with long, untidy hair. The name emphasises the feral, bestial nature of the hobs. One example of this type from the Highlands is the *peallaidh an spuit*, "the shaggy one of the waterfall," who was believed to live in caves behind the cascades. The *urisk* of Moraig waterfall in Argyll was understood to have a role regulating the flow of water over the preci-

---

302. Campbell, *Superstitions of the Highlands*, 191.

303. James MacDiarmid, "Fragments of Breadalbane Folk-lore," *Transactions of the Gaelic Society of Inverness* 25, (1901–2), 133; Dieckhoff, "Mythological Beings," *Transactions of the Gaelic Society of Inverness* 29, 241.

304. Watson, "Highland Mythology," *Celtic Review* 5, 51; Mackenzie, *Scottish Folk-Lore*, 185.

pice; apparently, he stopped it falling too quickly by dangling his feet in the flood.[305]

On the Isle of Arran, the child of the *urisk* is called the "Bleater," the *meileachan*, and is known on the island as a particular nuisance. In one instance, for example, it waylaid a farmer riding home at night and kept jumping up behind him on his horse. He managed to seize the being and held it tight until he got back to his farm, whereupon he locked it in his barn. Eventually the creature's mother came to set it free—something the man was happy to do—and as the pair left, he heard her ask her offspring whether it had revealed to the human "the virtue of egg water or the root of nettle." Similar knowledge is mentioned in connection with an *urisk* that was driven away from a farm by leaving it a coat in cold weather. The farmer's wife declared she would not miss it, for it had never disclosed "the virtue of the root of bur and what substance is in the sweat of an egg." Evidently, there is some magical property in an egg's cooking water that's known to the faeries (it may be recalled that a mermaid had something similar to say about it), and on Shetland washing your face in the first egg laid by a chicken could bestow the second sight.[306]

Manx Hobs

On the Isle of Man, there are two equivalent beings to the English hobgoblin. The first, that most closely resembles its mainland cousin, is the *fynoderee* (a name that's also spelled *fenoderee* and *phynodderree*), a being that's known to live on about twelve farms on the island. They don't tend to enter the farmhouses themselves, nor come near to them unless food is left out. They are rarely seen because during the daytime they keep to the woods and glens. Manx folklorist Mona Douglas described him in these terms: "he is a faery being who is said to have the body of a goat and the head and shoulders of a

305. MacDougall, *Folk Tales and Fairy Lore,* 295-308; James Browne, *A History of the High-lands and of the Highland Clans,* vol. 1 (Glasgow: A. Fullerton & Co., 1838), 106; Camp-bell, *Superstitions of the Highlands,* 197; Watson, "Celtic Mythology," *Celtic Review* 5, 48; David MacRitchie, *The Testimony of Tradition* (London: Kegan Paul, Trench, Trübner & Co., 1890), 159; MacDiarmid, "Fragments of Breadalbane Folklore," 133.

306. W. M. MacKenzie, *The Book of Arran* (Arran: Kilbrannan Publishing, 1914), 277, 280, 284; Burgess, "Some Shetland Folk-lore," *Scottish Review* 25, 102.

man; he may perhaps be called a sort of mythical goat." This further example of a hob being compared to a satyr or faun is a reminder of their "beastly" character.[307]

The *fynoderee* is a very typical hob. He has been compared to a domestic brownie and a troll combined. He is said to be bigger and broader than a man, extremely hairy, clumsy, and repulsive with knock-knees. Despite his appearance, he can run very quickly and is a great worker, being immensely strong. At the same time, he's also very dim. By way of illustration, the *fynoderee* of Bride parish, working on his own, cut two whole fields of corn in one night and then rounded up a flock of sheep, penning them along with several hares; in like manner, the *fynoderee* of Gordon tried to fetch water in a sieve.[308]

Several proofs of the *fynoderee's* strength are attested. Manx people point to a huge stone that was carried from the beach to a building site by one. In another incident, he met a blacksmith and asked to shake hands. The smith prudently placed a plough share in the *fynoderee's* grip: it was squeezed like putty.[309]

The *fynoderee* is friendly towards people, for the most part, and will labour tirelessly, threshing grain overnight, gathering in hay before a storm, or rounding up sheep during a blizzard. Nevertheless, like many of his kind, he is sensitive of criticism and will reject human clothes if they're given to him, although in his case it doesn't seem to be principle so much as practicality. For one thing, he is so hairy that garments are unnecessary in any case; over and above this, clothes can make him ill. In one famous story he expresses his disgust with the gift of suit by complaining:

---

307. Gill, *A Manx Scrapbook*, chapter 4, 193; Douglas, "*Restoring to Use Our*," 22.

308. Leney, *Shadowland in Ellan Vannin*; Morrison, *Manx Fairy Tales*; Moore, *The Folk-lore of the*, chapter 4.

309. Train, *Isle of Man*, vol. 2, chapter 18; Jenkinson, *Jenkinson's Practical Guide*, 91; Douglas, "*Restoring to Use Our*," 22.

"Cap for the head—alas, poor head!
Coat for the back—alas, poor back!
Breeches for the breech—alas, poor breech!"[310]

The *fynoderee's* response in this case was to abandon the farm for the soli-
tude of Glen Rushen. This would have been a disaster for the farmer, because
it is said that the luck of a house resides in the sprite and, with his departure, all happiness and prosperity will also be gone. Mona Douglas has sum-
marised the *fynoderee's* position as "a being who keeps all the unruly inhabitants of the unseen world in something like order, and holds the human
inhabitants of the Island under his protection." Some authorities believe that
Manx agriculture as a whole has declined along with the waning belief in and
respect for the *fynoderee*.[311]

The second Manx hob is called the *glastin* or *glashtyn*. This sprite has one
form as a horse (as was described earlier) but also as a lamb, a pig, and even
as a water bull or *tarroo ushtey*, but he will mostly be seen as a large, hairy,
naked man (though females are also known), simple and coarse and prone
to grudges. An example of their stupidity is the regular story of a *glashtyn*
herding in the flock of sheep with which he also—with very great trouble—
rounded up a hare.[312]

There are seemingly two separate types of *glashtyn*. One is semi-domesti-
cated, living in pools in rivers near to the farms where it works. The sprite is
good natured and helpful to those whom he favours. He is very strong, being
able to thresh a whole stack of corn in a single night and will also tend grain
drying in kilns overnight. In return for their labours, people would bank up
the cottage fire for them to enjoy at night but would never speak to them. The
glashtyn, like so many of his kind, doesn't like to be given clothes and doesn't
like to be overseen. One on a farm at Barra that was engaged in drying grain

---

310. See, for example, Briggs, *Dictionary of Fairies*, 170, or Train, *An Historical and Statistical
Account*, vol. 2, 148.

311. Evans-Wentz, *The Fairy-Faith in Celtic Countries*, 129; Douglas, "*Restoring to Use Our*,"
22; Train, *Isle of Man*, vol. 2, 138; William Harrison, *Mona Miscellany: A Selection of
Proverbs, Sayings, Ballads, Customs, Superstitions, and Legends, Peculiar to the Isle of Man*
(Douglas, Isle of Man: The Manx Society, 1869), 173.

312. Roeder, *Manx Folk-Tales*, 25; Spence, *Fairy Tradition in Britain*, 84–85.

realised that a man was spying on him, and he snatched the offender and threw him into the hot kiln as well. Fortunately, some kindly faeries intervened and pulled him out.[313]

The second type of *glashtyn* is wild-roaming. He has very unpleasant habits, such as trying to carry off women, but he can be scared off by throwing hot turves at him. The *glashtyn* at Braddan haunted the churchyard there and was described as being short with an evil, hairy face. If you wanted to pass the spot, you had to bow three times to appease him.[314]

What I think is particularly striking about this group of beings is how many of them are semi-wild sprites, often with a parallel reputation for violent acts, and yet they're entrusted with a farm's valuable assets. Of course, the farmers don't recruit them; the faery cowherds are generally inherited or volunteer themselves, but it is nonetheless a curious relationship. The spirit of the wilderness accommodates itself to the human subjugation of the landscape.

Goblins & Dwarves

So far, I have discussed the many varieties of hobgoblins, usually a more pleasant and amenable sprite that, despite its size and strength, can live amiably and helpfully in proximity to humans. Strip away the "hob" prefix, which has some connotations of shambling stupidity, and what's left are the goblins, creatures whose whole nature comprises the worst elements of the aggravated hob.

A goblin tends to imply a bad-tempered, if not an outright malevolent, sprite. The name isn't an English one, however, it's borrowed from French *gobelin*, and ultimately from Greek *kobalos*, denoting an evil spirit. The German *kobold*, which can be translated as "knocker," a mine faery, is also derived from the same source. The word first appeared in (written) English usage in about 1325 and was initially used to mean a devil or demon, although it was

---

313. *Yn Lioar Manninagh*, vol. III; Moore, *The Folk-lore of the*, chapter 4; Roeder, *Manx Folk-Tales*, 26.

314. Moore, *The Folk-lore of the*, chapter 4; Roeder, *Manx Notes & Queries*, 98; "Glashtin," Isle of Man—Paranormal Database Records, Paranormal Database, accessed May 22, 2020, www.paranormaldatabase.com/isleofman/mandata.php.

later demoted to something slightly less malign and more mischievous.[315] "Goblin" became interchangeable with a number of other words: for example, in the romance of *Melusine* from 1500 one may read of "Many manere of things, the which somme called Gobelyns, the other ffayrees, and the other *bonne dames* or good ladies."[316] A century later in Fairfax's *Godfrey of Bulloigne*, there's a comparable grouping of supernaturals: "The shriking gobblings each where howling flew; the Furies roare, the ghosts and Faeries yell."[317] By 1713 Thomas Tickell was able to describe "Our own rustical Superstition of Hob-thrushes, faeries, goblins and Witches." The labels have become virtually identical, so that today a goblin is often nothing more or less than a bad faery.[318]

Goblins are regarded as solitary and ill-tempered. We should be grateful that they choose to live in isolation from human communities, because they are very dangerous to encounter. Examples include two malign beings of the Scottish Borders. The Red Caps live in old ruins; anyone caught by bad weather when out on the road who takes shelter in the crumbling structures risks being killed. The Red Cap has been described as resembling a well-armed and armoured old man who has large teeth and eyes. He wears a red cap which he dyes in the blood of his victims. It is hopeless to attempt to fight him off, but reciting a passage of scripture or making the sign of the cross will drive him away. Very similar is the Powrie or Dunter who also dwells in ruined pele towers. This goblin isn't so actively violent; instead, he makes a sound like the stamping of flax or the grinding of grain; if this gets louder or lasts longer than normal, it foretells some tragedy.[319]

Difficulties similar to those found with the word goblin arise with the term "dwarf," which largely fell out of English folklore usage after the Anglo-Saxon period. Within Britain, the word "dwarf" was then reallocated for use to describe certain medical conditions because the category of creature

---

315. See, for example, Rossell Hope Robbins, ed., *Historical Poems of the XIVth and XVth Centuries* (New York: Columbia University Press, 1959), 28.

316. See Jean d'Arras, *Melusine*, vol. 68, ed. A. K. Donald, EETS edition, 1895, 4.

317. Edward Fairfax, translation of Torquato Tasso, *Godfrey of Bulloigne; or, The Recoverie of Jerusalem*, 1600, IX, xv, 162.

318. Tickell, *The Guardian*, April 15, 1713.

319. Henderson, *Notes on the Folk-lore*, 253, 255.

known as the dwarf does not exist in folk belief. Dwarves feature strongly in the folklore of Germany, but they only became familiar in Britain again through the Brothers Grimm and the much more recent work of J. R. R. Tolkien.

That said, a descendent of the original word, *dweorg*, lingered in the north, being used to describe some sort of being that should more properly be labelled a hobgoblin. (It also survives in Dorset, in the south of England, in the form "derrick," describing a pixie-like being.) There is a story from the Simonside Hills in Northumberland in which a lost shepherd spends a tense and unhappy night with a local *duergar*, sharing a hut during bad weather. The *duergar* resents his unwelcome companion and passes the time trying to trick him into falling off a cliff edge which he has concealed with glamour. The shepherd's peril is only revealed in the light of the morning when his hut-mate has vanished.[320]

The *hobyahs* of Perthshire appear to be some kind of goblin or dwarf-like being. There is only one story about them, in which they seem to be unpleasant creatures. An old couple lived with a young girl in a flimsy hovel made of hemp stalks. One night the *hobyahs* came with the intention of tearing down the insubstantial shelter and eating the occupants. Luckily the family's dog barked and scared them off. This was repeated several nights running, but sadly the old man misunderstood the reason for the dog's yelping, and he killed it. The next night the girl was kidnapped and carried off in a sack to the *hobyah* lair. Fortunately, a man out with his dog found her the following day and freed her whilst the *hobyahs* slept. He put the dog in the sack instead so that, in the evening, when the *hobyahs* opened the bag expecting to eat the girl, they were instead eaten themselves.[321]

Further north, the *fridich nan creag* of the Highlands are small goblins or gnomes that live inside rocks and subsist upon the crumbs and drops of milk that are dropped by human households when they are eating, cooking, or milking. If a family are too tidy and do not allow the sprites this small share

---

320. R. J. King, "Folklore of Devonshire," *Fraser's Magazine* 8 (1873): 773; Frederick Grice, *Folk Tales of the North Country: Drawn from Northumberland and Durham* (London: T. Nelson & Sons, 1944), chapter 38.

321. Joseph Jacobs, *More English Fairy Tales: Collected and Edited by Joseph Jacobs* (London, Putnam, 1922), 127.

of their food, they will find other sustenance, usually by taking cattle, sheep, and horses through apparent accidents.[322]

Conclusions

The hobs are, of all the faery beasts, the most animalistic. Many of the faery beasts possess beast-like form, but do not act consistently with their outward appearance.

The hobs are beasts of burden, simple creatures of brute strength and instinct. Yet, while they are a force of nature, they are also a part of nature. Their attachment to certain farms can be likened to the local flora and fauna; the hobs are one with the local environment. It is for this reason that we would wish to foster their good will: the favour and assistance of a hob can be of immense material benefit.

---

322. Carmichael, *Carmina Gadelica*, vol. 2, 295.

Chapter 9

BOGIES

In this chapter, I discuss a broad category of supernatural creatures whose exact place in the taxonomy of Faery can be hard to fix. They may sometimes look almost human, inclining us to label them as faeries, but they can just as often appear as hounds or as other animals. Many of them have a single function—usually to scare or to warn us—which makes them less than true faeries, with their rich and complex society. For these reasons I include all the bogeys, bogles, boggarts, and others in a single group of "bogies" under the overall heading of "faery beasts."

Names & Classification

The problem of defining bogies has been with us for centuries. Tudor poet Thomas Churchyard wrote about them collectively in 1592:

"Of old Hobgoblings guise
That walkt like ghost in sheetes

> With maides that would not early rise
> For feare of Bugs and spreets."[323]

Although they do share features with ghouls and spirits, there are many characteristics shared by these beings with the faes that argue for their inclusion with the "faery beasts." Sir Walter Scott characterised these creatures very well as "freakish spirit[s], who [delight] rather to perplex and frighten mankind, than either to serve, or seriously to hurt them."[324] In addition, whatever form these bogies may take, there are certain common characteristics that are found consistently across all forms, uniting them as a family as well as demonstrating their membership of the wider faery race. This may well be why poet Samuel Rowlands in 1612 lumped together a wide range of supernatural beings, describing how:

> "Great store of Goblins, Faeries, Bugs, Night-mares,
> Urchins and Elves, to many a house repaires."[325]

Once, the people of the British Isles identified a host of different bogies, many very localised and each no doubt with their own characteristics and habitats. For most of us, all we have now are the enigmatic names, from which we may try to distil some scant information about their natures. We know, for example, of Boggy-bo, tints, hodge-pokers, bygorns, bomen, flay-boggarts, and alholders. Part of this ignorance derives from something that seems to be alluded to in Churchyard's rhyme. There is a clear suggestion from him that—even at the turn of the seventeenth century—credence in bogles and hobgoblins had largely disappeared and that they survived in popular culture largely as a joke and as a means of scaring children into

---

323. Churchyard, *A Handful of Gladsome Verses*, 1592.

324. Walter Scott, *Minstrelsy of the Scottish Border: Consisting of Historical and Romantic Ballads [...]*, vol. 1 (Kelso: James Ballantyne, 1802), 181.

325. Samuel Rowlands, *More Knaves Yet?*, 1612.

behaving themselves. I'll give attention separately to the diminution of these sprites into mere bywords for "things that go bump in the night."[326]

A huge variety of these related faery creatures exist, whose affinities and connections are reflected in their very similar names: bugs, bogles, bogies, boggarts, bug-a-boos, and others. Across the British Isles there is a host of connected names, the *bwg* and *bwgan* of Wales, their versions of the English hobgoblin and bugbear whose names seem to have been borrowed into English as "bug." These names derive from *bwgwl* (threat) and *bw* (terror) and are also related to our "bogle," the Gaelic *bocan*, and the spirits called puck, *pwca*, *bucca*, and *bokie*.

This dense web of scary beings is by no means unique to Britain. In German there are related words such as *spuk* (a spook, bug, or hobgoblin) and *bögge* and *bogglemann*. Ireland has its *pooka*, and much further afield in Lithuanian there are *baugus* (terrific) and *bugti* (terrify), and in Maharatta, from India, *bagul*, a boggle. Very evidently, the Indo-European peoples from deep in their history have been terrified by bogeymen during the night. Scottish shepherd poet James Hogg therefore caught the essence of the bogie family when he spoke of "the gomral [stupid] fantastic bogles an' spirits that fley [scare] light-headed fok up an' down the country..."[327]

In light of the wealth of names that exist, a final word on terminology is necessary here. The names for the many types of bogies and other such faery beasts are very far from fixed or precise, and we should not worry overly about categorising these supernatural creatures correctly. Uncertainty is understandable: we are dealing with beings that have been glimpsed only briefly and which have caused alarm and horror in the witnesses, meaning that careful descriptions are unlikely ever to be forthcoming. This sense of doubt is compounded by the fact that the bogles can change shape, so that determining their core identity and appearance can be extremely difficult. Separating bogles from boggarts and shucks from padfoots can seem a hopeless task. The names chosen may be down entirely to local taste or the preference of the folklorist

---

326. Lists of British faeries are found in Scott, *Discoverie of Witchcraft*, book 7, chapter 15 and Michael Aislabie Denham, *The Denham Tracts*, vol. 2, ed. Dr. James Hardy (London: David Nutt, 1895), 77–80.

327. James Hogg, "The Wool-Gatherer," in *The Brownie of Bodsbeck; And Other Tales,* vol. II (Edinburgh: William Blackwood, 1818), 140.

who first recorded the apparitions. Accordingly, we shouldn't try to insist upon strict and consistent divisions between hobs and brags and goblins. They're not scientific terms, and we shouldn't try to pretend they are; they're just convenient labels for an otherworld we still don't understand very well.

Common Bogie Traits

What ties together all the strange creatures in this second part of the book—and what associates them with the better known faes, mermaids, and pucks? As we examine the many different types of bogey and boggart, you may repeatedly notice similar patterns of behaviour or of responses to humankind.

Fear

These creatures were, as a class, seen as malevolent and terrifying. This is confirmed by a rhyme from the Isle of Man in which an unfaithful lover is cursed, successively, with injury from the water bull, the night steed, the "rough satyr" (that is, the *glashtyn*), the faery of the glen (*ferrish ny glionney*), and with bogles. Pity the two-timing partner who faces this supernatural assault.[328]

A bogie in the shape of a white dog was known to haunt a crossroads near the village of Brigham in the East Riding of Yorkshire, alarming all those nocturnal travellers who passed by. Creech Hill in Somerset was the abode of a "bullbeggar," another variant upon the bogie, but one that seems in most places to have very early on been demoted to a bugaboo to scare children. The Somerset example was a black figure that chased or attacked those crossing the hill at night. It could grow to enormous size and was believed to be associated in some way with two bodies dug up on the hill during quarrying.[329]

Humans fear bogies not just because they are supernatural and unknown, but because they can be extremely violent. At Mulgrave Wood near Whitby was to be found a violent and ill-tempered sprite called Jeanie. Locals were unsure whether to call her a bogle or a faery but, certainly, she didn't like to be called by the name she'd been allotted. One man who did was pur-

---

328. Harrison, *Mona Miscellany*, 65.

329. Nicholson, *Folklore of East Yorkshire*, 79; Tongue, *Somerset Folklore*, 121.

sued viciously by her; she killed his horse, and he only escaped by crossing a stream.[330]

In Scotland March 29 was once celebrated as "Bogle Day." Just as faeries and other sprites are believed to roam abroad on Halloween, it looks as though on this day of the year the assorted Scottish goblins had the run of the countryside, free to behave as they wished.

Portents & Protection

When these beings manifest themselves, it is very often for a particular purpose, such as to predict some death or disaster or to draw a person's attention to concealed riches. By way of illustration, the being known as "Silky" at Black Heddon in Northumberland acted in many ways like a typical domestic brownie or hobgoblin—tidying an untidy house or disarranging a neat one—but she disappeared forever once a skin filled with gold fell through the ceiling of the old manor house.[331]

Silky also behaved like a sort of guardian spirit, appearing at night on the darkest part of a road in dazzling splendour and then accompanying a rider for a while until the route improved. Many other bogies will undertake tasks for humans, whether that is by performing domestic or agricultural chores or by giving them specialist knowledge, such as healing abilities. Silky gets her name from her rustling dress and, in this, she seems to be related to banshee-like protective spirits.

Many bogies can be a nuisance rather than a benefit. Silky, for all her goodwill, would make horses freeze with terror, and it was often necessary to carry a sprig of rowan in order to dispel her influence. Similar measures need to be taken against plenty of other bogies, either to prevent their mischief or to defend against their aggression. Throughout the chapter that follows, you will also encounter procedures for "laying" or exorcising these creatures. A fascinating example of this aspect comes from Arkengarthdale. A man laid a bogle in his cottage by opening his Bible, lighting a candle and then pronouncing the injunction "Now then, you can read, or dance, or do as you like." The bogle was

---

330. Atkinson, *A Glossary*, 56; Arthur H. Norway, *Highways and Byways in Yorkshire* (London: Macmillan, 1899), 146; Walter White, *A Month in* Yorkshire (London: Chapman and Hall, 1861), 104.

331. Henderson, *Notes on the Folk-lore*, 268.

observed to vanish in the form of a grey cat and wasn't seen again for many years. However—as will often be found to be the case—the banishment was not permanent. One day the man met the bogle again on the stairs—and this spelled his doom. Soon after the encounter, he left the house to go to his work in the mine and died in an accident.[332]

Bawling Bogles

Another common feature of bogles and boggarts is the noise they make. They will announce themselves with their shrieks and yells. Sometimes there is no purpose to this bellowing other than to alarm people living in the vicinity, as appears to be the case with the Mickleton Hooter or Belhowja in Gloucestershire, or else to annoy and inconvenience them, as with Jack o' the White Hat at Appledore in Devon who would shout "boat ahoy," summoning the ferryman across the mouth of the Torridge River, only for there to be no prospective passenger waiting. Nonetheless, omens are often read into the barks and howls these creatures emit.[333]

Several of these vociferous beings are known. At Sennen Cove, in the far west of Cornwall, the "hooper" is known for the whooping noise it made. In otherwise fine weather a dense fog bank settles on the reef of rocks just outside the harbour, cutting the quay off from the open sea, and at night a dull light may be seen inside the cloud and the cries of the hooper will be audible. The reason for the hooper's arrival is, it seems, to act as a warning against storms coming in from the Atlantic. If you ignore the augury and head out to sea regardless, you will never be seen again. At Claife, on the shore of Lake Windermere in the Lake District, the "Crier of Claife" was heard summoning the ferrymen from Bowness on the opposite shore, rather as at Appledore. The voice was disembodied and there was never a passenger waiting when the boatmen rowed across; often, they would return pale and speechless with horror and would die within a short time. The Crier was laid in a nearby quarry in Tudor times.

On the Isle of Man, a similar sprite called the *dooiney-oie* or night caller performs the same function. He's been called a "banshee," because he some-

---

332. Henderson, *Notes on the Folk-lore*, 268, 247.

333. J. B. Partridge, "Notes on Folk-lore," in *Folklore* 27 (1916): 308.

times seems attached to a single family, although he isn't predicting death. Rather, if his dismal howls of "Hoa! Hoa!" are heard during a winter's night on the coast, it is a sure sign that storms are approaching in the Irish Sea. Because of his warnings, the Manx people have regularly avoided considerable loss: fishermen were able to get in their nets, lines, and pots and farmers could shelter their flocks. Other writers have associated the night man with particular locations around the island, such as the glen at Ballaconnell in Malew parish and a cave on Cronk-y-Thonna. As with all faery beings, it is wise not to affront him: some men who once insulted the *dooiney-oie* promptly found themselves pelted with stones from an invisible source, and any group of boys who have tried to creep up to his cave to get a glimpse of him invariably end up with sprained wrists and ankles. The worst injury he can inflict is the shock caused by his very loud shouting.[334]

Lastly, mention should be made of the "Long Coastguardsman" of Mundesley in Norfolk, who at midnight on cloudy nights will walk along a stretch of the coast, singing and laughing in the wind whenever a storm is raging. Unlike the previous two sprites, the coastguard seems to mark bad weather rather than to forewarn of it.

Moral Purpose

The Scottish shepherd poet James Hogg said of bogies that "they are a better kind o' spirits, they meddle wi' nane but the guilty; the murderer, an' the mansworn, an' the cheater o' the widow an' the fatherless, they do for *them*." As an illustration of this moral function of the bogie class, there is the tale of a poor widow from Reeth whose neighbour stole some candles from her. The thief soon found himself haunted by a bogle; he tried shooting it, but it had no body that could be wounded. The next day it came to him, warning, "I'm neither bone, nor flesh, nor blood, thou canst not harm me. Give back the candles, but I must take something from thee." It plucked an eyelash, which may seem harmless enough, except that his eye "twinkled" for ever after that day.[335]

---

334. Train, *Isle of Man*, vol. 2, chapter 18; Gill, *A Manx Scrapbook*, chapter 4—Malew; S. Morrison, "Dooinney-Oie, The Night-Man: A Manx Folk-Tale," *Folklore* 23 (1912): 342; Henry Irwin Jenkinson, *Jenkinson's Practical Guide to the Isle of Man* (London: Edward Stanford, 1874), 40.

335. James Hogg, "The Wool-Gatherer," 140; Henderson, *Notes on the Folk-lore*, 247.

Appearance

The shape-shifting tendencies of bogies have already been mentioned. Their propensity for assuming different forms is part of the source of our problem in defining bogies and in separating out the different types of bogie. One folklore writer has said that there is nothing more uncertain than the manner in which a boggle manifests itself. "Any shape, human or animal or composite, any unaccountable noise, may be a boggle." Animal shapes are preferred, but these range from dogs and horses to cats or even rabbits. As will be seen in the next section, this mutability can be taken to extremes.[336]

Formless Bogies

As will be discussed, many of the different classes of bogie are able to use magic to appear in a number of different forms, but there are some that have such anomalous manifestations, or no fixed shape at all, that they deserve separate discussion.

Cloth-Like Bogies

A bizarre but persistent feature of reports is of encounters with beings that are neither human-like nor animals. Although we have grown used to the idea of apparitions that may be lights, encounters with supernatural beings that look like rolls of cloth is extremely surprising and disorientating. Nonetheless, these cases are common enough for us to conclude that it is a genuine aspect of faery. Moreover, they have been experienced for centuries: a report from Byland, North Yorkshire, dates to before 1400 and describes the apparition of a four cornered spinning sheet.[337]

In Lancashire, people have often met with the Holden Rag, a boggart that resembles a scrap of white linen, hanging in a tree at Holden near Burnley. If anyone tries to remove the rag from the tree, it will shrivel up and then vanish with a flash of light. The rag may also appear as a large black dog and cause a nuisance; it can blight crops and cattle and create vexation around farmsteads.

---

336. Jeremiah Sullivan, *Cumberland & Westmorland, Ancient & Modern: The People, Dialect, Superstitions and Customs* (Kendal, John Hudson, Jos. Dawson, and Jas. Robinson, 1857), 155–6.

337. Simon Young, "The Mysterious Rolling Wool Bogey," *Gramarye* 8 (Winter 2015): 11, https://www.academia.edu/24973729/Young_The_Mysterious_Rolling_Wool_Bogey.

The boggart was eventually laid under a rock— "so long as a drop of water runs through Holden Clough, which has never been dry since." At Norton near Darlington a supernatural being was seen that transformed from a white heifer to a roll of Irish linen and then into a white female figure.[338]

The "Picktree Brag" at Pelton in Durham has had a variety of manifestations, including four men holding up a white sheet, in which form it was considered a premonition of a death. The padfoot seen near Leeds has sometimes looked like a woolpack, which will roll on the ground before vanishing through a hedge. A female sprite found in Petty Lane, Glowrowram, near Chester-le-Street in Durham, would, if approached, collapse and spread out on the ground like a sheet or a pack of wool before disappearing. The apparition would terrify riders and milkmaids out late and could even upturn carts.[339]

Following people disconcertingly at night is a common bogie habit—and it's one practiced by the cloth-like types just as much as the black dogs and horses I'll describe in due course. Yorkshire poet Thomas Shaw described a faerie being called Will of Delph who:

"If you on errands went,
He'd catch you in the dark
And like a sheet of wool,
Come rolling close behind."[340]

What is consistent in all these apparitions is the fact that they move and that they will transform as the witness watches. Other examples are even more free-ranging and exotic. The troubled ghost of Lady Howard was believed to haunt the area between Okehampton Park and Fitzford House in Devon. She ran back and forth between the two as a great black hound, a calf,

338. Longstaffe, *The History and Antiquities,* 15; Simon Young, "In Search of the Holden Rag," *Retrospect* 35 (2017): 3–10. https://www.academia.edu/38310291/Young_In_Search_of _Holden_Rag

339. Cuthbert Sharp, comp., *The Bishoprick Garland: Or, A Collection of Legends, Songs, Ballads, &c, Belonging to the County of Durham* (London: Nichols, and Baldwin & Cradock, 1834), 41; Henderson, *Notes on the Folk-lore,* 270, 273; William Brockie, *Legends & Superstitions of the County of Durham* (Sunderland: B. Williams, 1886), 74–75.

340. Thomas Shaw, "Narrative of Shantooe Jest," in *Recent Poems, on Rural and Other Miscellaneous Subjects* (Huddersfield: J. Lancashire, 1824), 130.

a coach of bones, a greyhound, and "a woolsack full of eyes, rolling along." At Cowley's Corner in Oxfordshire in 1837, farmer George Andrews was riding his horse when he saw a thing looking like a woolpack that was rolling over the fields from the Corner towards a fishpond. Other people passing there had glimpsed something looking like a calf, a sheep, a naked man, and a flash of lightning.[341]

These bizarre entities are seen across the length and breadth of Britain. As mentioned in part 1, one of the many forms that the Highland water horse can assume is that of a tuft of wool and, you may recall from earlier, it is said that the *bochdan* feels like a bag of wool—shapeless and weightless—if you try to fight it.[342]

At Creagan in Argyllshire there are stories of something called *an sac ban*, the white sack, which once again seems to have been some sort of supernatural piece of material. It was said to look like a bag but to be mobile: it chased people, it could wrap itself around a person's feet so that they tripped up and then it would get on top of them, flatten them, and kill them. In Galloway the "seckyban" was known, plainly sharing its name with the Highland version. This southern sack would roll ahead of people in the road, and any house outside which it stopped would soon experience a death. Normally the sack should be white, but a black version of the "sacbaun" or "sedgeband" has also been reported. A similar apparition was met by the grandfather of Dorset poet William Barnes when out riding: a rolling "fleece of wool" entangled itself in his horse's legs, after which the poor animal was permanently lamed.[343]

Rolling Bogies

The previous paragraphs grouped together objects which observers compared to man-made materials. There have been other sightings, though, in

---

341. Elias Tozer, *Devonshire & Other Original Poems; With Some Account of Ancient Customs, Superstitions, and Traditions* (Exeter: Devon Weekly Times, 1873), 90; Percy Manning, "Stray Notes on Oxfordshire Folklore," *Folklore* 14 (1903): 65.

342. John Campbell, *More West Highland Tales*, trans. John Mackay, vol. 1 (Edinburgh: Oliver & Boyd, 1940), 203; Campbell, *Witchcraft and Second Sight*, 181, 220.

343. Campbell, *More West Highland Tales*, vol. 1, 488; Trotter and Trotter, *Galloway Gossip-Eighty Years Ago* (1901), 231.

which the fae creatures resembled more natural substances. Once, during the 1930s, a woman taking a walk on the Cornish coast encountered a creature she described (perhaps for want of an alternative) as a "pisky" that changed into "a long furry black roll, which gambolled about on the grass and then disappeared." One day during the early 1940s, a woman out for a ramble in rural Kent saw a small furry ball rolling up a slope towards her. It briefly opened when it drew close to where she was sitting to reveal a being, whom she again labelled as a "pixie," within—and then it disappeared. Odd as these incidents sound, they're not wholly unknown within Faery.[344]

Devon pixies have been said to move around like "balls of fern or heather, swept before the wind," and a Welsh sprite called the *pwca* looks like a handful of grass blowing along. A shepherd at Benderloch in Argyll saw a large bundle of ferns rolling down a hillside before falling over a waterfall and disappearing. This might have been nothing more than what it appeared to be—foliage propelled by the wind—but he knew that it was really "Black Donald," the devil, or—we might say—a malign spirit of some description. Observers have struggled to find the right names for what they have witnessed, but given how unlike conventional pixies and faeries these beings were, I think they are better classed as "bogeys" along with the other rolling, organic apparitions.[345]

It isn't just soft shapes that can come rolling at you. At Hellsgill, Nether Auchinleck, in Clydesdale, a sprite in the shape of the outer rim of a cart-wheel would come bounding down the brae, heading straight for any night-time traveller. Just as it looked to be about to collide with its victim, the wheel would vanish with an eldritch laugh. Other such Scottish "wheels" have been reported. You may recall from earlier how a *fuath* scared off a man on Skye who had been fishing during spawning time, against social norms, by turning into something that looked like a mill wheel. At Lag nam Bocan (Bogle's Hollow) on South Uist, a woman saw an iron car wheel rim rolling along the road. A comparable—and equally inexplicable—incident occurred at Mynydduslwyn in Gwent: a reddish, grey object, round like a bowl, was encountered rolling back and forth across a lane. The witness believed it was

---

344. Johnson, *Seeing Fairies*, 28, 236.

345. *Choice Notes & Queries* (London: Bell and Daldy, 1859), 35; Richard John King, "The Folk-lore of Devonshire," *Fraser's Magazine* 8 (1873): 781; Campbell, *Superstitions of the Highlands*, 303.

a living thing, because it grew larger and smaller as it moved; he enquired what in God's name it was, and the apparition instantly disappeared. Perhaps it's significant that both the nuggle and the *shoopiltee* discussed in chapter 5 are said to have tails resembling waterwheels.[346]

Amorphous Beings

If animated rolls of cloth or wagonless wheels were not alarming enough, there are supernatural entities that can take on forms even more shapeless and strange. It's very possible that some of the references to fleeces may in fact be trying to describe these creatures.

A well-attested amorphous Scottish being is the Morag, which lives in Loch Morar near Lochaber. This creature has been described as a "huge, shapeless, dark mass"; when it surfaces on the lake it might be mistaken for a small islet. Its appearance may be a source of terror, but its primary purpose was to mark the death or departure of a member of one of the local clans, and it can, accordingly, be the cause of great distress in the neighbourhood. The Morag is unusual in that she is seen in broad daylight and by a large number of people. Another witness described a "black heap or ball slowly and deliberately rising in the water and moving along like a boat waterlogged." It has to be admitted the other sightings portray her in far more conventional terms: for example, "the lower portions of her body are in the form of a grilse (salmon) and the upper in the form of a small woman of highly developed breasts with long flowing yellow hair." She is, therefore, a meremaid—very beautiful but timid—and she rushes about in great distress because of the impending loss that her appearance forebodes. In contrast, a witness in 1968 described something that was lacking "eyes or anything like that. It was a snake-like head, very small compared to the size of the neck—flattish, a flat type of head. It was very dark, nearly black. It looked as if it was paddling

---

346. C. T. C. S., "Popular Superstitions of Clydesdale," *Edinburgh Magazine* 3 (1818): 156; Campbell and Hall, *Strange Things*, 263; Jones, *A Relation of Apparitions*, 9; Goodrich-Freer, "Powers of Evil in the Outer Hebrides," *Folklore* 10, 273.

itself along." In this manifestation, the Morag sounds more like the plesiosaur by which the Loch Ness monster has been explained.[347]

There seems to be a lot of overlap between the more conventional water horses and kelpies and these shapeless bogies. Once, on the Scottish island of Raasay, a blacksmith, whose daughter had been abducted and killed by a water horse, managed to trap and kill the monster using heated irons. When he inspected the corpse of the animal afterwards, he said it resembled only grey turves or a soft mass like a jellyfish. A closely related account concerns a man from Tubernan in the Highlands who decided to catch the kelpie of Moulin na Fouah and then take his bound prize to the inn at Inveran to boast of his achievement. Equipped with a dog to help corner the beast and an iron needle and awl to help subdue it, he succeeded in his mission and led his burdened horse to the inn in triumph. However, when he arrived, the kelpie had dwindled away to nothing but a lump of jelly.[348]

There are related sprites in England. From Oxford, in or before 1916, comes an account of "Boneless," a big, shapeless shadow that slips along beside and behind people in the dark, terrifying them. A later report from Somerset seems to be a very similar entity, although it resembled a white bank of fog but very concentrated. It slides and slips along the ground, engulfing people and animals in its path in an icy, damp, and stale-smelling cloud as it passes. Finally, one Lancashire boggart manifested itself as "a column of white foam, like a large sugar loaf, in the midst of a pond."[349]

The culmination of these weird tendencies is another Scottish being. From Shetland, it is called simply "It." This entity lacks any fixed form: some have described a large lump like a jellyfish, others a bag of wool, yet others an animal without legs, or a human without a head. It could move incredibly quickly, though it lacked legs or wings, and it made no sound and yet conveyed meaning to people. It seemed indestructible too: an attempt to kill

347. "Morag, the Monster of Loch Morar—1," The Carmichael Watson Project, University of Edinburgh, Blogger, December 22, 2011, http://carmichaelwatson.blogspot.com /search?q=morag; "Morag, the Monster of Loch Morar—2," The Carmichael Watson Project, University of Edinburgh, Blogger, December 26, 2011, http://carmichaelwatson .blogspot.com/2011/12/morag-monster-of-loch-morar-2.html.

348. Campbell, More West Highland Tales, vol. 1, 209; Campbell, Popular Tales, vol. 2, 204.

349. P. P., "Folklore of Lancashire," Choice Notes & Queries—Folklore, 188–189.

and bury it apparently failed, as the entity rose up in a glowing mist and then spun off into the sea.[350]

Summary

All faery beings have the ability to be shape-shifters, and many of the faery beasts deploy the power as a means of tricking or trapping humans. Bogies are especially known for being able to take on new forms and for the astonishing variety of shapes they can assume. My last example (from 1883) underlines this but does not fit into any of the categories so far suggested. A Suffolk "goblin" was known for harassing (and even scaring to death) horses along a certain stretch of country road. It could look like a dog, a cat, a donkey, or another horse, but it particularly favoured appearing as a brown paper parcel.[351]

Land Fuathan

In part 1, I mentioned the family of terrifying beasts called *fuathan*. Some of these are intimately associated with rivers and bodies of water; others are not so clearly water sprites, but many of them are notable for their shape-shifting abilities so, accordingly, are described here.

Bochdan

A *bochdan*, whatever shape it takes, is an inherently terrifying type of *fuath*. This fear can be compounded by several additional factors. They may make unearthly sounds, such as the clanking of chains, horrific cries, loud whistling, or the sound of someone being throttled. They add to this effect by appearing in churchyards or at lonely fords or on isolated roads. In most cases, seeing a *bochdan* foretells a sudden or violent death at the location where the apparition occurs.

There are several traditional protections against *bochdan* and their kin. All over the Hebridean island of Eriskay regular blessings took place to protect against *fuathan*; for example, annual masses were held at Creag Shiant (the Faery Rock) at Baile to keep the resident goblin in check. If a person

---

350. Briggs, *Dictionary of Fairies,* "It"; Saxby, *Shetland Traditional Lore*, chapter 9.

351. M. H. James, *Bogie Tales of East Anglia* (Norwich: Pawsey & Hayes, 1891), 47–48.

is chased by a *bochdan*, they should try to reach the seashore, because the "black shore" below the line of the seaweed is safe from all faeries and fae beasts. As ever, these land beasts are unable to cross flowing freshwater either. However, if you aren't near a stream or the sea when a *bochdan* assails you, you may need to fend it off. The *bochdan* are averse to iron, as are all their kind, but it will be necessary to partly draw your knife before you meet the sprite, otherwise you'll never be able to get it out of its sheath. If you're asked by the sprite what it is you have on you to defend yourself, you should never name it directly: use a phrase such as "my father's sister," and this will guard the blade against being enchanted. Finally, you can draw a protective circle around yourself, using a stick or a knife, and pronounce the words "the cross of Christ be upon this." This will be an insurmountable defence.[352]

If it comes to a fight with a *bochdan*, humans very often find themselves at considerable disadvantage. Their opponents seem like bags of wool, soft and insubstantial, but at the same time they can overpower a man. If you are accompanied by a female dog or horse, you may find your difficulties doubled because they will turn against their owners, the only remedy to which is to draw blood from one of the animal's ears or to bind it with your belt.[353]

Brollachan

In one of its manifestations, the *bochdan* is nothing but a dark moving object—a shape without recognisable form that can maul men and dogs horribly. This amorphousness is the essential quality of the *brollachan*, a creature said to be the child of a *fuath*. The *brollachan* has eyes and a mouth but otherwise it is simply a dark mass. Because it lacks any definite form, it will try to possess animals and steal their bodies for a while. Any creature possessed by the *brollachan* will be recognisable because it will darken in colour and have red eyes, but the host body will soon wither and die and the possessor will need to move on. In spite of their fearsome nature, *brollachans* aren't apparently very clever: the best-known story about the monster follows the "ainsel" plot. All the being could say was "me" and "you;" when a man burned it so as to keep it at a safe distance, the outraged *fuath* mother wanted

---

352. Goodrich-Freer, "The Powers of Evil in the Outer Hebrides," *Folklore* 10, 261.

353. Campbell, *Witchcraft and Second Sight,* chapter 5.

to know who'd injured her child and was told only "me" and "you"—hearing which, she gave up seeking a culprit to punish.[354]

Other Land Fuathan

There are numerous other land *fuathan* about which relatively little is known, except that many of them are shape-shifters. Amongst them are the *beithir*, a snakelike being that lurked in caves and corries; the *cearb* or "killer," and the *fachan*, a one-armed, one-legged, one-eyed monster who might be armed and was (we must assume) dangerous. A relation of the *fachan* is the *fahm* of Glen Airn. This is an ugly little monster who frequents the mountain peaks in that vicinity. Perhaps fortunately, he's only seen at daybreak, as he has an evil and dangerous nature. He can shrink his body and enlarge his head until it's twice as big as the rest of him, and he can kill his victims by making their heads swell up and burst. Any creature that crosses the *fahm's* track before sunrise is sure to die. The name *fahm* derives from the Gaelic *famhair*, meaning "giant," a true example of which is the *ferla mhor* or "big grey man" who is sometimes seen—or heard—deep in the Scottish mountains.[355]

The *direach* of Glen Etive is very similar to the *fahm* (as, too, is the *bochdan* in one of its manifestations), but it can also be seen as a headless man, a billy goat, and a black dog who accompanies a traveller for part of his journey. Without doubt, part of the danger of *fuathan* is the fact that they can assume so many shapes—a pig, a dog, or even a length of coiled rope—so that you may never know when they are present. At the same time, it is very easy to summon them and fall into their power. In the Outer Hebrides, it was said that you should never call your dog by name after dark because then a *fuath* would come and would call away both the dog and its owner, who would have to follow.[356]

---

354. Campbell, *Witchcraft and Second Sight*, 189 (Islay), 208 (Schiehallion); Campbell, *Popular Tales*, vol. 2 no. 37, 203; Briggs, *Dictionary of Fairy Tales*, "Brollachan."

355. James Hogg, "Night The Second," in *The Queen's Wake: A Legendary Poem* (Edinburgh: Andrew Balfour, 1815), 68.

356. Briggs, *Dictionary of Fairies*, "Direach"; Goodrich-Freer, "The Powers of Evil in the Outer Hebrides," *Folklore* 10, 265, 273.

Puck

Thanks to William Shakespeare's *A Midsummer Night's Dream*, Puck is probably one of the most famous faery beings in the world. In fact, by the time he appeared in the play, he was already well known within England. Around the turn of the sixteenth century, several ballads and other publications appeared, attesting the popularity of this spirit, who was also known affectionately as Robin Goodfellow. He ceased to be merely "a puck" and came to rank with other named faeries such as Oberon and Mab. Oddly, this national success seems to have come at the expense of being recalled at local level. There are now almost no folktales about him, as opposed to the "literary" records.

Puck is a bogie (his name is a variant upon "bug"), and he displays many of the traits of the bogies to be described in this chapter. For example, in the play *Wily Beguiled*, Robin Goodfellow claims that he plays "the Bugbeare, wheresoere I come" and in *More Knaves Yet?* he has huge saucer eyes, typical of many bogie beasts.[357]

Even more bogie-like are Puck's habits of pranks and nuisance, mischief he often inflicts by changing shape. One Elizabethan poet rhymed about "bogges ... [and] pretty little pogges, / As Monkies, Owles and Apes"[358] and it is very likely that he had Robin in mind. Puck can look like different people (including a disabled beggar, soldier, old woman, tradesman, minstrel, young maid, and fiddler), or can appear like an ox, a crow, an owl, a raven, a hound, a hog, an ape, a fox, a hare, and a frog. He can also transform into inanimate objects, such as trees and stools, the better to play his tricks.[359]

Puck became famous precisely because of his rich and varied character. Besides his bogie-like traits, he was known to behave like a Will of the Wisp, and I examine this aspect in chapter 12. He was also recognised as a sort of hobgoblin, prepared to labour in a house or farm. In this guise, I might have included him with the "helpful boggarts" (see later, especially the story of the

---

357. W. W. Greg, ed., *Wily Beguiled*, 1606, Malone Society, 1912, line 479; Rowlands, "Of Ghosts and Goblins," in *More Knaves Yet?*.

358. T. Churchyard, *A Handful of Gladsome Verses*, 1592, first stanza.

359. *A Midsummer Night's Dream*, II, 1; *Robin Goodfellow—His Mad Pranks and Merry Jests*, 1628; *The Ballad of Robin Goodfellow*; *The Pranks of Puck*; Jonson, *The Devil Is an Ass*, 1616, I, 1.

Levenshulme boggart who's called Puck), but I chose instead to include him with the hardworking hobs in the last chapter.

Boggarts

"Stars are shining, moon is breet,
Boggard won't come oot toneet."[360]

Boggarts are a species of bogey universal to Lancashire and believed to live primarily in holes and caves but also to haunt dells, ponds, gates, and wells, from all of which they will only emerge at night. There is a Boggart Hole in Pendle Forest and, near to Manchester, there is the famous Boggart Hole Clough (or valley). There used to be dozens of boggarts attached to localities around the county, many with their own highly memorable names—Matty Kew, Old Moss, Thrasher, Young Grange Bump, and the Clough Spout Clogger. As this very brief list only begins to illustrate, there are many "rural boggarts" linked to localities like bridges, woods, lanes, and—most particularly—steep sided valleys with streams, but there are also "domestic boggarts" associated with old houses and mansions.[361]

Boggart Origins
One writer has suggested that boggarts arise from three different sources: there are those that embody the ghosts of murder victims, such as a headless boggart seen at Whitegate Lane in Blackpool; there are those that appear to be the souls of those suffering punishment for their mortal sins; and, lastly, there are those that function as banshees—warning of imminent death within certain families. Thus, the boggart of Clegg Hall near Rochdale was related to the murder of two orphan children there; even after the Hall was demolished in 1620, the angry spirit persisted—hence a saying: "It always keeps coming again, like the Clegg Hall boggart." At Kersal Hall, the murder of the English occupier by the incoming Normans was reputed to have given rise to the boggarts, who in due course took revenge on the French usurper. A boggart in the form of a black dog at

---

360. Traditional Lancashire saying.
361. *Notes & Queries*, series 4, vol. 5, 156.

Radcliffe Tower was linked to a girl murdered there. Overall, it's clear that many boggarts are ghosts who have acquired many of the powers of goblins.[362]

Appearance

Boggarts can change both their size and their shape. One seen by a boy at Frandley in Cheshire during the 1880s appeared first as a little old man but then silently swelled bigger and bigger until the boy fled in terror. This boggart kept his human shape; others may be witnessed as animals (such as the unalarming sounding group of little cats reported from Lancashire), as skeletons, or as monsters—which may include a headless woman. At Elland in West Yorkshire the boggart was called the Long Wall Mouse—a name suggestive of its appearance but not of its reputation for bringing bad luck to those who saw it. As I described earlier, the "Holden Rag" was, indeed, a piece of material. At Longridge in Lancashire, a boggart was encountered in the form of a woman carrying her own talkative head in a basket. Terrifying as this is in itself, worse was the fact that the boggart would pursue victims, hurling her head with snapping jaws after them. Luckily, as is so often the case, this particular apparition could not cross flowing water.

As this last example suggests, boggarts were often found haunting stretches of road. At Fairfield and Ashton in Lancashire the boggart assumes the shape of a woman dressed in white or black silk and glides along in front of travellers on the road before vanishing. A West Yorkshire man who joked about whether or not a companion engaged in mending a road near Todmorden had seen any boggarts was straight away felled by a heart attack. These bogies aren't tied exclusively to highways, though: the ancient stone circle at Arbor Low in Derbyshire is also said to be frequented.[363]

362. William Thornber, *An Historical and Descriptive Account of Blackpool and its Neighbour-hood* (Blackpool: Smith, 1837), 332; John Harland and T. T. Wilkinson, *Lancashire Legends, Traditions, Pageants, Sports &c, [...]* (London: Routledge, 1873), 11, 42, 192.

363. *Choice Notes & Queries—Folklore*, 188; James Bowker, *Goblin Tales of Lancashire* (London: W. Swan Sonnenschein & Co., 1878), 131; John Harland and T. T. Wilkinson, comps., *Lancashire Folk-lore* (London: Warne & Co., 1867), 54; John Billingsley, *West Yorkshire Folk Tales* (Stroud: The History Press, 2010), 41.

Evil Boggarts

The majority of boggarts are unfriendly and unpleasant beings. The more malicious of these creatures will attempt to pull people down into their underground lairs, as with the boggarts of Hellen Pot and Hurtle Pot near Chapel-le-Dale, both in Yorkshire. At the Bee Hole area of Burnley there used to be a boggart who lurked in wait for solitary people. It was said to have once killed a woman there and then to have hung up her skin on a rose-bush. The boggart at Horbury near Wakefield also attacks the unwary; it is hairy with glowing eyes and is reported to be icy to the touch.[364]

Other boggarts seem to be more likely simply to alarm travellers. For instance, at Bunting Nook in Norton outside Sheffield, a boggart haunts the place where three roads meet and has been a particular terror to children passing by there. In this guise, as I'll describe later, the boggart very much resembles many of the supernatural black dogs that lurk along Britain's highways.

Helpful Boggarts

Boggarts are not all bad by any means. Some will take on the labouring roles usually performed by brownies and hobs. They can work for free for humans and make them rich.

The helpful boggart at Hackensall Hall near Fleetwood in Lancashire assumed the shape of a horse, it was said, solely so that it could enjoy a warm stable and a hot fire at night. However, unlike the hobs, most labouring boggarts do not seem to have expected any sort of recompense at all; in fact, it's said that thanking or acknowledging the boggart is just what you *shouldn't* do.[365]

They may appear looking like large horses and, in that disguise, will work well for farmers and hauliers if they are well used by them. If they are mistreated or neglected though, the boggart will cry out loudly in complaint. At Levenshulme in Lancashire, a boggart (who is termed Puck, King of the Faeries) helped out an elderly farmer with his reaping and gleaning, but a falling out occurred between them when the man half-seriously questioned whether the boggart had tired out his best horses whilst getting in the har-

---

364. Roberts, *Folklore of Yorkshire,* 101; Sabine Baring-Gould, *Yorkshire Oddities, Incidents, and Strange Events* (London, Methuen and Co., 1900), 334.

365. Harland and Wilkinson, *Lancashire Folk-lore,* 58.

vest overnight. In consequence of these careless words, the crop ended up back in the fields, and the peevish boggart refused to do any more tasks in the fields. Nonetheless, Puck carried on doing the household chores until he overheard a neighbour asking the farmer whether he missed the boggart's help with the farmwork. The man confessed he did—and invoked a blessing upon him. With a shriek, Puck abandoned the farm entirely.[366]

Unfortunately, it is most common for boggarts to combine both desirable and alienating qualities. The boggart of Syke Lumb farm near Blackburn was known as a very hard worker when he was content—he would milk the cows, bring in the hay, fodder the cattle, harness the horses, load carts, and stack harvested crops; when he was irritated by some casual remark or insult, he would smash the cream jugs and prevent the butter churning, interfere with stock, such as setting them loose (or even driving them to the woods), make it impossible to get hay out of the stack, upset loaded carts, and pull off bed-clothes and drag hapless sleepers down the stairs.[367]

The boggart resident in the farm at Boggart Hole Clough, mentioned ear-lier, had fewer redeeming qualities than that at Syke Lumb. He undertook small domestic tasks, such as churning and scouring pots and pans, and he could be very merry, playing with the children and joining in the laughter and jollity at Christmas. Nonetheless, his interminable pranks were very wearing—he'd put buckets up chimneys and would crack table legs. He'd scare the domestic servants and worry the farmhands, frighten the children, and drive everyone to bed early to avoid him. He became more and more presumptuous, snatching the children's bread and butter out of their hands and interfering with their porridge, milk, and other food—for example, put-ting spiders in the buttermilk and cinders in the bread. In the same manner, the sole occupation of the boggart at Greenside seemed to be disturbing the people in the house he shared with them: he would drum on an oak chest,

---

366. Bailey and England, *Lancashire Folk Tales*, 91; Thornber, *An Historical and Descriptive*, 333; Bowker, *Goblin Tales of Lancashire*, 52.

367. Charles Hardwick, *Traditions, Superstitions, and Folklore (Chiefly Lancashire and the North of England) [...]* (Manchester: Ireland & Co., 1872), 127.

shake the bed hangings, and drag off the sheets during the night. These japes were unquestionably trying, but they were not intended malevolently.[368]

Nuisance Boggarts

It is when domestic boggarts turn wholly against their former masters that the real problems come, and life can become miserable, if not intolerable. It's been suggested that an angry boggart is in fact little different from the modern idea of a poltergeist. In West Yorkshire some homes were so notorious for the trouble caused by the vexed household sprite that they came to be known as "boggart houses"—quite a few of these can still be found, for example at Midgeley, Luddenden, Brighouse, Elland, and Leeds. Some "boggart chairs" are also known, stones on which the boggarts would sit outside these houses. Misbehaving boggarts seem to have caused such a nuisance in West Yorkshire that the little town of Yeadon took desperate measures—the "town book" records payments expended on boggart catchers.[369]

In fact, even helpful hobs might spend their leisure time elsewhere, scaring innocent travellers. There was a tradition that boggarts would disguise themselves as stones on moorland tracks, deliberately to trip up passersby. Animals, especially horses, can see them better than people, and often when they rear up unexpectedly it's because they have "taken the boggart"—they've spotted one, even if it doesn't look like a boggart to the human observer. Another trick of the beings was to shrink to the size of a flea and then to scare horses by speaking inside their ears.[370]

BANISHING BOGGARTS

When boggarts become an unbearable nuisance, one solution is to "lay" them: to cast them out or imprison them in just the same manner in which a troublesome ghost might be expelled. In the county of Lancashire, the boggarts have become especially confused with ghosts, and one story from Over Darwen illustrates how the ancestors, the unsettled dead, and Faery have

---

368. Hardwick, *Traditions, Superstitions, and Folklore*, 128; Harland and Wilkinson, *Lancashire Folk-lore*, 54.

369. Sugg, *Fairies: A Dangerous History*, 141–153.

370. Roberts, *Folklore of Yorkshire*, 98; Billingsley, *West Yorkshire Folk Tales*, 37–39; Bailey and England, *Lancashire Folk Tales*, 94.

all merged into one: a boggart was said to haunt an ancient burial tumulus in the area and, as late as the 1860s, children passing would take off their shoes and clogs for fear of awakening the dreaded being. People who have committed suicide after love affairs, who have been murdered or executed, or whose deaths were otherwise dramatic often seem to have been prime boggart material.[371]

EXORCISING BOGGARTS

Sometimes religion can be used to drive out a boggart. This may happen almost unconsciously or accidentally, as in the story of the Blackley Boggart. His pranks included souring the milk, scaring the stock, and driving off customers for the farm's produce, and eventually the farmer decided to quit the farmhouse and move elsewhere. Then, in response to the neighbour's enquiry about their departure, the farmer thanked God that they were leaving. This banished the boggart forever.[372]

The last account plays upon the common aversion that all faery beings are supposed to have for any aspect of the Christian religion. Sometimes, though, a much more formal religious rite is required to get rid of a boggart, and these cases in particular highlight the fact that the difference between boggarts and ghosts is not always very clear and that the places they frequent can often be the sites of murders or burials. The Lancashire boggart known as the Gatley Shouter seems in many respects to be a repentant ghost, who remained on earth regretting the number of the customers he had cheated during his life as a grocer. The unsettled spirit was laid by the parson with prayers, Bible passages, and a chalk circle: the sprite tried to return to the graveyard where it lurked, but the ritual was too strong for it. The boggart called "Old Scrat" at Brindle in Lancashire was a mischievous being who never did any great harm, but he was laid one day for an ill-judged prank. Old Scrat used to like to jump up onto carts and stop them; one time he did this with a hearse, and the furious vicar promptly exorcised him. The so-called "Lumb Boggart" of Bradwell in Derbyshire was exorcised by a local

371. Hardwick, *Traditions, Superstitions, and Folklore*, 141.

372. Bailey and England, *Lancashire Folk Tales*, 93.

Baptist and cast into a pool in the form of a fish after the residents of the house it had haunted could no longer put up with its nocturnal terrors.[373]

Certainly, very many bogies seem to be nothing but ghosts—as with the famed Jemmy (James) Lowther of Lowther Hall in Westmorland. He had been notorious in life, and after death continued to cause a nuisance until he was laid forever under a large rock by a Catholic priest. A similar story is told of a man called Shepperd, from Appleby. He, too, was laid by a priest under a rock, but within a few decades he was reputed to have emerged from under the stone in the guise of a large white horse and to have gone into the stream nearby.[374]

Only the combined prayers of an entire Lancashire village managed to lay the nuisance boggart called the Gatley Shouter. At Rowley Hall in the same county prayers alone were not enough; a headstone also needed to be set up at the junction of two streams. In the north of Scotland, the only way to terminate the nuisance caused by the bogle of Auld-na-Beiste was to organise a religious service which consecrated the spot where he lurked. The ceremony was repeated annually until the bogle finally took the hint and gave up his haunting completely.[375]

Laying Boggarts

Exorcisms are expressly religious ceremonies. Boggarts can also be banished using magical techniques.

There are still quite a few spots identified in Britain where boggarts have been laid—for instance under a laurel tree at Hotheshall Hall near Ribchester. Milk is regularly poured on the tree roots, both for the benefit of the plant and to prolong the spell. The boggart of South Clock-House used to annoy residents by pulling off their bedclothes or by sitting unnervingly in a yew tree in the shape of a huge white-robed figure. It was eventually laid beneath that same tree.

In Written Stone Lane, Dilworth, Lancashire, there is a stone slab which measures around nine feet by two feet by one foot, upon which is inscribed

---

373. Harland and Wilkinson, *Lancashire Folk-lore*, 54.

374. Sullivan, *Cumberland & Westmorland*, 159–160.

375. Bailey and England, *Lancashire Folk Tales* 93; Bonning, *Dumfries & Galloway Folk Tales*, 57; Sutherland, *Folk-lore Gleanings*, 93.

"Rauffe Radcliffe laid this stone to lye for ever, AD 1655." It's believed that this was done to lay a boggart who had haunted the lane and scared travellers. A local farmer later decided to ignore Radcliffe's wishes (and warning) and took the slab to use as a counter in his buttery. It took six horses several laborious hours to drag the rock to his farm and, after the stone was installed, nothing but misfortune followed. No pan or pot would ever stay upright upon it, eventually persuading the avaricious man to return the slab whence it came. It took only one horse a short while to pull the rock back, and once it was restored, the disturbances promptly ceased. In County Durham, Hob Headless, who haunted a highway, was laid under a large slab of stone for ninety-nine years and a day; rather as in the Dilworth case, it was said that the rock was not a safe place to sit. At Grislehurst in the county of Lancashire a boggart was laid in spectacular manner, in a grave under an ash and a rowan tree and along with a staked cockerel. The method didn't work, though, as in 1857 the creature was still reported to be terrifying locals at night. Perhaps because of these partial successes there was the parallel belief that only Catholic priests could successfully lay or outwit boggarts, often by imposing impossible tasks upon them, such as spinning a rope from the sands of the River Ribble before they could be released. It's to be observed that, despite resorting to a priest of the "old religion" in these cases, the remedies employed were not church rites but magical tricks.[376]

Tricking Boggarts

Notwithstanding their malign reputations, boggarts can sometimes be overcome simply by outwitting them. Quite a few of them seem to be very slow on the uptake. There is a well-known story of a farmer whose field was claimed by a boggart. They reached a settlement of their dispute whereby, in alternate years, they agreed to have what grew above and below ground. In the first year the boggart chose to take the "bottoms" of the crops—and the farmer planted wheat. In the following year, he planted turnips. Eventually,

---

376. For Dilworth, see Ian, "The Written Stone, Dilworth," Mysterious Britain & Ireland: Mysteries, Legends & the Paranormal, January 30, 2013, www.mysteriousbritain.co.uk /folklore/the-written-stone-dilworth/; Hardwick, *Traditions, Superstitions, and Folklore*, 131; Harland and Wilkinson, *Lancashire Folk-lore*, 56.

too late, it dawned upon the boggart what a bad deal he'd made, and he abandoned the farm in frustration.

Indeed, the fact that some boggarts seem to be a little slow-witted was exploited in a couple of the layings. At Holden Clough in Lancashire the boggart who'd inflicted nightly disturbances promised not to return so long as there was ivy on the trees—forgetting that it is an evergreen. A comparable trick was played at Hollin Hey Clough where the undertaking was to stay away as long as there were green leaves growing in the clough. The "hollin" of the name is a holly tree, and the valley is full of them and green all year round.[377]

KILLING BOGGARTS

Laying or exorcism may not work long term, and sometimes it doesn't even work immediately. Some bogies don't seem to be in the least perturbed by priests and incantations. Orton, near Kirkby Stephen in Westmorland, was plagued by a bogie that took the shape of a glowing light and would harass late-night travellers. A Methodist preacher was brought in to lay the sprite, but all he seemed to achieve was to get hit on the back of his head with his own hat. Fortunately, there may be other options in such intractable cases.[378]

Two boggarts made a nuisance of themselves around a farm at Gorsey Bank in Shropshire, not doing any great harm but constantly disturbing the inhabitants. Worn down by this, the farmer called in the parson to lay the pair, but they couldn't be banished. As is so often the case in these situations, the family then decided to remove itself instead. They did so but were dismayed to find that the bogeys followed them, bringing a salt box that had been left behind. In this case, rather than reach an accommodation with the sprite as is the usual outcome in these "we're flitting too" tales, the family acted more decisively. They made up the fire, invited the two boggarts to sit before it, and plied them with beef and ale. Just when the bogies were relaxed and off guard, they were thrown into the fire and held in the flames with pitchforks until they were burned to ashes.

---

377. James McKay, "The Evolution of East Lancashire Boggarts," *Transactions of the Burnley Literary & Scientific Club* 6 (1888): 113–127; Harland, *Lancashire Folklore*, 55.

378. Sullivan, *Cumberland & Westmorland: Ancient & Modern*, 162.

Despite all that's been said, there's some evidence that all the great effort of moving house or staging religious ceremonies would have proved unnecessary if people had been patient. Between Droylsden and East End there was a boggart who used to appear regularly in the form of a rabbit or dog, or bear. The growth of factories in the area appears to have been what banished him, as he has not been seen for nearly two hundred years now.[379]

Padfoots

The bogey called padfoot, which haunts the environs of the Yorkshire cities of Leeds and Wakefield, has several forms, but it always has large padding feet and moves quickly and lightly. It can appear as a beast the size of a small donkey, with black shaggy hair and eyes like saucers, and it will follow people along roads at night or waylay them in narrow places. If you try to speak to it or strike it, the bogie will have power over you and might drag you all the way home.

Sometimes the padfoot takes the form of a white dog with huge eyes but an insubstantial body. At other times, it is something larger than a sheep but with long smooth hair. Sometimes it gives a terrible howl, sometimes the padfoot is accompanied by the sounds of chains.

Seeing the padfoot might be a premonition of a death, not least because the encounter itself might prove fatal. The padfoot that haunted Horbury has been seen as a pale hound that can walk on its two hind feet; one man who found it obstructing his route tried to strike it with his stick and found that the blow passed right through the dog, which continued to sit and stare at him unnervingly. He turned and ran all the way home, but then took ill and died.

Other padfoots are reported from Staffordshire, where they are particularly linked to graves which they guard (for example at Swinscoe, Bradnop, and Ipstones); there is also some link with springs, as with the padfoot of Indefont Well at Ipstones.[380]

---

379. Harland and Wilkinson, *Lancashire Folk-lore*, 55.

380. Henderson, *Notes on the Folk-lore*, 273; W. P. Witcutt, "Notes on Staffordshire Folklore," *Folklore* 52, no. 3 (1941): 126.

Kows

The word "kow" is completely unfamiliar to us now, but it formerly implied some sort of malicious spirit. For example, in the Scots poem "The Cursing of Sir John Rowll" maledictions are wished upon those stealing the knight's hens and eggs. His curses include a brownie that can "play kow, Behind the claith, with mony mow"—that is, dressed up in a sheet with lots of grimacing.[381] Another Scottish writer describes a woman fleeing "from a shelly-coated kow," relating this creature to the coastal sprites who were examined in chapter 5.[382]

Very similar to the padfoot in its polymorphous nature is the Hedley Kow, which haunts Hedley near Ebchester. This bogie is notoriously mischievous, but it is not malignant. It might appear as a bundle of sticks lying in the road; if someone picks up the bundle of firewood, it will get heavier and heavier until they have to stop for a rest—at which point the bundle will become animated and shuffle away laughing.

The Hedley Kow would torment milkmaids on farms in various ways: it might assume the form of a cow and lead her on a chase round and round a field; when caught it would misbehave in the milking parlour, kicking over the pail and then slipping its tether and running off laughing; lastly, it might imitate the voice or the appearance of farm servants' lovers. Amongst the kow's other cruel pranks were giving all the cream to the cats, unravelling knitting, and breaking spinning wheels. If a man was trying to set out to fetch a midwife for his wife, the Kow would hinder him; if he was returning with the midwife, the Kow might try to make the horse bolt or buck. It has also been known to appear at farmhouse windows, tormenting the woman in labour inside, but if you go outside with a stick to drive off the prankster, you'll end up with a beating yourself. Where a person was riding alone at night, the kow would appear just ahead of them on the road. The solitary rider would try to catch up, hoping for company in the dark, but the horse

---

381. John Rowll, *Sir John Rowll's Cursing (Heir Followis the Cursing of Sr. Johne Rowlis, Upoun the Steilaris of His Fowlis)* with an Introductory Note by David Laing (Aberdeen, 1822), lines 101–2.

382. Allan Ramsay, *The Gentle Shepherd,* Act I, scene 1, in *Bell's British Theatre*, vol. 9, 1780.

ahead would always speed up until they were racing madly across the countryside, at which point the Kow would cackle mockingly.[383]

Brags

Another variant on the bogie sprite is the "brag." Four especially famous ones are known. That at Pelton in Durham, known as the Picktree Brag, has several forms. It might be encountered as a calf wearing a white scarf round its neck and with a bushy tail; however, other witnesses have met with a coach horse or a jackass that would trot along in front of them before stopping at a pond and whinnying or would try to unseat the rider into the pond. The brag has also been seen as four men holding up a white sheet and as a naked, headless man. On one occasion, its appearance marked a death.[384]

The Portobello Brag, which appears around Birtley in County Durham as a donkey, will also try to throw people into bogs or gorse bushes and will then gallop off, apparently celebrating its conquest and their misfortune. The Hylton Lane Brag is to be met with on the highway to Sunderland in the form of a donkey, a horse, or a woman. Its habit is simply to walk with a traveller but nothing more. Lastly, the Humbleknowe Brag is found at a farm near Sedgefield, where it will disturb the occupants either by making it sound as though all the stock have got out and are running wild or by battering against the doors and windows.[385]

Bocain

The *bocain*, *baucan*, or *bochan* of the Scottish Highlands is very like the bogies of the rest of Britain—a nuisance and a source of alarm rather than a real threat to life and health. They tend to lurk in isolated places—such as mountain roads and lonely fords.[386]

On the Hebridean island of Lewis one of these bogles was to be found in the hollow named after it: Lag-a'-Bhocain. This creature's habit was to fight any travellers that passed that way, wrestling with them and throwing them

383. Henderson, *Notes on the Folk-lore*, 270; Oliver, *Rambles in Northumberland*, 101.

384. Sharp, *The Bishoprick Garland*, 41; Henderson, *Notes on the Folk-lore*, 270.

385. Thomas Wilson, *The Pitman's Pay and Other Poems* (Gateshead: William Douglas, 1843), 95; *Brockie, Legends & Superstitions,* 53–55.

386. Campbell, *Witchcraft and Second Sight*, 220.

down violently. Eventually it met its match, though. A man resolved to vanquish the *bocain* and set out deliberately to fight it, trusting in his strength and skill rather than any magical powers. His confidence was well placed, and he overcame the bogie and held it down, forcing it to speak and to tell its story, after which humiliation it was never seen again. A *bocain* can only speak to you if you address it first and, if you do ask it a question, it's wise always to ask it "in the name of God."[387]

So many locations were infested with *bocains* that the practice on Lewis was for travellers always to carry a copy of the Latin New Testament with them. This measure was considered to be a complete protection against the bogies' assaults—as is so often the case with faery beings.[388]

It's reasonable to suppose that the *boodie* of the Buchan district in the northeast of Scotland is another relative of the *bocain* and the bogie. These phantoms have been described as "something other than ghosts." They have no fixed shape and can shift form from minute to minute, at first appearing as a cloud of black smoke, then perhaps turning into something resembling two huge wooden boards that slap together as they swell. The main and constant feature of the *boodie*, without doubt, is the extreme terror which it induces in witnesses.[389]

Barguests

Barguests (or bargheists) tend to haunt tombs and ancient burial barrows and are known by the loud and terrible cries they make. This association with ancient monuments and graves is very strong indeed. Barguests often manifest as huge chained dogs, but they've also been seen as donkeys, calves, and pigs. The derivation of the name is disputed; some think that it means a "borough or town ghost" but barguests are very far from being urban-only phenomena. Some interpret the name as "gate-ghost," and it's certainly true that most seem to be rural, and some have even been known to help with farmwork and assist with other human activities, as we shall see.[390]

---

387. Campbell, *Witchcraft and Second Sight*, 220; MacKenzie, *The Book of Arran*, 273.

388. Malcolm MacPhail, "Folklore from the Hebrides," *Folklore* 7 (1896): 400, 402.

389. Milne, *Myths and Superstitions*, 13.

390. John Roby, *Traditions of Lancashire*, vol. 1 (London: George Routledge and Sons, 1872), 376.

The barguest is known for its low roar, which is widely regarded as a presage of death—as is its mere appearance in a locality. Thus, the example found at Oxwells near Wreghorn in Leeds only appears when any notable person in the community has died. It takes the form of a large black dog, the size of a donkey, with blazing eyes the size of saucers, and all the other dogs in the vicinity will follow it in a pack, barking and howling. Any person who gets in the barguest's way on such an occasion will receive a blow with its paw that will prove fatal. A very similar barguest is known at Egton in Yorkshire, appearing just in advance of a local death. At Yaddlethorpe in Lincolnshire the barguest is believed to be associated with a spot where a staked body was found buried; at Northorpe in the same county the black dog barguest haunted the village churchyard. Curiously, though, a wizard was said to have lived nearby who would transform into a dog and then bite the cattle in the fields.[391]

The barguest (or ghost) that haunts Glassensikes near Darlington has taken many forms: headless men and women (some of whom vanish in flames), white and black dogs, white cats, and even rabbits. In the shape of a large black dog, often pulling chains along with its feet, it has noiselessly followed travellers along on a road and even barred their way. A man walking home at night near Grassington in Yorkshire heard chains rattling and tried to escape what he felt sure was a barguest by crossing a bridge. To his profound dismay, this particular bogie followed him over the running water and, when he got to his home, he found a large beast, bigger than a sheep, and woolly, lying across the threshold. Desperate to get inside, he raised his stick to it, but the sprite turned its eyes upon him—they were as huge as saucers with red, white, and blue rings within them that shrank to a dot in the centre. The beast only moved when the man's wife inside the cottage came to open the door.[392]

391. Thomas Parkinson, *Yorkshire Legends and Traditions, as Told by Her Ancient Chroniclers, Her Poets, and Journalists* (London: Elliott Stock, 1888), 139; Sullivan, *Cumberland & Westmorland, Ancient & Modern,* 157; Henderson, *Notes on the Folk-lore,* 275; *County Folk-lore* 5, 52, 54.

392. Parkinson, *Yorkshire Legends and Traditions,* 127, 131; Longstaffe, *The History and Antiquities,* 13–14; William Hone, *The Every-day Book and Table Book […],* vol. 3 (London: William Tegg, 1878), 655.

Not all barguests are seen as living wholly outside human society. The one known as the Capelthwaite, that was to be found around the borders of Yorkshire and Westmorland, lived in a barn at Cappleside Hall and, although it could appear as any sort of four-legged animal, it was most often encountered as another black dog. In this shape it would assist on farms by driving in the sheep. Like many hobs and brownies, it was said to be so enthusiastic in this work that it would occasionally round up a hare as well. Whilst some farmers were favoured, most just suffered mischief from the Capelthwaite, and so it was eventually laid in the River Bela by the vicar of Beetham. A black dog known as Hairy Jack was said to live in an old barn at Grayingham in Lincolnshire too.[393]

In Northumberland, barguests are said particularly to favour the company of midwives. They will accompany them to the houses they have to visit, sometimes in the shape of dogs, sometimes looking like monkeys or small, deformed men. Once the midwife is inside assisting her patient with the childbirth, the barguest chatters at the window or imitates the cries of the woman in labour. In the city of Newcastle, the dog went further. If it laughed when the midwife reached her destination, she knew that all would go well; if the hound howled, she knew she would face problems.[394]

Not everyone can see a barguest nor, presumably, many of the other bogies I have been describing. Only those with second sight have this (mis) fortune, although anyone else who touches them at the right time will also have the horror revealed to them.[395]

Bugganes

The Isle of Man equivalent to the bogie or boggart is the buggane. Like many of their species, they have been described as "polymorphous creatures." They can be encountered as a strong man with big eyes, a black monster, little stacks of hemp or corn, or sacks of chaff; they might appear as cows, pigs, dogs, or black cats—albeit ones that might suddenly swell to the size

---

393. Henderson, *Notes on the Folk-lore*, 275; *County Folklore* 5, 53.

394. Oliver, *Rambles in Northumberland*, 98.

395. James Orchard Halliwell-Phillipps, *A Dictionary of Archaic and Provincial Words [...]* (London: John Russell Smith, 1865), n.p.

of a horse. Their main habit is to block roads to travellers, although luckily a blessing or some other holy words will dispel them.[396]

Even odder and more puzzling variants of the buggane are reported from around the island. In Malew parish the "Big Buggane" was once seen looking like a large man shining all over, as if he was dressed in an oilskin coat. At Grenaby, the buggane called Jimmy Squarefoot has a pig's head and face with two large tusks and has been known to charge at passersby on the highway and even to carry off people to a cave. Another "pig buggane" menaces travellers on the highway at Lezayre. The Kione Dhoo (black head) buggane takes the form of a horse. Gob-ny-scuit gully in Maughold parish is haunted by a buggane in the shape of a man with a cat's head and fiery eyes. This last example is an especially mischievous creature, for it likes to vex the locals. It will tear the thatch off haystacks, blow smoke back down chimneys, deposit soot in the inhabitants' food, and push sheep over the edge of cliffs. Lastly, at Spooyt Moor in Patrick parish the buggane tends to be seen as a big black calf that crosses the road in front of a traveller with the sounds of chains being rattled and then plunges into a pool. In his human form he tried once to abduct a local girl; he threw her over his shoulder and carried her off towards his lair, which was the cave behind a nearby waterfall, but she was luckily able to cut the strings of her apron and escape his clutches.[397]

There was quite a strong moralistic streak in at least some of these creatures. The buggane of Glen Maye tried to throw a lazy housewife into a waterfall because she postponed her baking until after sunset. Had she not cut loose the strings of her apron to escape, she would at the very least have had an icy soaking. The *buggan ny Hushtey* lived in a large cave near the sea and had no liking for lazy people, it was said. Nonetheless, this work ethic was paired with a sense of pity for the less fortunate. When Poor Robin of nearby Chou Traa lost his faithful dog and a barrel full of buttermilk through a cruel prank, the buggane took care of him by bringing in the cows, lighting the fire, and boiling the kettle, ready for when he came home. The loss of his faithful companion at the same time made Robin depressed, so that he slept poorly, got up late, and fell behind with his farm tasks. Late one evening

---

396. Roeder, *Manx Folk-Tales*, part 1, 28.

397. Gill, *A Manx Scrapbook*, chapter 4; Gill, *A Third Manx Scrapbook*, chapter 3; Douglas, *"Restoring to Use Our,"* 21.

when he was still out in the field ploughing by the light of a lantern, the buggane made the plough horse bolt through a hedge. It was found dead the next day, near to the entrance to the buggane's cave—and this provoked the villagers into blocking the hole and then placing a stone cross there to bar the buggane's passage.[398]

For all this criticism, some manifestations of the buggane were helpful to humans; there is a very clear crossover here with the *dooiney-oie* whom I mentioned earlier. The being that lived in *Towl Buggane* (the Buggane's Hole) at Gob-ny-Scuit would shout a warning before stormy weather, enabling local farmers to get in their harvests in time. He was just as likely, though, to give these warnings when no storms were due, just to tease the locals.

The Scottish version of this sprite, the *bauchan* or *bogan*, is a slightly pleasanter character. In one story from Lochaber a farmer had a love-hate relationship with the *bauchan* who lived in the vicinity. They often used to fight each other, but at the same time the *bauchan* would gather fuel for the farm in bitter weather and helped the family move house. When the farmer had to leave his land because of the Highland clearances, the *bauchan* travelled with him to the United States and (in the shape of a goat) helped clear the new land he settled.[399]

Another *bauchan* was known at Morar on the mainland coast facing the Isle of Skye. It was called the *colannn gun cheann* or "headless body" and would waylay and maul men on their own at night—women, children, and groups of people were never assaulted. Eventually, it killed the local laird's son, and he resolved to destroy it. He fought the creature alone. The battle raged all night until finally the *bauchan* was subdued; fearing the coming dawn it asked to be freed. This was allowed, on condition that it leave the district for ever.[400]

Bugbears

Regardless of how terrifying these creatures may have been when we first encountered them, some have lost their capacity to shock and have been

---

398. S. Morrison, "The buggane ny hushtey—a Manx Folktale," *Folklore* 34 (1923): 349.

399. Campbell, *Popular Tales*, 1860, vol. 2, 91.

400. Briggs, *Dictionary of Fairies*, 79; see, too, the version in Campbell, *Witchcraft and Second Sight*, 191.

demoted to "nursery sprites" whose primary function is to scare children—to get them into bed and to keep them there once they've been tucked in. The sprite called Mumpoker is one such, and quite a few of the boggart family have suffered this fate. Another example is the Suffolk "clim," a sort of imp that inhabits nursery chimneys and was sometimes called down to take naughty children away.[401]

The "bogey-man" is now a generic phrase for such empty horrors, and "bugbear" now denotes something that's more of a source of irritation than terror. Indeed, some groups of sprites seem to exist solely to ensure that children behave and stay safe. These include "Jack up the Orchard" from Shropshire, whose name and function scarcely need explanation and, from further north, Churn Milk Peg and Melsh Dick whose presence dissuades boys and girls from going into nut groves. From Eyemouth in Berwickshire comes mention of "the bogle in the Billy-Myre, / Wha' kills our bairns a'." Scaring children away from the dangerous bog has evidently become his sole function. In Yorkshire homes, Knocky Boh was a being who lived behind the wainscoting, tapping on it to terrify the infants. The last element of his name is highly significant: it takes us back to bugs and boggarts.[402]

This process of devaluation has been going on for a long time. By the mid-seventeenth century, "bullbeggars" had been reduced to a "mere nursery scare word," which had no really precise meaning and simply suggested any kind of bugaboo that might terrify children. Examples of similar scare words are found in George Gascoigne's play *The Buggbears*, which is a translation from Tasso dating to about 1565. He lists:

401. *County Folk-lore* 3, 85.

402. Wright, *Rustic Speech and Folk-lore*, 198; George Henderson, *The Popular Rhymes, Sayings, and Proverbs of the County of Berwick; With Illustrative Notes* (Newcastle-on-Tyne: W. S. Crow, 1856), 2–3.

"puckes, puckerels, hob howlard, bygorn and Robin Goodfel-
low...
Pickhornes, hob Goblin, Rawhead, bloudiebone the ouglie,
Hagges, Buggbears and hellhoundes and Hecate the nightmare."[403]

What we have here is a roster of former monsters, mostly now reduced to names for parents to conjure with—they are an undefined shape lurking in the shadows of a darkened bedroom, they are a sound in the corner of a nursery, they are something unsafe and uncertain. Other such bugbears whose identities and functions are today almost completely forgotten are *scarbugs, caddies, mock beggars, bugabos, tom-pokers, snapdragons,* and *todlowries.*

Occasionally a few scraps of information give us a better picture of the decline of these creatures into bedtime stories. Raw Head and Bloody Bones was a half-human, half-animal sprite that lived in disused coal pits in the Black Country area of Staffordshire. It was a very dangerous being, but it would from time to time emerge from the abandoned mines and go door to door at nearby cottages, begging for food and other things. By late Victorian times this monster dwindled to not much more than a name used to scare children away from the mouths of the pits.[404]

The Scottish equivalent of these *bugbears* are the bodachs in the far north of the country. They sound a little more ferocious and intimidating than their English kin, but they perform the same functions. They are consistently seen in the vicinity of places where children would be at risk: for example, the *bodach an smeididh,* "the beckoner," tries to lure the unwise and the unwary into danger. The *corra-loigein* looks in windows at night, scaring children and trying to steal them away. This *bodach* can only enter a house if it is invited

---

403. Henk Dragstra, "'Bull-beggar': An Early Modern Scare-Word," in *Airy Nothings: Imagining the Otherworld of Faerie from the Middle Ages to the Age of Reason [...],* Karin E. Olsen and Jan R. Veenstra, eds. (Leiden: Brill, 2013), 192; Gascoigne, *The Buggbears,* in Richard Warwick Bond, ed., *Early Plays from the Italian: Edited, With Essay, Introductions and Notes by R. Warwick Bond* (Oxford: Clarendon Press, 1911), 84–157, act 3, lines 57, 70.

404. Charlotte Sophia Burne, "Staffordshire Folk and Their Lore," *Folklore* 7 (1896): 371.

inside in some way; parents therefore stress how important it is for children to be very quiet after dark.[405]

Conclusions

Bogies, in all their forms, are a baffling species of faery beast. They are, on the whole, terrifying—but not uniformly so. Many seem to exist solely to instil horror and dread in us, but some confound this description by providing us with assistance or warnings. Most baffling of all, though, is the sheer variety of forms that bogies can take. Many will be seen as large dogs, but they can also show themselves as horses, donkeys, cows, pigs, cats, goats, pigs, rabbits, and hares. I will turn next to discuss daemon dogs and other fae animals, and it may well seem extremely difficult to determine when a faery beast ought to be classed as a "barguest," a "black dog," or as a fae donkey choosing to appear in canine form. Given that a supernatural hound is a supernatural hound however it's labelled, it may not matter very much, except that there are distinct differences in temperament between the different groups. That said, I think we must trust the experience of generations. People who have had encounters with these beasts over the centuries knew when they were dealing with a brag, a padfoot, a boggart, a *fuath*, or a *direach*. It seems simplest and wisest to accept their designation—and leave it at that.

---

405. Campbell, *Witchcraft and Second Sight,* 187.

Chapter 10

DAEMON DOGS

Canine form is something often taken by faery beasts, especially bogies, but they may vary this with other more benign shapes like ponies and calves. It can be hard to determine with many of these cases what the "natural" or "normal" form of these beasts may be. However, there is a group of beasts which are consistently met as canines, which I examine in this chapter. Although folk tradition separates "black dogs" from "shucks" and "shugs," there is no clear division of the categories, and the difference can be as much regional as anything. No general name exists for all these beings either so, for convenience, I'll call them the daemon dogs.

Hounds are naturally a more frightening prospect than livestock (even bulls), because of the threat of being mauled, and the British Isles are full of these menacing beings. Most are encountered singly, but there is also a very strong tradition of hunting packs of spectral dogs that are often experienced flying in the night sky.

Faery Pets

Just as the faes have their own livestock, they have their own dogs, which are kept for hunting and as guard dogs. These hounds are recognisable by their size, fearsome nature, unusual colour, or bark. Their baying may be very loud, and the sound of their running like the galloping of horses. In one reported case, the mere sound of a faery dog on the roof of a byre was enough to cause the cattle within to die of fright.[406]

Interestingly, on the Isle of Man, these dogs act as heralds for the faeries. The arrival of a little white dog is a sure sign that "they" are coming, and inhabitants know to leave the house tidy and go to bed. All in all, though, the faeries' dogs behave like any domesticated hounds: they are pets with owners, and they perform certain functions. This clearly distinguishes them from the "daemon dogs" I discuss here.[407]

The Nature of Fae Hounds

Our concern in this chapter is with supernatural dogs that exist entirely on their own. They may have many very typical "faery" traits to their character or behaviour, but they operate entirely independently of faery-kind, often engaged in conduct or seen in places which would never concern conventional faeries.

An example from Alfriston in Sussex illustrates the complex nature of some fae hounds. The village has two daemon dogs, one of which is black and is seen running through the streets on the night of a full moon. The second dog is white and has a reputation as an omen of death or other misfortune. The story is that the dog and its master were robbed and murdered by some farmworkers. Dog and master were hastily buried by them beside a road, and for seven years the dog appeared on Midsummer Eve. Then the road was widened, and the remains were found, at which point they received a proper burial. This dog therefore seems to have three functions—like many bogies, it is a ghost that marked where the hidden corpses lay and, once that issue was resolved, it remained as a more general ill omen.[408]

---

406. Campbell, *Superstitions of the Highlands*, 141; see too MacGregor, *The Peat-Fire Flame*, 37.

407. See my *Faery*, chapter 5; Campbell, *Popular Tales*, vol. 1, 47, no. 23; Evans-Wentz, *The Fairy-Faith in Celtic Countries*, 122.

408. "Running Hound," Black Shuck, Hellhounds, and Other Black Dog Reports, Paranormal Database, accessed May 13, 2020, www.paranormaldatabase.com/reports/shuckdata .php; "White Dog," Black Shuck, Hellhounds, and Other Black Dog Reports, Paranormal Database, accessed May 13, 2020, www.paranormaldatabase.com/reports/shuckdata.php; "Black Dogs in Sussex," Ghostly Black Dogs, Sussex Archaeology & Folklore, accessed May 25, 2020, http://www.sussexarch.org.uk/saaf/blackdog.html.

Furthermore, from Scotland to Cornwall, these faery hounds share consistent common features that show that they are more than just the ghosts of dead dogs. There are several hundreds of these creatures known across Britain, although they are commonest in the south of England, most particularly in East Anglia and in the southwest.

Classification

Many folklore writers have examined the black dog mythology and have tried to categorise and classify the many apparitions in some rational way. The "barguest" has been defined as a malevolent shape-shifting creature (a bogle, as I discussed earlier), in contrast to the "true black dog," which usually only appears in canine form and will often be protective and helpful to humans. These fae hounds can be noticeably shaggy and dark, and they may be as large as a calf or a donkey, but they are never seen as an actual calf or donkey, as is the case with the barguest. Other writers differentiate between daemon dogs and those dogs that are ghosts—either of humans or of dogs. Lastly, folklorist Katherine Briggs cut through all this and suggested that we might just distinguish between benevolent and dangerous types. There's a lot to be said for this very simple analysis; communities in the past have applied a range of labels, many of them regional, none of them necessarily precise or consistent. Witnesses confronted with abnormally large dogs at night have seldom had the presence of mind or opportunity to carefully enumerate their qualities and behaviour. There's a danger, therefore, of trying to overanalyse our sources.[409]

Appearance

What sets these faery hounds apart tends to be their size and their colour. They are usually ebony, although white and yellow examples are known, and they are frequently larger than the "average" hound. Witnesses have often stressed that the animal they saw was strikingly big for a dog; sometimes they are so large that they have to be compared to other mammals. The yellow hounds have often been mistaken for lions; other comparisons have been with bears, deer, donkeys, horses, ponies, cows, and—most often—with calves

---

409. Ethel H. Rudkin, "The Black Dog," *Folklore* 49 (1938): 111–131; Theo Brown, "The Black Dog," *Folklore* 69 (1958): 175; Edwin Sidney Hartland, ed., *English Fairy and Folk Tales,* (London: Walter Scott, 1890), 234–44; Briggs, *British Folk-Tales and Legends: A Sampler* (London: Granada, 1977), 115.

and bullocks. Two white dogs, both the size of polar bears, were witnessed leaping over railway engines at Great Yarmouth in 1859. A black dog seen at Geldeston in Norfolk grew larger and smaller, swelling from the size of a large hound to bigger than a horse and then back again; in contrast, a hound at Barnby in Suffolk shrank from the size of a Labrador to that of a cat.[410]

The size could be intimidating on its own, but there was often more to alarm the observer. Between Baschurch and Yeadon in Shropshire a headless black dog was seen at the spot where a man was allegedly murdered. Nearly a tenth of faery dogs are reported as lacking heads—the absence of fangs being scant comfort to witnesses. Grantown in Moray suffered from the presence of a dog the size of a pony, its fur tinged green and its head either strangely small or absent. At Grinton in Swaledale in Yorkshire, the reverse apparition was encountered: near the gates of Cogden Hall a dog's head without any body would terrify travellers.[411]

It's quite common for black faery dogs to be hybrid creatures. At Melton in Suffolk the hound had a donkey's face; a man who tried to catch it was bitten on the hand before the creature simply vanished. A dog seen at Creag-an-Ordain, near Lochinver, had a human face instead, which is probably even more distressing. The dogs might transform their shape too: at Hallen in Bristol a large inky-coloured dog used to emerge from a hedge, turn into a donkey, and then rear up onto its hind legs. There is, in fact, a curious link between donkeys and dogs. At Coate in Wiltshire a white donkey was often observed in the place where a huge jet-black dog would also appear. This hound never moved; its eyes would grow larger if you threw stones at it, and seeing it predicted a death. As already described, a large black dog haunted the lane leading to the churchyard of Geldeston in Norfolk, but a donkey was also reported to appear in the vicinity.[412]

---

410. *Norwich Mercury,* January 25, 1860; James, *Bogie Tales of East Anglia,* 9–11; R. R., "Barnby Fears Its 'Headless Hound,'" *Eastern Daily Press,* January 17, 1968.

411. Burne, *Shropshire Folk-lore,* 105.

412. "Donkey Faced Dog," Suffolk—Paranormal Database Records, Paranormal Database, accessed May 25, 2020, https://www.paranormaldatabase.com/suffolk/sufpages/suffdata .php?pageNum_paradata=10&totalRows_paradata=336; "Black Shuck, Hellhounds, and Other Black Dog Reports," Paranormal Database, accessed May 25, 2020, www .paranormaldatabase.com/reports/shuckdata.php/; "Geldeston Area, Norfolk," Shuck-land, accessed May 25, 2020, https://www.hiddenea.com/shuckland/geldeston.htm.

Even a normal canine head could be disfigured by abnormal eyes: many are glowing; they are often red, or bright yellow, orange, or white; they are very frequently "the size of saucers" or even bulging. It's fascinating to note that Robin Goodfellow himself, in 1612, was portrayed with "eyes as broad as sawcers." This suggests that this feature has long been regarded as being typically supernatural and was by no means restricted to daemon dogs. Additionally, quite a number of hounds had only the one eye. That haunting Parson Drove in Cambridgeshire was the size of a calf and possessed one huge yellow eye.[413]

There are two other regular aspects to these hounds. Bone-chilling howls or ominous barks are reported, as are glowing mouths or fiery, sulphurous breath. If the hybrid hound of Creag-an-Ordain barks three times or more, disaster is sure to follow, and exactly the same is said of a faery hound seen on Cladach a Chrogain beach on Tiree. Hearing the donkey-sized black hound of Southery howl at midnight on May 29 will prove fatal for you within twelve months.[414]

The shag dogs of Birstall in Leicestershire have a glow about their jaws; an albino pack at Wellington in Somerset breathes flames. During the early 1890s at Rocklands in Norfolk a farmer driving a horse and cart found a huge dog blocking the road. He rashly tried to push forward past the hound, but when the cart touched it, the air was filled with waving flames and a hideous stink of sulphur. The farmer died a short time afterwards. Not far away at East Flegg, villagers have reported that wherever the local daemon dog has passed is found to be scorched, as if there had been a fire on the spot. At Castle Acre in Norfolk in the 1970s a grey hound was seen that produced sparks as it moved. This detail is especially intriguing when compared to reports from Stowmarket (further south in Suffolk). It is said there that, after faery visitors have been in your house, "on going upstairs sparks of fire as bright as stars used to appear under the feet of the persons who disturbed them."

413. Samuel Rowlands, *More Knaves Yet?*, 1612.

414. "Black Shuck, Hellhounds, and Other Black Dog Reports," Paranormal Database, accessed May 25, 2020, www.paranormaldatabase.com/reports/shuckdata.php/; "B869, Between Stoer and Lochinver—Human-Faced Dog," Paranormal Database, accessed May 25, 2020, https://www.paranormaldatabase.com/m/detail.php?address=1330; Walter Henry Barrett, *Tales from the Fens*, ed. Enid Porter (London: Routledge & Kegan Paul, 1963), 136–9; "Near Ruins East of the Town—Wolfhound Howls and Doom Follows," Paranormal Database, accessed May 25, 2020, https://www.paranormaldatabase.com/m/detail.php?address=542.

It looks as if sparks generated whilst walking are an especial feature of the supernatural beings of East Anglia.[415]

It's not clear why chains are so commonly heard, but they also seem to be highly characteristic of these supernatural dogs. At Bishops Cannings in Wiltshire a headless dog drags chains across the churchyard at night. Another runs between Letton Hill and Pimperne in Dorset, dragging the links along behind. Not far away at Stourpaine, another dog (albeit invisible) drags its chains through the village square; here it's said to be the ghost of a dog that escaped from mistreatment.[416]

A hound as a big as a cow, with yellow eyes and lolling tongue, is reported to haunt Godley Green in Cheshire. It pads along beside walkers, howling, and emitting a sound of chains, but it is quite insubstantial. If you try to touch or strike it, your blow will pass right through it, unimpeded. This "ghostly" quality is quite common, but it means, of course, that hounds can pass straight through walls, gates, and other obstacles. They are able, too, to appear and disappear instantaneously, although at Bardwell in Suffolk a hound was seen during the early 1980s that materialised progressively, beginning with its gleaming eyes. Equally, they can be shot at or cars can collide with them without there being any sign of an injured hound or any damage to the vehicle.[417]

---

415. "East Flegg Area, Norfolk," Shuckland, accessed May 13, 2020, www.hiddenea.com /shuckland/eastflegg.htm; "Near Castle Acre, Norfolk," Shuckland, accessed May 13, 2020, www.hiddenea.com/shuckland/castleacrenear.htm; J. Hooper, "Demon Dogs of Norfolk & Suffolk," *Eastern Daily Press*, July 2, 1894; "Phantoms of the Night," *Norwich Mercury*, January 28, 1944; Francis Young, *Suffolk Fairylore* (Norwich, Lasse Press, 2019), 83, citing Arthur Hollingsworth, *The History of Stowmarket, the Ancient County Town of Suffolk [...]* (Ipswich: F. Pawey, 1844), 247.

416. "Headless Hound," Black Shuck, Hellhounds, and Other Black Dog Reports, Paranormal Database, accessed June 1, 2020, https://www.paranormaldatabase.com/reports /shuckdata.php?pageNum_paradata=1&totalRows_paradata=348; "Dog That Isn't There," Dorset—Paranormal Database Records, Paranormal Database, accessed May 15, 2020, https://www.paranormaldatabase.com/dorset/dorsdata.php?pageNum_paradata=10& totalRows_paradata=358; "Village Square, Heading Out Towards the Hills—Dog That Still Isn't There," Paranormal Database, accessed May 25, 2020, https://www.paranormal database.com/m/detail.php?address=8702.

417. "Yellow Dog," Manchester Ghosts, Hauntings and Paranormal Activity, Paranormal Database, accessed May 25, 2020, www.paranormaldatabase.com/hotspots/manchester .php; "Bardwell, Suffolk," Shuckland, accessed May 13, 2020, www.hiddenea.com /shuckland/bardwell.htm.

Whilst many witnesses report that black dogs lack solid, tangible bodies, this isn't uniformly the case. A white puppy seen at Stocken Hall in Rutland in one case squeezed between a mother and her daughter as they were both climbing a staircase. They couldn't see it, but they felt its body passing them. For some hours afterwards each felt a "burning chill" where the dog had touched their legs. A sense of intense cold as one of these hounds passes is quite often reported, in fact. Earlier, too, I mentioned the encounter with a barguest at Grassington: the man walking home heard chains brushing along the lane, but there was nothing at all to see.[418]

At Northrepps, in Norfolk, a two-headed black dog with eyes like saucers has been recorded. Men who saw it, but *not* women, would die within a year. Its most interesting feature (of several) was that it would sometimes turn into a ball of wool. In this form it very closely resembles several bogies described in the last chapter.[419]

Finally, many black dogs also display that classic faery trait of being unable to cross flowing water. At Selworthy, near Porlock in Somerset, a man's ghost was believed to be the origin of the typical terrible black dog that used to (quite literally) dog those travelling along the highway. Nevertheless, it could be escaped merely by passing over a watercourse. In Manchester in 1825 a hound that had haunted the highway was "laid" under the bridge crossing the river Irwell. Very probably the location was a part of the magic that contained the creature. I'll return to laying daemon dogs later.[420]

The Haunts of Daemon Dogs

Nearly a quarter of the black dogs are consistently sighted in the vicinity of a road or bridge. As well as thoroughfares, there is some close association with water courses and water sources. For instance, a now-lost well at Thornton, near Bradford in Yorkshire, used to be guarded by a large black hound with glowing red eyes and a huge tail which was known as "Bloody Tongue." To add to the horror of this apparition, it was sometimes accompanied by an

---

418. Jennifer Westwood and Jacqueline Simpson, "Rutland" in *Haunted England: The Penguin Book of Ghosts*, ed. Sophia Kingshill (London: Penguin, 2010), n.p.

419. Verily Anderson, *The Northrepps Grandchildren* (London: Hodder & Stoughton, 1968), 46, 153–4.

420. Tongue, *Somerset Folklore*, 109.

old hag with a lantern. Several other wells in the same county have their own spectral watchdogs too.

Other hounds' haunts include churchyards, ancient earthworks and standing stones, and more recent historic sites such as castles and old houses. At Formby in Lancashire, "Old Trash" is a black dog with glowing eyes who is seen to bound along the beach, leaving no paw prints in the sand. At West Kennet Long Barrow near Avebury in Wiltshire a hound appears at sunrise every Midsummer's Day, accompanied by a druid.[421]

A curious account from the Sussex village of Yapton describes how the villagers would once leave the doors of their homes open so that a ghostly black dog that haunted the village could roam freely. This was more out of fear of angering it than welcoming it into their homes as the dog would emit unearthly howls if it was not allowed to pass freely. What's most intriguing about this is that the faeries will cause similar disturbances if any house is built on one of their routeways and the doors aren't left open so they may come and go as they wish.[422]

Deadly Daemon Dogs

Given the size and colour of these wolflike monsters, the perfectly reasonable response of humans is to fear a mortal threat. This may be entirely justified. The Black Dog of Bungay is an excellent illustration of this. The event was reported nationally when on Sunday August 4, 1577, it suddenly materialised in the parish church of this small Suffolk town, terrorising the congregation at worship. The dog ran down the aisle of the church, seizing two people at prayer by their necks and killing them. Another man was clawed viciously on the back; the church door bore the marks of its talons as well. That same day, the dog also appeared at nearby Blythburgh, clawing the church door and, inside, killing three and burning one. These direct physical attacks are highly unusual though; normally black dogs rely on simply surprising and scaring

---

421. "Coastline-Dog with Glowing Eyes," Paranormal Database, accessed May 25, 2020, https://www.paranormaldatabase.com/m/detail.php?address=2416; "The Paranormal Gallery, Wiltshire, West Kennet Long Barrow," Paranormal Database, accessed May 13, 2020, www.paranormaldatabase.com/zenphoto/index.php?album=wiltshire/west-kennet-long-barrow/.

422. "Black Dogs In Sussex, Ghostly Black Dogs," Sussex Archaeology & Folklore, accessed May 13, 2020, www.sussexarch.org.uk/saaf/blackdog.html.

their victims—and this can be serious enough. A girl who saw the black dog of Aldreth Causeway died soon after from the shock of the experience and, from that date on, locals avoided the area at night, warning each other that "the dog'll have you, sure as harvest."[423]

Some faery dogs bear a distinct antipathy towards humans. There is one living in a cave on the Isle of Portland that springs out to seize unwary passersby and drag them into the sea, where they drown. At Gorleston in Norfolk a large black dog dragging chains met a man on the road and threw him over a hedge into a marsh, after dragging him for half a mile or so. He was so stunned by the experience that he lay out all night.[424]

Many of these deadly dogs don't need to bite or seize a victim to kill. Any sort of physical contact can prove to be fatal. A large white dog ran alongside two men walking at East Flegg in Norfolk. Only one could see the beast, which appeared to be friendly. It licked his hand, but he died within the year.[425]

Merely meeting a black dog can guarantee death or insanity in many places around England. One specimen, the size of a bear, haunts Troller's Gill in Wharfedale. If you stare into its huge yellow eyes, you are certain to die within days. The calf-sized dog of Wicken Fen kills even less directly—all those who merely catch sight of it will die and, in the same way, if you meet the "Wild Rider" with his pack at Weacombe in the Quantock Hills, you are bound to die. A similar ominous black dog with a matted, shaggy coat and green eyes roams Whitmore Park in Coventry at night. Local people avoid the area, since to see the dog is believed to mean that a death in the family will soon follow.[426]

423. "Blythburgh, Suffolk," Shuckland, accessed May 13, 2020, www.hiddenea.com/shuckland /blythburgh.htm; Christopher Reeve, *A Straunge and Terrible Wunder: Story of the Black Dog of Bungay* (Wichita: Morrow & Co., 1988), n. p.; "Blythburgh, Suffolk," Shuckland, accessed May 28, 2020; James Wentworth Day, *Here Are Ghosts and Witches* (London: B. T. Batsford, 1954), 21.

424. "Gorleston, Norfolk" Shuckland, accessed May 13, 2020, www.hiddenea.com/shuckland /gorleston.htm; P. de Lisle, "Tales & Traditions of Old Yarmouth," *Yarmouth Independent*, January 7, 1893.

425. Jennifer Westwood, "Friend or Foe? Norfolk Traditions of Shuck," in *Supernatural Enemies*, ed. Hilda Ellis Davidson and Anna Chaudhri (Durham, NC: Carolina Academic Press, 2001), 107.

426. Parkinson, *Yorkshire Legends and Traditions*, 127; Day, *Here Are Ghosts and Witches*, 24–5; John Harries, *The Ghost Hunter's Road Book* (London: Charles Letts, 1974), 69; Roy Palmer, *The Folklore of Warwickshire* (London, Batsford, 1976), 79.

Numerous hounds haunting villages in East Anglia have the same deadly deputation—either for the observer or for some close relative.[427] If you see the hound that haunts Reach, you may die within the year—or, alternatively, you will go mad within a fortnight. The dogs at Welney and Wicken can damage mental health as well.[428] Even where an encounter is not fatal or injurious, it is common for bad luck and financial loss to follow. Dogs with this reputation are known at Cambridge, Heveningham, and Overstrand.[429]

One miserable story from Chipping, near Lancaster, combines all these misfortunes in one. It tells of a dog that was met in the road, blocking the way on two successive bridges. As the unfortunate pedestrian approached, the dog glided backwards in front of him, emitting its awful howl. Finally, it blocked the doorway of the man's cottage, although it vanished when he tried to strike at it. Within days the man lost his son in a river, and his wife died of fever before he himself went mad.[430]

Annoying or assaulting one of these dogs is predictably dangerous. A farmer from Beckingham in Nottinghamshire was troubled by a large black dog with glowing eyes that used to cross his land, running from the churchyard to the marsh. He decided to block its route but fell down mad and nearly completely paralysed. In a comparable case from Aylesbury, a farmer got tired of meeting a large black dog in his path every time he went to milk his cows. Instead of going out of his way to avoid it, one day he struck out with his stick. The dog vanished, but the man fell down paralysed and was never able to speak again. Several places in England have stories of daemon dogs

---

427. Death, usually within a year, will strike you or a family member if you see the dog at Aslacton, Barnby, Cromer, Great Livermere, Great Massingham, Hadleigh, Hawkwell, Lessingham, Neatishead, Southery, Thorndon, or Winfarthing.

428. Day, *Here Are Ghosts and Witches*, 24–5; Harries, *The Ghost Hunter's Road Book*, 69; "Welney, Norfolk," Shuckland, accessed May 13, 2020, www.hiddenea.com/shuckland /welney.htm; "Wicken Area, Cambridgeshire," Shuckland, accessed May 13, 2020, www .hiddenea.com/shuckland/wicken.htm.

429. "Cambridge, Cambridgeshire," Shuckland, accessed May 26, 2020, https://www .hiddenea.com/shuckland/cambridge.htm; "Overstrand, Norfolk," Shuckland, accessed May 26, 2020, https://www.hiddenea.com/shuckland/overstrand.htm; "Hevengham, Suffolk," Shuckland, accessed May 26, 2020, https://www.hiddenea.com/shuckland /heveningham.htm.

430. Bowker, *Goblin Tales*, 27–36.

which disappear in dramatic flashes, and in one case reported from Hatfield Peverel in Essex, this burned to death a farmer, his horse, and wagon after the farmer had tried to strike the dog with his whip.[431]

Dreadful Daemon Dogs

Fortunately, many of these dogs are alarming but are not mortally threatening. At Micklow in Staffordshire, for example, a greyhound emerges from a hedge and accompanies late-night travellers for a distance before disappearing into a culvert under the road. The "Galley Trot" of Woodbridge in Suffolk was white and as big as a cow; if you ran away from it, it would inevitably pursue you. The village of Burgh, also in the south of Suffolk, suffered from the longer-term residence of another "Gally Trot." This was white and the size of a bullock, and it apparently lived in a bog within the parish. As with so many of this type of being, it was given to chasing and alarming locals, most particularly those that tried to escape.[432]

A very famous example of the breed haunted Wells-next-the-Sea in Norfolk during the sixteenth century. It is reputed to have attacked one man and then chased off the playwright Christopher Marlowe when he visited the area to investigate the truth of the shaggy dog story.

Fae Dogs & the Future

Like so many faeries and faery beasts, the sighting of a black dog can signify more than just a shock for the witness. The spirit of "Black Vaughan" of Hergest Court in Herefordshire was believed to return to his former home, haunting the lanes in the area as a black bull and overturning wagons and scaring riders at dusk; as a black dog accompanied by the sound of chains, he presaged a death in the Vaughan family. Another "banshee" dog is the white headless hound of Mistley in Essex, which is portent of a death in the Norman family.[433]

---

431. "Vanishing Hound," Black Shuck, Hellhounds, and Other Black Dog Reports, Paranormal Database, accessed May 13, 2020, www.paranormaldatabase.com/reports/shuckdata .php; "Hatfield Peverel, Essex," Shuckland, accessed May 13, 2020, www.hiddenea.com /shuckland/hatfieldpeverel.htm; Word-Lore: The *"Folk Magazine,"* (1926), 167.

432. "Burgh, Suffolk," Shuckland, accessed May 13, 2020, www.hiddenea.com/shuckland /burgh.htm; Edward Moor, *Suffolk Words and Phrases; Or, An attempt to Collect the Lingual Localisms of That County* (London: R. Hunter, 1823), 141.

433. Alasdair Alpin MacGregor, *The Ghost Book* (London: Robert Hale, 1955), 72.

Other dogs foreshadow a death to ordinary individuals. At Alveston, in Warwickshire, a ploughboy met a black dog on his way home on nine successive evenings. His final encounter was with a headless woman in a silk gown who rushed past him. The following day he heard of his sister's death and was convinced that the dog had been an omen. In the 1970s a woman living at Buxton in Norfolk was walking past the church when the clock struck four. A large black dog appeared beside her, which she tried to pat, but it almost immediately vanished again. A few days later, she learned that her brother had died at exactly that moment.[434]

Far away in Wiltshire a man saw a sable dog with huge fiery eyes sitting by the road as he walked towards Coate village, where his grandfather lay seriously ill. Before the man reached his destination, he met the undertaker walking the other way; his grandfather had just died. A similar ominous black dog with a matted, shaggy coat and green eyes roams Whitmore Park in Coventry at night. Local people avoid the area, since to see the dog means a death in the family. In Chelmsford in Essex, the connection between local black dog sightings and death is so well established that it is said of a dying person that "the Black Dog is at his heels."[435]

One summer evening during the 1940s, at Winfarthing in Norfolk, a woman was looking out of her window when she saw a large black dog approaching her cottage. It reached the garden gate but then vanished. Her grandfather died shortly afterwards, and the witness was convinced that the dog had acted as herald of his death. A man who lived at Clopton Green between Woolpit and Rattlesden in Suffolk in late Victorian times reportedly saw a "thing" with two saucer eyes the night before he died. It wouldn't move out of his way, instead growing

---

434. Palmer, *The Folklore of Warwickshire,* 79; "Buxton-with Lamas, Norfolk," Shuckland, accessed May 13, 2020, www.hiddenea.com/shuckland/buxtonwithlamas.htm.

435. Kathleen Wiltshire, *Ghosts and Legends of the Wiltshire Countryside,* ed. Patrick M. C. Carrott (London: Michael Russell, 1973), 4–5; Palmer, *The Folklore of Warwickshire,* 79; L. Newman and E. Wilson, "Folklore Survivals in the Southern Lake Counties and in Essex: A Comparison and Contrast," *Folklore* 63 (1952): 100; "Chelmsford area, Essex," Shuckland, accessed May 13, 2020, www.hiddenea.com/shuckland/chelmsford.htm.

bigger and telling him, "I shall want you within a week." The shock of a talking dog might well have been sufficient to kill him, regardless of its message.[436]

More generally, the monstrous black dogs with shaggy fur, drooping ears, and huge feet of Lancashire, often called a "trash" or a "skriker" (for the shrieking noise it made) were taken as more general omens of death (within a family or a group of friends) when they were witnessed prowling the byways around the parish church of Burnley. The skriker is probably heard more than it is seen, as it will tend to wander in woods emitting its piercing shriek. Both it and the trash may appear as a white horse or cow, but mostly they are met with as a large dog with very broad (possibly webbed) feet, shaggy hair, drooping ears, and large eyes. Their feet splash as they walk (hence the first soubriquet), and the being cries out piercingly as it walks backwards in front of you, vanishing the first instant your attention is distracted or, otherwise, plunging into a pool. If you try to strike the creature, your hand or stick will pass straight through it.[437]

The association between the hound and death or disaster is often more a circumstantial rather than a direct one. For instance, in 1929 a black dog was sighted at Halesworth in Suffolk the night before a row of cottages burned down. More recently still, the sighting of a black dog on the highway near Shap, high in the Lake District, always seemed to precede a fatal car accident. Lastly, two miners from Bradwell in Derbyshire were playing cards when one saw a large black dog sitting nearby, watching them. His companion could see no such dog, so it was plain that it was a supernatural experience. The man who saw the hound refused to go to work the next day; his companion carried on as normal—and was killed in a rock fall.[438]

---

436. "Winfarthing, Norfolk," Shuckland, accessed May 13, 2020, www.hiddenea.com /shuckland/winfarthing.htm; "Clopton (near Woodbridge), Suffolk," Shuckland, accessed May 13, 2020, www.hiddenea.com/shuckland/cloptonnearwoodbridge.htm; "Phantoms of the Night," *Norwich Mercury,* Jan. 28, 1944; "East Anglian Miscellany Upon Matters of History, Genealogy etc," reprinted from the *East Anglian Daily Times,* vol. 1 (1901), note 105.

437. Harland and Wilkinson, *Lancashire Folk-lore,* 91; T. T. W., "'Trash' or 'Skriker,'" *Notes & Queries,* series 1, vol. 2, 1850, 52; see, too, Bowker, "The Skriker," in *Goblin Tales,* 27.

438. Mark Henderson, "The Bradwell Dog," in *Folktales of the Peak District* (Stroud: Amberley Publishing, 2013), chapter 17.

Finally, as we've seen already, a few black dogs seem to behave like bogies and to act like ghosts or as memorials to those who have died accidentally or been murdered. In the East Anglian Fens and along the coasts in Norfolk, they seem particularly to mark drownings. Others have a role akin to banshees in certain families.[439]

Banishing Daemon Dogs

The more persistent and troublesome black dogs could always be laid. At Dean Prior, on the southern edge of Dartmoor in Devon, this was achieved by turning an unwelcome ghost first into a hound and then by leading it to a pool in a wood, where its allotted task was draining the pool beneath a waterfall using a perforated hazelnut shell. Not until this task was complete might the dog leave off.[440]

Water also featured in the laying of a bogie in the shape of the Cappelthwaite black dog at Beetham in Westmorland: with prayers and bible passages the vicar drove the animal into the River Bela, from which it has never since emerged. A dog at St. Dials near Cwmbran was laid by the simple means of hitting it on the head with a Bible, and the example that lurked around Grindlesford Bridge in Yorkshire was even easier to get rid of—you simply had to shout at it very loudly.

Helpful Hounds

Given their general nature, it is understandable why many communities would wish to be rid of a black dog, but they are not consistently malign or terrifying. A black hound seen near Soulbury in Buckinghamshire acted just like a friendly pet, running alongside a cart in playful fashion. It was only when a woman riding in the cart attempted to stroke it—and the dog vanished—that they appreciated what their companion on the road had been. During the Second World War a young airman met the large black dog, often seen at Swanton Morley in Norfolk, and reported a great sense of friendliness

---

439. Catherine Crowe, "Chapter 14," in *The Night-Side of Nature; Or, Ghosts and Ghost-Seers* (New York: Redfield, Clinton Hall, 1850), 319–344.

440. R. J. K., "The Pool of the Black Hound," *Notes & Queries*, 1850, vol. 2, no. 61, 515.

as it ran beside him as he cycled along, quite at odds with most witnesses' reports.[441]

More than being friendly, a number of faery hounds are positively helpful to humans. Dogs at Withington in Cheshire and at Birstall in Leicestershire were believed to appear to protect single women walking alone at night in those districts; a dog at Scunthorpe definitely guarded a woman from an assault by a group of men. A man was similarly protected from thieves in a wood at Brancepeth in County Durham, as was Bishop Petre at Ingatestone in Essex during the eighteenth century.[442]

Lost walkers were guided back to their path by a hound at Weacombe in Somerset. An element of seeing the future can plainly enter into this (as well as seeing into the minds of potential rapists and robbers): a man walking alone at night on a road at Bawburgh in Lincolnshire was scared off the carriageway by a huge hound with the usual eyes like burning coals. Just as he stepped off the road, a car came past driving without headlights. The man felt that the dog's menaces had actually saved his life.[443]

A fascinating experience is reported from Roudham in Norfolk from 1962. A man driving along the main road saw a large dog run onto the carriageway in front of him. He expected to hit the animal but, somehow, he avoided a collision, as if the dog had passed right through the car. He got home looking terrified but, ever since that night, he found he had acquired the second sight and was able to predict death and illness amongst his family and friends. It was as if the daemon dog's powers had been transferred to him during this near miss.[444]

Rather more frequently, the faery dogs guard hidden treasure. A large black hound keeps treasure hunters away from the Wambarrows in Somerset; at Kildonan in Scotland a two-headed dog guards a treasure at the bottom

441. "Swanton Morley," Shuckland, accessed May 18, 2020, https://www.hiddenea.com /shuckland/swantonmorley.htm.

442. Roy Palmer, *Folklore of Leicestershire and Rutland* (Wymondham: Sycamore Press, 1985), 197; Westwood, *Lore of the Land,* 88, 227.

443. "Gurt Dog," Black Shuck, Hellhounds, and Other Black Dog Reports, Paranormal Database, accssed May 26, 2020, https://paranormaldatabase.com/reports/shuckdata.php ?pageNum_paradata=13&totalRows_paradata=343; "Bawburgh, Norfolk," Shuckland, accessed May 26, 2020, https://www.hiddenea.com/shuckland/bawburgh.htm.

444. "Roudham, Norfolk," Shuckland, accessed May 18, 2020, www.hiddenea.com/shuckland /roudham.htm.

of a pool. A man who managed to drain the water away was visited by the creature during the night and was so terrified that, the next morning, he simply let the pool refill again. A third dog awaits you, sitting on a chest of treasure, below the ground at the foot of a standing stone near Murthly in Perthshire, and others are reported from Clopton in Suffolk and Ranworth in Norfolk.[445]

Lastly, at Uplyme on the Devon and Dorset border near Lyme Regis on the English south coast a black dog guided a man to hidden wealth. It appeared repeatedly in the farmhouse and finally led the farmer to a hoard of coins concealed in the thatched roof. Oddly, though, after bringing good fortune to this household, the dog moved to lurking in the lanes outside at night, swelling up until it was as high as the trees, scaring travellers with the sound of dragged chains, and bringing death to any who actually heard it.[446]

Other Daemon Dogs

Although black daemon dogs are a particular feature of the English country-side, they are not unique to that part of the British Isles.

Manx Hounds

The Isle of Man has its own black dogs too. These are called the *moddey dhoo*, which is merely Manx for "black dog." They are widespread across the island, haunting roads and lanes mostly, and sometimes appearing headless (as, for example, at Kinlye's Glen and Hango). The most famous example was known at Peel Castle in the seventeenth century. It used to appear at night and lie in the guardroom. The troops of the garrison eventually got used to its presence, although even so they would never swear in its presence nor were any

---

445. MacGregor, *The Ghost Book*, 71; Mackinlay, *Folklore of Scottish Lochs*, 181; Westwood and Kingshill, *The Lore of Scotland*, 97; "Ranworth, Norfolk," Shuckland, accessed May 18, 2020, www.hiddenea.com/shuckland/ranworth.htm; "Clopton (near Wood-bridge,) Suffolk," Shuckland, May 26, 2020, https://www.hiddenea.com/shuckland/cloptonnearwoodbridge.htm; "Somerset—Paranormal Database Records," Paranormal Database, accessed May 26, 2020, paranormaldatabase.com/somerset/somedata.php; "Unknown Pool—Two Headed Dog," Paranormal Database, accessed May 26, 2020, www.paranormaldatabase.com/m/detail.php?address=9084.

446. "Growing Hound," Devon—Paranormal Database Records, Paranormal Database, accessed May 26, 2020, https://www.paranormaldatabase.com/devon/devodata.php?pageNum_paradata=15&totalRows_paradata=398.

of them ever prepared to be left alone with the hound. Other Manx examples are agreed to be very large, shaggy, and black with "saucer eyes." They tend to haunt particular locations, where they will prowl up and down. They cannot be heard either breathing or walking, but from time to time their howls will be heard in the distance. Besides terrifying people and horses and occasionally pulling riders from their mounts, these hounds do not seem to do any great harm unless they are molested. Their howls are sometimes regarded as forecasts of calamity.[447]

There is another Manx faery dog, called the *coo ny helg* (the hunting dog) which is to be seen running in fields, or even on the road, in the evening. It is white with red ears or feet and, if you see it and say, "Shee dy row adhene" ("Bless the faeries") you will be endowed with good luck.[448]

Gwyllgi

In Wales, there is a very similar tradition of spectral hounds appearing to people, usually those walking alone late at night. In many places this creature is called the *gwyllgi*, also called the "dog of darkness" or the "hound of twilight" and it typically haunts lonely highways. The *gwyllgi* can paralyse travellers with the gaze of its blazing eyes. Either a mastiff will appear in a road, blocking the way, baring its teeth and barking fearsomely, or it may walk beside a traveller for a distance. Quite often these dogs will then turn into large bodies of fire. In one interesting story from Pembrokeshire, the mysterious hound is linked to a pair of standing stones, a common faery site. One passerby was thrown over a hedge by an unseen force there and never subsequently recovered his full health. A man who went to investigate the spot, taking his own dog with him, was confronted by a mastiff that terrified his own hound before it was surrounded by flames.[449]

Scottish Islands

This section concludes with a fascinating black dog story from Colonsay in the Hebrides. In this case, the dog—as big as a calf—is the hunting hound of

---

447. Gill, *A Manx Scrapbook,* chapter 4; Gill, *A Third Manx Scrapbook,* chapter 3; Waldron, *The History and Description of,* 23; Douglas, *"Restoring to Use Our,"* 16–17.

448. Douglas, *"Restoring to Use Our,"* 17.

449. Sikes, *British Goblins,* 168; Jones, *A Relation of Apparitions,* 16, 43, 70, 72.

a man called Macphie. Resting in a hut whilst pursuing game, a "dark object" (Gaelic *duthra*) (a *bean sith*) tried to enter and the dog fought it off. However, whilst it mauled and repulsed the faery woman, the dog was transformed in the process: its hair began to smoke and green fire began to flare from its mouth. Macphie decided to escape, but the dog seemed possessed with the woman's malevolent spirit and chased him; he had to kill it with two silver sixpences fired from his hunting rifle. As I have described, this hound is already halfway to being a daemon dog but needs the faery encounter to endow it with the full complement of terrifying features.[450]

Hounds of the Wild Hunts

A widespread and very long-established folk story in Britain concerns a "wild hunt" heard by witnesses in the skies above. There is a very clear parallel between this idea and that of the faery host, often called by the Gaelic name of *sluagh*, riding above the world, carrying off people and killing others—or their livestock—on the ground with elf-bolts. Nonetheless, there are also distinct differences. The aerial host is only found in Scotland and is closely related to the tradition of terrestrial faery raids: in both forms a cavalcade of riders progresses over the countryside, but hounds are absent. On the Isle of Man, faery hunts are a familiar part of the folklore; they closely resemble human foxhunts with riders following packs of hounds across the countryside, although the Manx faery hunts are, predictably, almost always sighted at night.[451]

An Anglo-Saxon source records hunters on black horses and goats following a pack of hideous black hounds with huge eyes, but generally in England the "wild hunt" comprises the baying daemon dogs with only one rider accompanying them—or none at all. The identity and nature of this rider is also uncertain. Mythological British figures Herne the Hunter, King Herla, and Wild Edric have all become linked to some perpetual and doom-laden pursuit across the heavens, but it is not uncommon for the rider to be identified as the devil or even as the Archangel Gabriel, although the com-

---

450. Campbell, *Superstitions of the Highlands,* 118.
451. On the *sluagh,* see my *Faery,* 198-9; on Manx hunts see Roeder, *Manx Folk-Tales,* 7–9.

mon name of "Gabriel Hounds" more probably derives from a medieval Latin word, *gabares*, meaning a corpse.[452]

The hunts were known across the British Isles by such names as the Yeth Hounds, Gabriel Ratchets (a ratchet is a type of hunting dog), the Seven Whistlers, Dando and his Dogs, or the Sky Yelpers. As this latter term indicates, the hounds were not usually seen on the ground but rather were heard, late at night or early in the morning, as if there was a great beagle pack high in the sky. The Gabble Ratchets of Derbyshire were said to be a pack of hounds led by an immense black dog and a rider, both of whom were wreathed in flames.[453]

Dogs of Doom

The presence of these hounds above a house was taken to be a sure sign that death or some other misfortune was soon to follow. There are recollections from South Yorkshire of an instance in which the hounds were heard around a house where, soon afterwards, a child was burned to death, and of a case where a man summonsed to visit a very sick relative was accompanied on his journey by the yelping of the hounds in the sky. When he reached the house, he found that the patient had just died. As was just described, the earthbound black dogs can perform exactly the same role. Generally, in the Sheffield area, it was believed that the hounds swarmed in the sky above the parish church and had men's faces.[454]

More generally, the hunt functioned as a premonition or warning. Colliers at Wednesbury in the West Midlands would sometimes hear the ratchets high in the air on their way to work. It is almost certain that their response on these occasions would have been to go home again, sure in the knowledge that a disaster was in the making at the pit. Closely related to this report is one from Leicestershire in which local colliers refused to go to work one day

---

452. G. Garmonsway, *The Anglo-Saxon Chronicle* (February 1127) (London: Dent & Sons, 1953), 258.

453. William Yarrell, "Gabriel Hounds," *Notes & Queries,* series 1, vol. 5, 596; James Britten, "Sheffield Folklore," *Notes & Queries,* series 4, vol. 7, no. 171 (1871), 299, and T. Ratcliffe, "Black Dogs: Gabriel Hounds," *Notes & Queries,* series 11, vol. 5, no. 120 (1912), 296.

454. Henderson, *Notes on the Folk-lore,* 129; Harland and Wilkinson, *Lancashire Folk-lore,* 58; T. Ratcliffe, "The Gabriel Hounds: The Seven Whistlers as Bad Omens," *Notes & Queries,* series 7, vol. 1, no. 11 (1886), 206.

in March 1855 because they had heard "the seven whistlers" in the air above them; not far away at Bedworth miners refused to enter a pit one day in September 1874 after the whistlers had been heard. At Bilston in Staffordshire if workers heard the whistlers at the mouth of the pit, they would stop work for the day, as disaster was plainly imminent. There is a fascinating report from about 1885 of nearby Rowley Regis Colliery Company prosecuting six miners for refusing to work in similar circumstances. In their defence, they pleaded the custom of the seven whistlers, and the court case was settled with an agreement that the men would only stop work if they felt sure an accident was threatened in their own pit and not some other one in the district. Fishermen shared this belief and would pull for shore if they heard the whistlers pass over, knowing that a storm would be approaching. The sound made has been compared to birds—or to children wailing.[455]

Hunting Souls

In other areas, these dogs were explained in more religious terms, with the hounds pursuing the souls of the damned or unbaptised. At Buckfastleigh in Devon, for example, it's said that Richard Capel of Brooke Manor was carried off by the so-called "whist hounds" after a lifetime spent terrorising the young women of the neighbourhood. These same hounds are heard hunting elsewhere on Dartmoor, at Dewerstone Rock and at Shaugh Bridge. The Dandy Dogs of Cornwall are notable for the fact that they weren't seen in the sky but always racing along the ground like a conventional hunt; more significantly, perhaps, a prayer could defeat them.[456]

Welsh Wild Hunt

The *Cwn y Bendith y Mamau* (faery dogs) of Wales were believed to be a pack of hounds with terrible howls; they're also known as the *Cwn Annwn* (the hounds of hell) or the *Cwn Wybir*, the sky hounds. They are white with red ears or blood red with fiery eyes. They seem to have three functions: they

---

455. William Yarrell, "Gabriel Hounds," *Notes & Queries,* series 1, vol. 5, 596; William Jones, *Credulities Past and Present; Including the Sea and Seamen, Miners, [...]* (London: Catto & Windus, 1880), 128; Burne, "Staffordshire Folk and Their Lore," *Folklore* 7, 370.

456. See Westwood and Simpson, *The Lore of the Land,* 182, and Hunt, *Popular Romances,* 220–3.

may hunt lost souls, whose crying will be heard as they are pursued across the sky, or they chase and terrorise live criminals. Their appearance thirdly foretells death: either the pack would follow the route to be taken by the next funeral procession, at the end of which they would gather in the churchyard, howling around the spot where the next grave would be dug, or they would pass over a house shortly before a death occurs there. If you are a wrong-doer who is the victim of their attentions, producing a cross (and presumably uttering a prayer or similar) will protect you.[457]

People would often fall silent for fear and seek shelter when the dogs were heard in the sky. The sound of their barking diminishes as they get nearer, so that in the distance they sound loud and deep, like a pack of bloodhounds, whereas nearer they resemble a pack of beagles. The hounds frequented crossroads and, if you met with them there, some people believed that they might give you a fatal bite or drag you away. Others deny that they have ever harmed humans or livestock. In fact, it is not even clear how solid they are: one once reportedly fell onto a gravestone in a churchyard but no one was able to catch the hound, even so.[458]

Shocks and Shugs

Shocks and shugs are difficult beasts to define. They are mainly a feature of the East Anglian counties of England, and they are shape-shifters. One folk-lore authority described the shuck as "not essentially a dog, but a shapeless monster" which is strongly reminiscent of the bogie called the *brollachan*, described in the last chapter. Certainly, whilst the shuck will appear most commonly as calf-sized dogs, it's also seen in the form of calves, goats and as an apelike being, which is the main reason for giving these shucks a separate section to themselves.[459]

The name "shuck" has very ancient roots. It comes from the Anglo-Saxon "*scucca*" (pronounced shooka), a word that seems to have had general conno-tations of evil or monstrous. In the Old English poem *Beowulf* it is one of the

---

457. Rhys, *Celtic Folklore: Welsh and Manx,* vol. 1, 216.

458. Owen, *Welsh Folk-lore,* 124; Jones, *A Relation of Apparitions,* 82; Sikes, *British Goblins,* 233.

459. Brown, "The Black Dog," *Folklore* 69, 176.

labels applied to the water monster Grendel (see chapter 2). This may explain why the "shuck" today is often associated with watercourses and bridges.[460]

The name shuck and its variants—shuck, shug, chuff, scarf, or skeff—have also become entangled and confused with the more standard English words "shaggy" and "shock," as in a "shock of hair." This rough pelt of black or white, ragged like a sheep's, is a distinguishing feature of the beast, as are its large and staring yellow eyes. The shuck known at Sulhouse is even more fearsome to behold, as it has a single blazing eye in the middle of its forehead. Some shucks are headless.[461]

Shucks are almost exclusively nighttime creatures and, what's more, it was said that they could only be seen by those "born in the hours of chime," that is—at eight, twelve, or four o'clock. This ability is evidently the goblin equivalent of the second sight with faeries.[462]

Dog Shucks

Roads are consistently the places where the shuck in its dog form is most often found. Their habit is to pad noiselessly along under the shadow of the hedges, unnerving pedestrians. The one known at Downham in Suffolk drags chains and smells of sulphur.[463]

At Irstead in Norfolk a ferocious shuck would bar the road to passersby but would pass right through them; at Geldeston, the black dog was sometimes as large as a horse, with fiery eyes and foaming jaws. It would follow travellers along the highway leading towards Bungay, growling fiercely if you tried to turn back and occasionally dragging a victim along by their clothes. On the coast of north Norfolk, between the churchyard at Overstrand and Sheringham, there was an "Old Shuck" who ran along a well-established route every evening at twilight. This dog was sometimes headless, with a white neckerchief covering the severed neck, or had large fiery, staring eyes. It was tangible as well as visible, being described as "rough, hard and shaggy,"

---

460. Young, *Suffolk Fairylore*, 29.

461. Walter Rye, "Norfolk Superstitions," in John L'Estrange, ed., *Eastern Counties Collectanea Being Notes and Queries [...]* (Norwich: Thomas Tallack, 1872), 2.

462. Morley Adams, *In the Footsteps of Borrow & Fitzgerald* (London, Jarrold & Sons, 1915), 187–192.

463. Rye, "Norfolk Superstitions," in *Eastern Counties Collectanea*, 36.

and its appearance predicted storms. Elsewhere in the east of Norfolk, the shuck that haunted Martham seems to have been linked to the churchyard. It was an immense example, with the obligatory black shaggy hair and burning eyes, and once so terrified a traveller that he fainted on the spot. He returned to the place the next day and found a mark on the grass between the graves that seemed to have been singed with gunpowder. There was another headless hound at Coltishall Bridge in the Broads whilst at Neatishead an aggressive cur appeared after dark, yet for all its snarling was as insubstantial as "a sheet of paper."[464]

In Cambridgeshire, north of Ely, a sighting of the black "shucky dog" was always taken as an omen of impending death. For instance, on the spot near Littleport where a rider drowned in one of the dykes, a dog could be heard walking, panting, and howling for its drowned master. Meeting the shuck foretells death within the year.[465]

Aside from the morbid connotations of the shuck, its sheer presence could be deeply disconcerting. The shuck of Methwold on the eastern edge of the Fens is a good example of the behaviour I'm describing here. It would never emerge fully from the shadows of the roadside, so that a lonely late-night traveller would only ever be aware of a shape whose red luminous eyes glowed in the dark. The shuck would walk softly when the pedestrian walked and would stop if she or he stopped. This unpleasant sense of being tracked slowly overwhelmed the victim until they were trembling and almost paralysed. Then they would make a precipitous flight—with the shuck loping steadily along behind. Some shocks are much more violent than others—at

---

464. Amelia Opie, *Memorials of the Life of Amelia Opie: Selected and Arranged from Her Letters, Diaries, and Other Manuscripts,* comp. Cecilia Lucy Brightwell (Norwich: Fletcher & Alexander, 1854), 225; "Overstrand, Norfolk," Shuckland, accessed May 26, 2020, https://www.hiddenea.com/shuckland/overstrand.htm; EST, "Shuck the Dog Fiend," *Notes & Queries,* 1850, vol. 2, no. 29, 467; John Glyde Jr., comp. and ed., *The Norfolk Garland: A Collection of the Superstitious Beliefs and Practices [...]* (London: Jarrold & Sons, 1872), 65; Robert Forby, *The Vocabulary of East Anglia; an Attempt to Record [...],* vol. 2 (London: J. B. Nichols and Son, 1830), 238.

465. Enid Porter, *Cambridgeshire Customs and Folklore with Fenland Material Provided by W. H. Barrett* (London: Routledge & Kegan Paul, 1969), 53–4; Rye, *Eastern Counties Collectanea,* 2; "Littleport, Cambridgeshire," Shuckland, May 18, 2020, www.hiddenea.com/shuckland/littleport.htm.

the very least throwing travellers down and bruising them, in the worst cases spraining ankles or breaking bones. One witnessed near Melton in Suffolk had a donkey's head and a smooth velvet hide; a man who tried to take hold of it was bitten on the thumb—and bore the marks until he died.[466]

Puzzlingly, Old Scarfe, the shug that lived in and around Old Yarmouth, could be stopped in its tracks by the simple measure of laying down straw in its path. That the remedy was so simple is perhaps lucky, as this beast used to be seen at night as a howling black dog the size of a goat, with horns, blazing eyes, and chains. It would roam the town, scaring road users and harming livestock.[467]

Monkey Shugs

Elizabethan poet Thomas Churchyard wrote the following very pertinent and informative lines concerning buggs and pucks:

> "Nay, better talk of bogges,
> That walkes in dead men's shapes:
> Or tell of pretty little pogges,
> As Monkies, Owles or Apes."[468]

The apelike manifestations of the shug are the most fascinating aspect of this being—and this is for two reasons: first, that in their anthropoid form they are the closest to humans (and faeries) and, second, because by their very exoticness, they seem more authentic. Whilst it is easy to conceive of a villager of the sixteenth or seventeenth century imagining a monstrous version of an everyday animal, the creation of something resembling a mammal which many might never have heard of, let alone seen, is more surprising. Nevertheless, these creatures were encountered across a wide area. At West Wratting in Cambridgeshire as recently as the early 1950s a police constable recounted a childhood experience when he saw the local "shug monkey,"

466. Charles Kent, *The Land of the "Babes in the Wood," or The Breckland of Norfolk* (London: Chatto & Windus, 1910), 111; Gutch, *County Folk-lore* 3, 84, 91.

467. "Great Yarmouth, Norfolk," Shuckland, accessed May 18, 2020, www.hiddenea.com /shuckland/greatyarmouth.htm.

468. Churchyard, *A Handful of Gladsome Verses,* 1592.

a black, shaggy animal that haunted the road leading to the next village of Balsham, and which he reported to be:

> "a cross between a big, rough-coated dog and a monkey with big shining eyes. Sometimes it would shuffle along on its hind legs and at other times it would whizz past on all fours. You can guess that we children gave the place a wide berth after dark!"[469]

At Melton in Suffolk "Old Shock" haunted local roads and footpaths, throwing down walkers. It has been described as a large dog or calf with "tea-saucer eyes," but it was also to be seen hanging on the bars of a toll-gate, making it resemble an ape. Nonetheless, it had a donkey's head and (in contradiction of the source of its name) a smooth velvet hide. This particular beast bit the hand of a man that tried to catch it. As is often the case, it was believed that its appearance foretold a death in the vicinity. These ape-like faery beasts are by no means limited to the eastern counties of England. In Surrey, in the south, the village of Buckland boasts a "shag," which is a monster like a huge ape, sometimes spotted sitting on a large rock in a lane and sometimes invisible. It would scare those riding or driving carts along the highway at night, just where it crossed a stream called the Shagbrook. A white lady has also been seen at the spot, tied to a story of a jilted girl who died of grief there. Lastly at Ranton, in Staffordshire in the north Midlands, there was a "man-monkey" who used to appear where the highway crossed a canal. This creature was black with white eyes and would emerge from beneath the road bridge, leaping on passing horses and terrifying them (and the humans with them). A man had apparently drowned in the canal there at some point in the nineteenth century.[470]

In the border counties of Scotland there lived a sprite called the Wag-at-t'-Wa that, although it is often compared to a brownie, is in fact a good deal more like a shug. It lived in the kitchens of farms, overseeing the work of the domestic servants but not actually undertaking any chores, unlike a brownie.

---

469. Day, *Here Are Ghosts and Witches*, 28; Harries, *The Ghost Hunter's Road Book*, 70.

470. Burne, *Shropshire Folk-lore*, 106; Westwood & Simpson, *Lore of the Land*, 712; "Buckland Shag," Surrey—Paranormal Database Records, Paranormal Database, https://www.paranormaldatabase.com/surrey/surrdata.php.

Whenever the pothook over the fire was free, the wag would swing there; he looked like an old man dressed in grey, except that he had long crooked legs and a long tail. In this respect, he sounds a lot more like a monkey hanging from the crook. The wag approved of children, happiness in a household, and lots of home-brewed ale. He would disappear if there was a death in a family, and a cross marked on the pot crook would seemingly lay him. Furthermore, it may be remembered from earlier that one of the forms of the Northumbrian barguest was as a monkey who accompanied midwives.[471]

Lastly, most intriguingly, we should take note of the Highland creature called the *fear liath mor*, the big grey man, who has only ever been seen high on mountains. He is said to be up to twenty feet in height, like a large ape with long arms and grey or brown hair. In many respects, of course, this faery monkey is the British equivalent of the yeti or sasquatch.[472]

Conclusions

Spotting fae dogs appears to be fairly easy. Many are obviously supernatural because of their size or some other feature, but at first sight many look like normal black or brown dogs. Even so, as they run along beside you as you walk, cycle, or drive, there will be something in the gait, in the strange silence, or in the atmosphere that is eerie and uncanny and that will convey to you the realisation that this is not a normal encounter.

Fae dogs have a mixed reputation: some are helpful, some are fearsome, some can be life threatening. Some mark or predict deaths; a few cause them; just a few bring good fortune. They may be readily recognisable by their huge size and terrifying eyes, but some are even more alarming due to their ability to transform into horses, cows, goats, or donkeys. They are fascinating apparitions, but not faery beasts you would willingly wish to meet.

---

471. Henderson, *Notes on the Folk-lore*, 256.
472. "Shaggy Creature," Cryptozoology Reports from the Paranormal Database, Paranormal Database, accessed May 18, 2020, www.paranormaldatabase.com/reports/cryptodata .php.

Chapter 11

FAE CATTLE AND OTHER BEASTS

In part 1, I examined the Scottish and Manx water beasts, the kelpie, water horse, and water bull. England has nothing as fearsome or as violent as these Highland beasts. There are, however, fae horses and cattle that share some characteristics with their northern relatives, but they are far milder in their general nature: alarming, admittedly, but not deadly.

It's important, too, to repeat here that these faery beasts are distinct from any livestock and domestic pets that might be kept by the faeries and mermaids. In fact, there should be no room for confusion, as in England there is very little tradition of faeries keeping their own farm animals; it is a feature primarily of the Scottish accounts. The faeries' farm animals may have some distinctive markings and a few of their own magical properties, but they are by and large just ordinary livestock reared by our Good Neighbours. An example might be the faery pig of the Isle of Man, a creature called *arkan sonney* in Manx—"the lucky piggy." This is a white pig with red ears and eyes that is capable of changing its size but can't change its shape. They are very attractive creatures, and having one amongst your swine herd will bring you luck. These faery pigs are most often seen by children at dusk in the Patrick area of Man. Another pig is said to appear around Glenfaba and wears a red hat.[473]

These cattle and other beasts the faeries own are simply livestock: they graze in herds and they give milk. This chapter is concerned with magical beings who may take the familiar form of livestock in the field but in no other respect resemble the habits or behaviour of farmyard beasts. As will be demonstrated, these fae animals can be quite unstable or changeable in form: the bogle called the Hedley Kow discussed earlier can appear as a cow or as a horse, amongst his other shapes. White geese and bears are known too: during the Civil War, for example, a headless bear was sighted at Worcester. These are all faery beasts in the truest sense, being endowed with supernatural powers and traits, and for that reason I shall also refer to them as "fae animals."[474]

Fae Cattle

Fae calves and bulls seem to exist mainly to instil fear into travellers without inflicting any great harm upon them. At Brigg in Lincolnshire the Lackey Causey Calf used to haunt a stretch of the highway between Brigg and Wrawby and would emerge at night and try to entice travellers into a small stream; it sometimes appeared headless. Another headless calf was known at Latchingdon in Essex. At Roxby a "shag-foal" (see later) that haunted Boggart Lane could also appear as a white calf; another calf would appear around twilight at Tupholme Priory. At Hethersett in Norfolk, creatures called "faines" lurked around a couple of local roads and would startle nighttime walkers by coming up behind them and whisking them briefly off their feet as they rushed past. The *faines* were calves with shining eyes like saucers; it was said that they could blow anyone near them off their feet. At Liphook in Hampshire a white calf appeared at night near a stream, making noise,

---

473. See my *Faery* chapter 5; Douglas, *"Restoring to Use Our,"* 21–22.

474. Richard Baxter, *The Certainty of the Worlds of Spirits Fully Evinced* (London: T. Parkhurst & J. Salisbury, 1691), 58; "Bogie Goose," Yorkshire—Paranormal Database Records, Paranormal Database, accessed May 26, 2020, https://www.paranormaldatabase.com /yorkshire/Pages/yorkdata.php?pageNum_paradata=1&totalRows_paradata=608.

appearing and disappearing and finally shrinking in size to that of a hen and vanishing.[475]

Several of these creatures seem to be associated with dead people and may even be their ghosts. The so-called "guy trash" of Yorkshire is an evil cow that foretells mortality. A fae cow at Millichope Hall in Shropshire was associated with a former squire who was unhappy about the handling of his will. He manifested as a flayed calf. Not far away from this creature, at Bagbury on the Welsh border, there existed a flayed bull, said to be the ghost of a former owner. It would appear at night with flaming eyes and roaring so loudly that sleep was impossible in the vicinity. This terrifying bull was eventually laid by a communal effort which involved driving it into the church at nearby Hyssington whilst the vicar read biblical passages. The creature progressively shrank until it was small enough to capture in a box, after which it was buried underneath the threshold of the church.[476]

These enchanted cattle can be linked to hidden riches in a range of ways. A calf at Hackthorpe Hall in Westmorland was guardian of buried treasure and led a farmer to a stone drinking trough for cattle under which a stash of gold was concealed. At Crosby Ravensworth in the same county, a great white bull patrolled a fortified stone tower, protecting the treasure hidden in the cellar of the ruin, and at Goodwood in Sussex a calf stood watch over gold buried in an ancient hill fort. Lastly, at Vayne Castle in Angus in Scotland, a monstrous ox violently chased some intruders out of a concealed dungeon where silver and gold were stashed, disappearing in a blaze of flames that sealed the entrance forever.

Fae cattle can help humans in another way. Once, a famine struck the Hebridean island of Lewis, but a white cow appeared from the sea and told islanders that they could come to her at the Callanish stone circle nightly, when she would provide each household with a pailful of milk. This went

475. Eliza Gutch and Mabel Peacock, comp., *Examples of Printed Folklore Concerning Lincolnshire* (London: David Nutt, 1908), 51, 53; *County Folk-lore* 5, 53; Walter Rye, *The Recreations of a Norfolk Antiquary* (Norwich: Holt, Rounce & Wortley, 1920), 28; "Boy Playing Flute," Hampshire—Paranormal Database Records, Paranormal Database, accessed May 26, 2020, https://www.paranormaldatabase.com/hampshire/hampdata.php?pageNum_paradata=4&totalRows_paradata=179.

476. Burne, *Shropshire Folk-lore,* 642, 107.

on for some time, sustaining the people when they would otherwise have starved, until a witch went to the cow with a sieve instead of a bucket. As her receptacle never filled, she milked the white cow dry and broke the spell. Similar accounts of saviour cows abused by witches are found elsewhere in Britain.[477]

At Norton near Darlington there was a supernatural white heifer that could transform into a roll of Irish linen. This apparition would then vanish, to be replaced with a "white lass." From the Scottish border villages of Bowden and Gattonside, there are very limited reports of a sprite called "cowlug" which, as its name suggests, was distinctive for its cow's ears. We know next to nothing about them, except that they were believed to be abroad in the district on one night a year in particular. Alscot Park near Stratford-upon-Avon, and its surrounding lanes, was the lair of a hideous being that was half-calf and half-man. The hybrid or shifting nature of these creatures fits with many of the other beasts that have been described so far.[478]

The Aerial Bull

Brief mention should be made of an unusual Scottish faery beast. Details of this particular creature are very scarce, but it is said to appear in the form of an ordinary black bull, except that it is made only of dark cloud. The creature descends from the sky on a strong wind on New Year's Eve and wanders on the earth's surface for a while before departing—for which reason it is also sometimes called the "New Year Bull."[479]

Fae Horses

The tradition of faery beasts in equine form is very old indeed. The thirteenth century historian Gervase of Tilbury wrote about a fae animal called the "grant," which looked like a yearling foal, except that it walked on its hind legs alone. It had very bright eyes, and its appearance in village streets was a

---

477. Westwood and Kingshill, *The Lore of Scotland,* 466.

478. Longstaffe, *The History and Antiquities,* 15; Aitken, *Forgotten Heritage,* 27.

479. MacCulloch, *The Highlands and Western Islands,* vol. 4, 331.

warning of some imminent disaster such as a fire. What was true in 1211 is still true today.[480]

There are faery beasts that are always encountered in the shape of a horse and others that seem to be able to vary at will. The Doonie of Nithsdale and the Borders may be seen as an old man, but sometimes he will appear as a brownie and at others as a pony. In Southern England, the "colt-pixy" is a faery who will periodically appear in pony form, leading horses astray and luring walkers into bogs in Hampshire. In contrast, the Somerset colt-pixy acts as a guardian of orchards and scares off apple thieves.[481]

Rather like the kelpie and *each uisge* in Scotland, there is some suggestion of a link between these supernatural horses and water: some examples were said, for instance, to appear where the River Trent flowed into the Humber, walking on the surface of the water on moonlit nights. Mostly, though, English fae horses seemed to spend their time scaring hapless locals, as was the case with Hazelrigg Dunnie of Northumberland, whose tricks included taking on the form of farmers' plough horses and then, having been yoked for a day's work, suddenly shedding his harness and galloping off at high speed.[482]

Tatterfoals

There is a particular type of enchanted horse that must be described separately, which is the "tatterfoal" or "shag foal." This is a good deal more like the kelpie of Scottish legend than many of the fae horses of England. It is a very old apparition, having been described as early as the first decade of the thirteenth century, and it was particularly found across Lincolnshire. The name derives from the animal's coat, which was distinctively shaggy or tatty, a feature which marks the transition from immature to mature horse. The foal would accost road users, perhaps merely blocking the way and scaring them, but sometimes trying to pull them off their mounts. For example, at Orgarth Hill in Lincolnshire there was a "rough-coated goblin horse" that would suddenly appear and keep pace with travellers, terrifying their own horses. The

---

480. Gervase of Tilbury, *Otia Imperialia: Recreation for an Emperor,* ed. and trans. S. E. Banks and J. W. Binns (Oxford Medieval Texts: Clarendon Press 2002), part 3, section 62.

481. Aitken, *Forgotten Heritage,* 27; Briggs, *Dictionary of Fairies,* "Colt-pixy."

482. Denham, *The Denahm Tracts, Folklore Society* 35, London, 1895, 158.

"Spittal Hill Tut" that haunted the hill outside Freiston in Lincolnshire was a fae horse which would also follow a rider for a distance before vanishing. On at least one occasion, though, it reared up and grabbed the rider with its forelegs, squeezing the breath out of him before letting him go. A closely related shaggy foal would scare pedestrians or drag drunken riders from their saddles at Barton on Humber. Several of these creatures are reputed to be linked to interred murder victims or to buried treasure at the spots they haunt. For instance, at Heage Hall in Derbyshire, the executed Mary Queen of Scots appears mounted on a brown horse whilst the spirit of a former squire who so mistreated his wife that she died appears with two inky black dogs or driving a coach and horses.[483]

Fae Donkeys

At Montford near Shrewsbury, a large dog haunted the highway, but this would also manifest sometimes as a fae donkey. Once, a man saw it lying by the roadside, and when he went to investigate and cautiously poked it with his foot, it rose up into the air like a cloud of vapour and vanished. At Fitz, also in Shropshire, the ghost of a woman who was robbed of the jewellery in which she had been buried has been known to appear in the form of a young horse called Obrick's or Obitch's colt. She might let people ride her and was even seen during daylight.[484]

At Geldeston in Norfolk there is another supernatural donkey, said to rattle chains and breathe fire. A nearly identical white donkey is known at Horning further north in the county; it has followed travellers at night and, if they tried to flee, would chase them with smoke and flames issuing from its nostrils. It is possible to see through the creature, and it disappears into the churchyard wall. Fae donkeys are also known at Roxby and Kirton in Lind-

---

483. *County Folklore* 5, 50, 55; "Mary Queen of Scots," Derbyshire—Paranormal Database Records, Paranormal Database, accessed May 26, 2020, https://www.paranormal database.com/derbyshire/derbdata.php?pageNum_paradata=7&totalRows_para data=268.

484. Burne, *Shropshire Folk-lore,* 105–6.

sey in Lincolnshire. On a mountain pass called Clagh Height on the Isle of Man, a donkey has been seen that transforms itself into a huge black dog.[485]

Fae Felines

The faeries have their own cats, which can be quite intimidating in themselves, but there is a separate tradition of monstrous supernatural cats as well. In Welsh legend, for example, there is the *cath palug*, a giant cat which is linked with water and becomes one of the "three plagues of Britain." King Arthur fights it in several stories—sometimes successfully, sometimes fatally.

In more recent folk tradition, white fae cats are reported from time to time: at Reeth in North Yorkshire an unnaturally large cat with fiery eyes lurks beneath the bridge over the River Swale. There is also a widespread story of "The King of the Cats," which follows a broadly standard plot. A person witnesses a cat's funeral and returns home to inform their spouse of the curious marvel they've seen. As the tale is told, their own cat shows unusual comprehension and interest, and at its conclusion will jump up, declaring, "That means I'm King of the Cats!" and disappear. In an interesting version from Argyllshire, a huntsman shoots a wild cat one day and, before it dies, is told to inform his kitten of its demise. The hunter does this—and the kitten declares, "That was my sister," swells to monstrous proportions, and kills him in turn.[486]

Haunting Hares

There are reports of fae beings that are seen as hares or rabbits, small animals which ostensibly are not especially alarming. However, they are always reputed to foretell deaths (as at Kidsgrove and Etruria in Staffordshire) or are associated with the sites of murders and, perhaps, other unpleasant events. Rabbits have been linked to places where bloodcurdling shrieks are heard, and there are reports of injuries inflicted on those who have tried to interfere

---

485. Adams, *In the Footsteps*, 190; Westwood and Simpson, The *Lore of the Land*, 499; *County Folklore* 5, 56; Day, *Here Are Ghosts and Witches*, 160; Gill, *A Third Manx Scrapbook*, chapter 2.

486. "Collecteanea," *Folklore* 27 (1916): 309; Katherine Briggs, *The Fairies in Tradition and Literature* (London: Routledge & K. Paul, 1967), 72.

with them: a man who attempted to catch the Etruria rabbit had his shoulder dislocated, for instance.[487]

I have described how boggarts and barguests may take on the shape of rabbits at times, but there are also sprites that appear in hare or rabbit form all the time. This ought not to surprise us especially, given that there are also quite a number of modern accounts in which faeries are met with in just this guise. Equally, witches in the guise of hares were a common element of folk belief. At Hoghton in Lancashire the fae link was further cemented because it was said that faeries and rabbits happily cohabited in the same warrens.[488]

At Bolingbroke Castle in Lincolnshire a fae hare would appear that ran between the legs of people, tripping them up, before vanishing in the dungeons of the ruined keep. Thetford Warren in Norfolk was haunted by a white rabbit with large flaming eyes that moved very quickly and was never caught. It was frequently spotted, but beyond the eerie experience, nothing ever came of merely seeing it. Matters were different, though, if anyone tried to hunt the rabbit: the foolhardy person was certain to be found the next day, mysteriously killed by their own gun. A very similar tale comes from Egloshayle in North Cornwall. A white rabbit haunted the churchyard there, appearing only on the nights of full moons and vanishing into the boundary wall; a young man tried to kill it but again died by his own weapon. A fae rabbit used to appear *inside* St. George's Church in York and always disappeared before it could be caught, whilst another in the graveyard of St. Mary's Church, Rochdale, was invulnerable to bullets, which passed straight through it. A white hare at Humbleton in Northumberland could also never

487. Westwood and Simpson, *The Lore of the Land,* 668, 663.

488. "Fairy Tunnels," Fairies and Little People, Paranormal Database, accessed May 26, 2020, https://www.paranormaldatabase.com/reports/fairydata.php?pageNum_paradata =6&totalRows_paradata=214.

be killed, whilst one at Cromarty Castle would vanish by evaporating in a cloud of smoke.[489]

Another white rabbit with shining eyes was seen regularly at Caistor in Lincolnshire during late Victorian times, but the purpose of its appearances was unknown. Matters were very different at Crank in Lancashire, where in the eighteenth and early nineteenth centuries a white rabbit was known to haunt the roads of the district, hopping alongside late-night travellers. Being joined on the highway by this companion was a sure sign of misfortune to follow; the creature was linked with a girl (and her pet rabbit) who had been murdered in the vicinity. At Wheal Vor tin mine near Helston in Cornwall it was believed that a fatal accident in the mine was presaged by the appearance of a white hare or rabbit in one of the engine houses. The miners declared that they had chased these apparitions until they were seemingly hemmed in, but they would still escape. Being of a superstitious nature, it was believed amongst miners that a white rabbit crossing your path on the way to work was likewise a warning not to descend into the pit that day.[490]

A white hare with bloodshot eyes appeared at Bardsea in Lancashire as companion to a "dobby" (a hob or brownie) who wandered the coast roads on stormy nights. They became associated with the tolling of the church bell after a parishioner had died, marking but not predicting a death in the locality.

489. *County Folk-lore* 5, 54; Kent, *The Land of the,* 89; Westwood and Simpson, *The Lore of the Land,* 517; "Northumberland—Paranormal Database Records," Paranormal Database, accessed May 26, 2020, www.paranormaldatabase.com/northumberland/nhumdata .php; "White Rabbit," Haunted Churches and Other Myths & Legends, accessed May 26, 2020, https://paranormaldatabase.com/reports/church.php?pageNum_paradata=26 &totalRows_paradata=672; "Rabbit," Yorkshire—Paranormal Database Records, Paranomral Database, accessed May 26, 2020, https://www.paranormaldatabase.com /yorkshire/Pages/yorkdata.php?pageNum_paradata=30&totalRows_paradata=753; "Hare," Northumberland—Paranormal Database Records, Paranormal Database, accessed May 26, 2020, https://www.paranormaldatabase.com/northumberland/nhum data.php?pageNum_paradata=3&totalRows_paradata=86; "Baum Rabbit," Lancashire— Paranormal Database Records, Paranormal Database, accessed May 26, 2020, https:// paranormaldatabase.com/lancashire/lancdata.php?pageNum_paradata=19&totalRows _paradata=554.

490. Westwood and Simpson, *The Lore of the Land,* 441; Terence W. Whitaker, *Lancashire's Ghosts and Legends* (London: Robert Hale Ltd., 1980), 194–196; R. Hunt, *Popular Romances of the West of England—Second Series,* 125.

Like many faery beasts, then, fae hares could foretell events to come. At Aird-rie, the Kerr family knew that the appearance of a white hare marked fast-approaching misfortune. On the island of Guernsey, a white hare was only seen in stormy weather. At Looe in Cornwall another such hare was regularly seen as it ran down the hill from the village of Talland and then disappeared in the vicinity of a public house; this was regarded as an ill omen.[491]

As recently as the 1940s, a magical hare that could not be killed was reported by two men out hunting partridges near Oakley in Bedfordshire. It was shot several times but there was never any trace of a body.[492]

Conclusions

All the fae animals have two consistent aspects. One is that (with only a couple of exceptions) they maintain their form: supernatural calves and ponies stay in that shape. It may be hard to take seriously the notion of an enchanted hare or foal and to approach it with the appropriate level of caution and respect—whereas a donkey with the body of a hound is instantly identifiable as strange and potentially dangerous. That said, the records of encounters indicate that witnesses tend to sense something eerie or uncanny, even with an animal as ostensibly harmless as a white rabbit.

Secondly, although they may disconcert, scare, and sometimes play tricks on humans, they do not put their lives in danger. It's true that they often mark a local death, and their appearance may even warn of mortal peril, but they will sometimes help people or guide them to good fortune.

---

491. Westwood and Simpson, *The Lore of the Land*, 389; "Hare," Reports of Haunted Inns from the Paranormal Database, Paranormal Database, accessed May 26, 2020, https://www.paranormaldatabase.com/reports/inns.php?pageNum_paradata=11&totalRows_paradata=427; "White Hare," Reports of Curses and Cursed Places in the UK and Ireland, Paranormal Database, accessed May 28, 2020, https://www.paranormaldatabase.com/reports/curse.php; Bowker, *Goblin Tales*, 152–158.

492. Laurence Meynell, *Bedfordshire* (London: Robert Hale, 1950), 139.

Chapter 12

WILLS OF THE WISP

Our last category of faery being is the will of the wisp, a sprite that appears as lights at night and leads travellers astray in the dark. The will often lacks any solid body at all. Whilst the true faeries can often be seen as points of light or glowing, in its classic form, the will of the wisp is nothing *but* a moving flame. Antiquarian Jabez Allies witnessed a will of the wisp at Powick, near the city of Worcester, in 1839. He described a blue light, as bright as an electric spark, that either rose and fell or moved quickly horizontally.[493]

Fear of the Dark

To fully appreciate the threat of the will of the wisp, it helps to understand our ancestors' attitudes to nighttime. In the pitch darkness of the hours before dawn, without any artificial light other than the torch or lantern you carried yourself, moonless nights would be potentially perilous and fearsome. John Fletcher, in his 1611 play *The Night Walker*, captures these terrors in the defiant words of his character Frank Hartlove:

---

493. Jabez Allies, *On the Ancient British, Roman, and Saxon Antiquities and Folk-lore of Worcestershire* (Worcester: J. Grainger, 1840), 409.

> "The night, and all the evil the night covers,
> The Goblins, Haggs, and the black spawn of darkness,
> Cannot fright me"[494]

Hartlove may have felt brave, but another character, Wildbraine, was not ashamed to admit how vulnerable he felt walking the streets of London at night, where he might be mistaken for a thief or other wrongdoer, whilst "in the country, / I should be taken for William o' the Wispe, / Or Robin Good-fellow." The lone light moving in the darkness ought to be an indication of a friendly fellow traveller, or of the refuge of a cottage, but it might often turn out to be false and could betray the wanderer.[495]

The will of the wisp was most memorably described by Milton in *Paradise Lost* as:

> "As when a wandering fire,
> Compact of unctuous vapor, which the night
> Condenses, and the cold environs round,
> Kindled through agitation to a flame
> —Which oft, they say, some evil spirit attends—
> Hovering and blazing with delusive light,
> Misleads the amazed night-wanderer from his way,
> To bogs and mires, and oft through pond or pool;
> There swallowed up and lost, from succour far"[496]

Another significance is given to wills of the wisp in parts of Somerset. There they are called "spunkies," and they are believed to be the wandering souls of children who died unbaptised. They assemble at certain churches on Midsummer's Eve to gather together that year's new ghosts and, at Hallow-een, they guide these spirits to their funeral services. Interestingly, further southwest into Devon and Cornwall, it is the pixies who are thought to be the souls of newborn infants and who are sometimes seen as moths. Tiny

---

494. John Fletcher, *The Night Walker, Or, The Little Thief,* in *Beaumont and Fletcher,* ed. A. R. Waller (Cambridge: University Press, 1909), act 3.

495. Fletcher, *Night Walker*, Act 3.

496. John Milton, *Paradise Lost,* 1667, book 9, lines 634–642.

size and a flickering, flittering nature appear to be the common features that may have given rise to this idea.[497]

Types of Sprites

The name of this phenomenon varies from region to region. In some parts of Norfolk, for example, the flitting lights are called "hyter" or "hikey sprites" (*hyte* having the meaning of crazy). The *hyter sprites* are widely regarded as rather more beneficent beings than some of their kind. There is considerable doubt within the county whether to call the sprites faeries, bogies, or wills of the wisp, but they are well known to be connected with the perils of the night. More and more, it seems, they have been co-opted by parents as another sort of bugbear (see chapter 9) that will scare naughty children inside when it's dark and away from marshy areas and streams. They may appear as tiny men or as flickering blue flames.[498]

Other East Anglian names included Lantern Men, Jenny Burnt Arse, and Syleham Lamps (from a place where they were especially notorious, appearing like balls of light over the Broads). Other names used around Britain include Friar Rush, Mad Crisp, Dicke a Tuesday, Jacky Lantern, Kitty with a Wisp, Kit with the Canstick, and Gyl Burnt-Tayle. In this latter case it's likely that the name "Jill" is derogatory, denoting a loose woman—very much as with the lascivious Jilli Ffrwtan faery of Wales. A very common name is Hobby Lanterns, Hob o'Lantern, or Hoberdy's Lantern, all of which clearly associate the lights with hobs and hobthrusts (see the discussion of Puck later). The Welsh form of the sprite was known as the *ellyllddan*, which simply means "elf fire." In Lancashire the apparition was known as Peg o' Lantern, and a well-known example was regularly sighted hovering over the marshland of Edge Lane, east of Manchester city centre.[499]

Mention should be made of the similar, but unrelated, phenomenon called the "corpse-candle" (*canwyll corph* in Welsh). This is another moving light, but it has a single purpose, to predict a death, and it may be seen on or

---

497. Tongue, *Somerset Folklore*, 122.

498. Ray Loveday, *Hikey Sprites: The Twilight of a Norfolk Tradition* (Norwich: R. Loveday, 2009), 12–27.

499. Harland and Wilkinson, *Lancashire Folk-lore*, 53; John Brand, *Observations on Popular Antiquities: chiefly Illustrating the Origin of Our Vulgar Customs, Ceremonies, and Superstitions*, vol. 3 (London, G. Bell, 1900), 395.

near the body of a dying person, or with their spectre, as well as separately, perhaps at the place where the person will die.[500]

The Hinky Punk of the Somerset-Devon border behaves like a will of the wisp, even though it is said to be corporeal—a strange one-legged and one-eyed creature with a lantern, luring the unwary into morasses or over abysses. The "punk" element of the name might appear to link this modern sprite to Shakespeare's famous character, but in fact the word is an abbreviation of "spunk" or "spunkie" as used in Scotland (the *pinket* of Worcestershire is likely to be related as well). The term "spunky" denotes a kindling substance—tinder or touchwood—and has the sense of sparky. As for "hinky," this word may be related to "hike" (to swing) and "hikey" (a swing) or to "hite," to run up and down aimlessly. In Somerset, a "hity-tity" is a seesaw, all of these dialect words being suggestive of the constant dancing motion characteristic of these lights (and reminding us, too, of the "hyter" or "hikey" sprites of Norfolk).

Leading Astray

The main point of the will of the wisp is a very faery one—it is to mislead people, almost invariably those travelling during the hours of darkness. Most particularly in summer (although the Hobby Lanterns of Dunwich were seen only in the last quarter of the year, between September 29 and December 24), they appear in meadows and marshes—or flying along rivers and hedges—looking like wisps of straw alight. Sometimes the light is the colour of a bright candle, sometimes it might be red. Using the best comparators he had available to him, a rural witness from Suffolk in late Victorian times described the local Hobby Lanterns as being as "bright as two candles." The lights called Jack o' Lantern at Alderfen Broad in Norfolk are often seen "rising up and falling, and twistering about, and then up again. It looked exactly like a candle in a lantern."[501]

---

500. Sikes, *British Goblins*, Book 2, chapter 9.

501. Camilla Gurdon, "Folklore from South-East Suffolk," *Folklore* 3 (1892): 558; Westwood and Simpson, *The Lore of the Land*, 488; Day, *Here Are Ghosts and Witches*, 153; "Marshland Between Alderfen and Neatishead, Known as Heard's Holde—Heard's Lantern," Paranormal Database, May 26, 2020, https://www.paranormaldatabase.com/m/detail .php?address=7702.

Wills of the wisp draw those who are travelling towards them so that they stray from their route and end up lost and wandering desperately through bogs and brakes. Then the light they have been following suddenly disappears, and the person finds themselves abandoned—exhausted, wet, and scratched. Mostly this is pure mischief, but sometimes these incidents end fatally, with people drowned in rivers and pools. Because of this risk, at Aymestrey in Herefordshire the custom up to the late eighteenth century was to ring the church bell at dusk as a guide to late travellers. Nearby Pokehouse Wood on the River Lugg was allegedly infested with faeries and wills of the wisp, and the man who paid for the bell ringing had himself apparently spent a whole night led astray amongst the trees. It is significant to note that the wood's name may be linked to Puck, another name for Robin Goodfellow, and a sprite who is renowned for his malicious pranks—such as leading travellers astray (see later).[502]

In the east of England, it was believed that these sprites would be drawn to any human carrying a lantern for their protection and would maliciously smash it and extinguish the light. Rather like the knockers in tin and coal mines, they also objected to whistling and generally took reprisals against those who offended, mocked, or insulted them. They demanded respect and were violent to any whom they felt withheld it or who underestimated their powers. In such situations, the only thing to do was to lie prostrate and hold your breath.[503]

The spunkie or Willy the Wisp of the Scottish Lowlands would appear as sparks at a person's feet and then race ahead of them like a candle, or else would seem like a light in a window near at hand—but then continually recede as the traveller advanced. The spunkie has been known to be seen at sea, too, often leading boats onto rocks: at Buckhaven in Fife, a will of the wisp seen along the coast would lure walkers into marshes and boats offshore onto the beach. In the Scottish Highlands, the idea of the will of the wisp doesn't seem to have been so clearly identified and the so-called "ghost lights" tended to be ascribed to other beings such as the *bodach*, the *cailleach*, and even the *dulan*, what we might translate as an "elemental."[504]

---

502. Ella Mary Leather, *Folklore of Herefordshire* (Hereford: Jakeman & Carver, 1912), 48.

503. Day, *Here Are Ghosts and Witches*, 156–157.

504. Stewart, *Popular Superstitions*, part 5; *County Folk-lore* 7, 34; James Cargill Guthrie, *The Vale of Strathmore; Its Scenes and Legends* (Edinburgh: William Patterson, 1875), 100.

The nuisance and terror caused by wills of the wisp were considerable. Humans disliked them—and so did livestock. They could make horses shy and overturn the carts they were pulling. Draught animals were particularly harassed if their owner doubted or mocked the existence of the will of the wisp. In such cases, further revenge might be exacted by following the victim home and then dancing around his home, shining in at the windows and adding a sleepless night to the miseries already inflicted. The Jack o' Lantern known in the Horning district of Norfolk would try to knock riders from their mounts. Such is the terror inspired by the "Shiners" of the fen region near Methwold that people will refuse to go out at night except in the direst necessity.[505]

Helpful Sprites

These sprites are not solely associated with tricks and inconvenience, nonetheless. In Cornwall, there are pisky-like beings called Jacky Lantern and Joan the Wad, who will tickle her victims but, if invoked correctly, can also guide them home with her straw torch during bad weather. Their assistance also seems to bring good luck, and charms and door knockers in the shape of Joan (a naked woman) used to be popular in the county.

The same was the case over the border in Devon: Dartmoor miners believed that digging wherever a will of the wisp was seen would lead you to a profitable mineral lode. In the same county it is possible to summon a will of the wisp to you by repeating the prescribed charm:

> "Jack o' the lantern, Joan the wad,
> Who tickled the maid and made her mad,
> Light me home the weather's bad."[506]

In another version of this rhyme, Jack and Joan are offered a "crub" for their help and protection. For this promise of a crumb, the will of the wisp will come to your aid and guide you home, although the experience might admittedly prove to be pretty alarming and leave you ill for weeks. In some other cases, the sprites would volunteer their guidance out of pure goodwill. One Devon man, from the days of his youth, was always guided home in the

---

505. Day, *Here Are Ghosts and Witches,* chapter 9; Kent, *The Land of the,* 111; Rye, *Eastern Counties Collectanea,* 3.

506. Jonathan Couch, *The History of Polperro, A Fishing Town […]* (Truro: W. Lake, 1871), 134.

dark by the Jack o' Lanterns, never being led astray nor scared. His only pre-caution was that he always thanked them for their trouble.[507]

In the Yorkshire Dales there's a story of a will-of-the-wisp-type sprite called Peg o' Lanthorn. She is, unusually, visible as a beautiful but very sad young woman, rather than merely being seen as the flame of the candle within her lantern, and she has been credited with at least one good deed. A man who had been seized by the Hellen-Pot Boggart and was being dragged towards the mouth of the bogie's pothole was released when Peg passed between them and the opening. The boggart sank into his lair, and the light from the lantern passed on. Perhaps, of course, her plan was to lure the trav-eller to a doom of her own designing, because she then led the man across the open moorland for some distance. Luckily—or perhaps purposely—they passed a lonely farmhouse where he was able to find shelter.[508]

Puck

Pucks—and for that matter, the piskies of the southwest—will from time to time behave like wills of the wisp, emphasising yet again the fact that it's hard to draw hard and fast boundaries between supernatural entities. The activ-ities of wills of the wisp are very evidently a form of "pixy-leading," and it's also clear from early texts that in this activity Puck, Robin Goodfellow, and the *ignis fatuus* (the fool's fire) are very much indistinguishable. In Worces-tershire, a person who follows a will of the wisp is said to be "pook-led," and *The Life of Robin Goodfellow* of 1628 invokes:[509]

> "All those that news desire
> How you saw a walking fire.
> Wenches, that doe smile and lispe,
> Use to call me Willy Wispe."[510]

507. William Crossing, *Tales of the Dartmoor Pixies: Glimpses of Elfin Haunts and Antics* (Newcastle upon Tyne: F. Graham, 1890), chapter 4; Rosalind Northcote, "Devonshire Folklore, Collected Among the People Near Exeter Within the Last Five or Six Years," *Folklore* 11 (1900): 212.

508. Baring-Gould, *Yorkshire Oddities*, 332.

509. See Spence, *The Fairy Tradition in Britain*, 17: "poake-ledden."

510. Halliwell, *Life of Robin Goodfellow*, "How Robin Goodfellow led a company of fellows out of their way," in *Illustrations of the Fairy Mythology*, chapter 6, 120.

The *Ballad of Robin Goodfellow* similarly has Robin tricking those out late on the roads:

> "Sometimes he'd counterfeit a voice and travellers call astray,
> Sometimes a walking fire he'd be, and lead them from their way.
> Some call him Robin Goodfellow, Hobgoblin or mad crisp;
> And some again doe term him oft, by name of Will the Wispe."[511]

Puck may mislead by calling out with false voices or by mysterious lights. He appears as an "idle" or "false" fire, which, as Milton described, would be seen "Hovering and blazing with delusive Light." Victims will stray from the road; lose their bearings; blunder through hedges, clumps of bushes, and bogs; and end up in ponds and water-furrows, stuck in mire and clay, at which point, Puck will desert them with derisive laughter.[512]

In Wales, *pwca* is a tiny figure with a lantern who will lead walkers toward cliff edges at night. As soon as victims realise their danger, Pwca blows out his candle and disappears with a laugh.[513]

Whether Puck *is* the will of the wisp or merely impersonates it, is very hard to determine. Given his predilection for shape-shifting, it may be best to conclude that he has temporarily taken on this sprite's guise for his amusement.

Getting Rid of Wills of the Wisp

If you are led astray by a will of the wisp, you will need to escape from its influence to return to safety and to find the right path again. If the Hobby Lanterns of Dunwich in Suffolk have misled you into the marshes behind the beach, you are said to be "will-led," and the remedy (exactly as with

---

511. *Ballad of Robin Goodfellow*, chapter 7, in Halliwell, *Illustrations of the Fairy Mythology*, chapter 7, 155.

512. *The Pranks of Puck,* verse 3 in Halliwell, *Illustrations of the Fairy Mythology,* chapter 8, 165; Fletcher, *The Faithful Shepherdess,* 1608, Act 1, 1, Act 3, 1, https://emed.folger.edu /sites/default/files/folger_encodings/pdf/EMED-FS-reg-3.pdf; Milton, *Paradise Lost*, Book 9, lines 634–9; Drayton, *Nymphidia*, lines 291–7, in Halliwell, *Illustrations of the Fairy Mythology*, chapter 13, 195.

513. Sikes, *British Goblins*, 20–24.

pixy-leading) is to turn a garment. Taking off a sock and turning it inside out, or reversing a jacket or hat, is sure to undo the will of the wisp's spell.[514]

The Jack o' Lantern at Alderfen in Norfolk was considered to be the ghost of a drowned criminal and was, accordingly, the subject of an attempted laying by three gentlemen. The spirit was "read down" by reciting biblical verses until it had shrunk sufficiently to be caught in a bottle and bound.[515]

In many parts of Britain, simple environmental change has reduced the nuisance caused by wills of the wisp by reducing or eliminating the conditions they preferred. Readers may recall land reclamation has had very much the same effect upon the water bull of the Isle of Man (see chapter 4 earlier).

Conclusions

Wills of the wisp are a fascinating and awe-inspiring phenomenon. Nor should the will of the wisp be thought of as entirely a being of the past. Despite much agricultural improvement and drainage, there is still plenty of marshy moorland in Britain, and sightings can still occur in these places. Ella Leather recorded that there were many seen on the Black Mountains in the early 1900s and, during the mid-1960s, people confessed that they were afraid to venture onto the moors near Warleggan in Cornwall because of the dancing red, white, and blue lights that would lead them into peril. As recently as January 2010, at Shingle Street on the north Norfolk coast, a couple reported seeing a greenish glowing ball dancing over the marshland there.[516]

Although their appearance is generally mischievous and there are risks involved, approached correctly, with suitable respect, the wills of the wisp may be prepared to grant you a safe journey and even good fortune.

---

514. Grace Haddow and Ruth Anderson, "Scraps of English Folklore," IX (Suffolk), *Folklore* 35 (1924): 355.

515. Westwood and Simpson, *Lore of the Land*, 488.

516. Tony Deane and Tony Shaw, *The Folklore of Cornwall* (Stroud: The History Press, 2009), 90; see, too, Charlotte Dacre's poem, "Will of Wisp."

FINAL THOUGHTS: PERILOUS PLACES AND THREATENING THINGS

I started this book by asking whether or not these supernatural beasts that I have described ought properly to be labelled "faery." As I have explained, there are very many common themes and, indeed, stories, that apply to both the conventional faeries and to the faery beasts. There is astonishing diversity too: the variety of types of faery beast is—aptly—mind-boggling (a word that is, of course, derived from "bogle"). Nevertheless, despite the many shapes, sizes, and species they can assume, there is clearly a single nature that unifies them as a category and that unites them with the faeries. Their aversion to iron, to rowan, or to holy scripture, their knowledge of the future, and their complex relationship with death and the dead are just a few examples of that common identity.

Faery is a dangerous place: it can be risky for humans to spend time with faeries or in faeryland. Worse still, that unearthly peril can spill over into our own world. There are plenty of faery beasts whose sole interest is to inhabit the deserted or neglected parts of our environment, there to lie in wait for the unwise and the unwary. Of course, the faery folk have likewise intruded upon and occupied our world. In what respect are the beasts different, therefore?

I think the key distinguishing feature of the beasts is this: The faeries live in communities and have their own ways of life; they will interact with humankind, but they can, quite adequately, live entirely separate from us. In contrast, faery beasts are (by and large) solitary; their *only* interactions are with humans, and these are predominantly hostile. Only very rarely do faery beasts intervene in our lives to warn or to help us. Our deepest and most satisfying interactions have always been with the merfolk, and even these are far more limited and infrequent than contacts with the faery folk. Nevertheless, all these faery beasts can appear with a purpose. Merfolk and bogies like the buggane will warn of storms approaching; meremaids, the *bean-nighe*, fae horses and rabbits, and the Wild Hunt can all warn of impending disaster. As well as the *bean-nighe* and banshee, whose special function this is, the appearance of very many of the bogies, daemon dogs (especially those of the Wild Hunt), and fae animals foretells of imminent death. It benefits us to pay attention to the beasts' intrusions into our world. One way or another, being alert can protect us, whether that is because we escape harm by one of the beasts or because it is acting as a portent.

Mostly, though, the faery beasts' purpose is to menace and to threaten us. For this stark reason, they should never be underestimated or doubted. Even those creatures that are prepared to live and work in proximity to humans— the hobs and *gruagachs*—should never be taken for granted: they are quick to take offence and, when this happens, they can become vengeful boggarts who make our lives a misery.

Given the potential danger of most of these faery beasts, it is important to know how to deal with them. Throughout the book I have highlighted the simple, practical measures that may be taken to defend yourself. If though, for some reason, you feel that a particular beast won't leave you alone and is making life a misery, there are still tried and tested remedies available. As I have highlighted, all of these beasts can be laid (or exorcised or banished): this has been proven to work for hobs, bogies (including boggarts and barguests), black dogs, fae animals like the trash, and wills of the wisp.

For all their menace, though, the faery beasts are both rich and strange. The study of their varied forms and habits is full of fascination, because it has much to tell us about ourselves. The beasts ensnare us by playing upon our worst traits—upon our greed, laziness, lust, impatience, and our overwhelming curiosity. They are able to threaten us because we allow them to do so: we are in a rush to get somewhere and travel late; we are in a rush to finish chores and will take any steps to save ourselves time and trouble; we want to get rich quickly. We allow the faery beasts into our world through our own ill-judged actions—and they exact the charge.

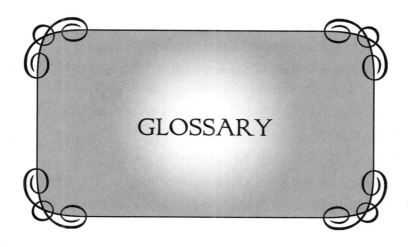

GLOSSARY

Ainsel: this is a label for a common theme in faery stories. A human encounters a faery being and is asked his or her name. Cannily, the reply is "my ainsel" (my own self). Soon after, whether accidentally or deliberately, the faery being is injured. It runs off to complain to a parent or friends but when asked "who hurt you?" has to answer "ainsel"—myself. As there's no one else to blame, there's no one to be avenged against, and the human escapes punishment.

Asrai: a water sprite of the English Midlands.

Banshee or bean-sidhe: an Irish and Scottish female faery particularly tied to certain families.

Baobhan sith: a faery hag on the Highlands.

Barguest: a boggart in dog form.

Bean-nighe: a faery woman seen washing clothes in a stream.

Biasd na srogaig: a type of unicorn from the Scottish Highlands.

Bocan: a Highland bogie or poltergeist.

Boggart: a brownie gone bad who only plays pranks and does harm.

Bogie: (also boggle, bogle, or bug) a mischievous or dangerous spirit.

Boobrie: a Scottish water horse, bull, or bird.

Brag: a calflike boggart.

Brollachan: a shape-shifting and dangerous bogle.

Brownie: a domestic faery of the east and north of England and Lowland Scotland. It lives on farms and in houses and undertakes chores.

Bugbear: a boggart or bogle now mainly used to scare children.

Buggane: a Manx boggart.

Bwca/bucca: a Welsh/Cornish faery, related to "Puck."

Cabbyl ushtey: the Manx name for the "water horse."

Caillagh: a Manx hag.

Cailleach: the Gaelic for a supernatural hag.

Caointeach: (pronounced koniuch) a Highland banshee; her name means "keener."

Ceffyl y dwr: the Welsh water horse.

Crodh mara: faery cattle that come from the sea.

Crodh sith: faery cattle.

Cwn Annwn: Welsh "hell hounds."

Cwn Wybir: Welsh "sky hounds."

Cyhyraeth: the Welsh equivalent of the Scottish keener.

Dandy Dogs: a pack of faery hunting hounds.

Doonie: a Scottish wild faery who appears as a horse or as an old woman.

Dwarf: not a British being; a German and Scandinavian goblin.

Each uisge: Gaelic, meaning "water horse," a creature living in pools and lochs.

Elf: the Old English/Anglo-Saxon name for the being we now tend to call a faery.

Elf-bolt/elf-shot: flint arrows fired by the elves.

Fae: meaning enchanted, magical, supernatural, or linked to faerykind. Used in this sense in this book. Can also mean "a faery."

Faery: capitalised, the word is used in the book to mean faeryland or the otherworld; otherwise it is a noun denoting one of the inhabitants of faeryland. As an adjective, as in "faery beasts," the word describes an enchanted or supernatural state.

Fahm: a deadly Highland bogle.

Finfolk: on Orkney, the merfolk, who live in *"Finfolkaheem."*

Fenoderee/phynoderee: the Manx equivalent of the brownie.

Fuath: a dangerous Highland bogie.

Gabble Ratchets: a supernatural pack of hounds.

Gallytrot: a bogle that appears in the shape of a horse.

Glaistig: a hairy female faery of the Scottish Highlands.

Glashtyn: a Manx faery related to the Scottish *glaistig.*

Gnome: an invented word, meaning a small, dwarfish being.

Goblin: a type of bad faery.

Gruagach: a hairy Scottish Highland being, rather like a brownie.

Gwartheg y llyn: Welsh "lake cattle."

Gwrach y rhybin: the Welsh banshee.

Gwragedd annwn: Welsh faery women who live under lakes—the singular is *gwrag.*

Gyre-carlin: the faery queen in Fife who has links to spinning.

Gywllgi: a Welsh supernatural hound.

Habetrot: a faery woman especially linked to spinning thread.

Hobgoblin: hobs and lobs are a general class of beings in England, which include the pucks and the brownies.

Hyter sprite: a type of tiny faery from East Anglia.

Kelpie: a water monster of rivers in the Scottish Highlands.

Kow: a boggart that takes horse form.

Loireag: pronounced "loryack;" she is a water sprite of the Scottish Highlands associated with spinning.

Maighdean mara: Gaelic, meaning simply "mermaid."

Moddey dhoo: on the Isle of Man, a supernatural black dog.

Njugl: a Shetland water horse/monster.

Nuckelavee: a water monster of Orkney.

Padfoot: a boggart that takes dog form.

Puck: an Old English name for a hobgoblin.

Red cap: a malevolent goblin of the Scottish Borders.

Roane: seal folk of the Hebrides.

Sea-trow: on Orkney and Shetland, trows (faeries) who were banished from land to live in the sea.

Selkie: Scottish seal folk.

Shellycoat: a Scottish water horse with shells instead of fur.

Shock or shug: a black faery dog.

Shoopiltee: a Shetland water horse.

Sidh/sith: pronounced "shee" and respectively the Irish and Scottish Gaelic words for "faery."

Sluagh: pronounced "slooa" and meaning the faery host that rides through the skies at night.

Tacharan: a water horse of the Scottish Highlands; very tiny.

Tangie: a sea horse of Orkney and Shetland.

Tarbh uisge: Gaelic, meaning "water bull," an animal found in freshwater.

Tarroo ushtey: the Manx equivalent of the Scottish water bull.

Tatterfoal: a bogle in the shape of a young foal seen in the east of England.

Urisk or uruisg: a brownie-like being of the Scottish Highlands.

Will of the wisp: a sprite like a flame or light that misleads nighttime travellers.

Yr hen wrach: "the old hag" in Welsh.

BIBLIOGRAPHY

"A remarkable case of fantasy," *The Times*, November 22, 1856, 12.

Adams, Morley. *In the Footsteps of Borrow and Fitzgerald*. London: Jarrold & Sons, 1915.

Addy, Sidney Oldall. *Household Tales with Other Traditional Remains Collected in the Counties of York, Lincoln, Derby, and Nottingham*. London: Nutt, 1895.

Aitken, Hannah. *A Forgotten Heritage: Original Folk Tales of Lowland Scotland*. Edinburgh: Scottish Academic Press, 1973.

Allies, Jabez. *On the Ancient British, Roman and Saxon Antiquities and Folklore of Worcestershire*. Worcester: J. Grainger, 1840.

Anderson, Verily. *The Northrepps Grandchildren*. London: Hodder & Stoughton, 1968.

Anon. *Folklore and Legends: Scotland*. W. W. Gibbings, 1889.

Anon. "Faery Tales." *Celtic Review* 5 (1908): 155–170;

Anon. *The Two Lancashire Lovers*, 1640.

Atkinson, John C. *A Glossary of the Cleveland Dialect: Explanatory, Derivative, and Critical*. London: John Russell Smith, 1868.

Atkinson, John C. *Forty Years in a Moorland Parish: Reminiscences and Researches in Danby in Cleveland*. London: MacMillan & Sons, 1891.

"Bardwell, Suffolk." Shuckland. Accessed May 13, 2020. www.hiddenea.com /shuckland/bardwell.htm.

Bailey, Jennie, and David England. *Lancashire Folk Tales*. Stroud: The History Press, 2014.

Baring-Gould, Sabine. *Yorkshire Oddities, Incidents, and Strange Events*. London: Methuen and Co., 1900.

Barrett, Walter Henry. *Tales from the Fens*. Edited by Enid Porter. London, Routledge & Kegan Paul, 1963.

Barton, Ingrid. *North Yorkshire Folk Tales*. Stroud: The History Press, 2014.

"Baum Rabbit." Lancashire—Paranormal Database Records. Paranormal Database. Accessed May 26, 2020. https://paranormaldatabase.com /lancashire/lancdata.php?pageNum_paradata=19&totalRows_paradata =554.

"Bawburgh, Norfolk." Shuckland. Accessed May 26, 2020. https://www .hiddenea.com/shuckland/bawburgh.htm.

Baxter, Richard. *The Certainty of the Worlds of Spirits Fully Evinced*. London: T. Parkhurst & J. Salisbury, 1691.

Billingsley, John. *West Yorkshire Folk Tales*. Stroud: The History Press, 2010.

"Black Dogs In Sussex." Ghostly Black Dogs. Sussex Archaeology & Folklore. Accessed May 13, 2020. www.sussexarch.org.uk/saaf/blackdog.html.

"Black Rock—Mermaid." Paranormal Database. Accessed May 7, 2020. www .paranormaldatabase.com/m/detail.php?address=1469.

"Black Shuck, Hellhounds, and Other Black Dog Reports." Paranormal Database. Accessed May 25, 2020. www.paranormaldatabase.com/reports /shuckdata.php/.

Blakeborough, Richard. *Wit, Character, Folklore & Customs of the North Riding of Yorkshire: With a Glossary of over 4,000 Words and Idioms Now in Use*. London: Henry Frowde, 1898.

Blind, Karl. "New Finds in Shetlandic & Welsh Folk-lore." *Gentleman's Magazine*, no. 252 (1882), 353–371, 476–480.

"Blythburgh, Suffolk." Shuckland. Accessed May 28, 2020. www.hiddenea
.com/shuckland/blythburgh.htm.

"Bogie Goose." Yorkshire—Paranormal Database Records. Paranormal
Database. Accessed May 26, 2020. https://www.paranormaldatabase.com
/yorkshire/Pages/yorkdata.php?pageNum_paradata=1&totalRows
_paradata=608.

Bottrell, William. *Traditions and Hearthside Stories of West Cornwall.* Vol. 1.
Penzance: Beare and Son, 1870.

Bowker, James. *Goblin Tales of Lancashire.* London: W. Swan Sonnenschein
& Co., 1878.

"Boy Playing Flute." Hampshire—Paranormal Database Records. Paranormal Database. Accessed May 26, 2020. https://www.paranormaldatabase
.com/hampshire/hampdata.php?pageNum_paradata=4&totalRows
_paradata=179.

Brand, John. *A New Description of Orkney, Zetland, Pightland-Firth and
Caithness, Wherein, [...].* Edinburgh: W. Brown, 1883.

Brand, John. *Observations on Popular Antiquities: Chiefly Illustrating the
Origin of Our Vulgar Customs, Ceremonies, and Superstitions.* Vol. 3.
London: G. Bell, 1900.

Briggs, Katharine. *A Dictionary of Fairies: Hobgonblins, Brownies, Bogies,
and Other Supernatural Creatures.* London: Penguin Books, 1977.

Briggs, Katharine. *British Folk-Tales and Legends: A Sampler.* London:
Granada, 1977.

Briggs, Katharine. *The Fairies in Tradition and Literature.* London: Routledge
& K. Paul, 1967.

Britten, James. "Sheffield Folklore." *Notes & Queries.* Series 4, vol. 7, no. 171
(1871).

Brockie, William. *Legends & Superstitions of the County of Durham.* Sunderland: B. Williams, 1886.

Brown, Theo. "The Black Dog," *Folklore* 69 (1958): 175–179.

Browne, James. *A History of the Highlands and of the Highland Clans*. Vol. 1. Glasgow: A. Fullerton & Co., 1838.

Bonning, Tony. *Dumfries & Galloway Folk Tales*. Stroud: The History Press, 2016.

Broome, Dora. *Fairy Tales from the Isle of Man*. Harmondsworth: Penguin, 1951.

Buchan, Peter. *Annals of Peterhead, From Its Foundation to the Present Time [...]*. Peterhead: Buchan, 1819.

Buchanan, Robert. *Ballads of Life, Love, and Humour*. London: Chatto & Windus, 1862.

Buchanan, Robert. *The Poetical Works of Robert Buchanan*. Vol. 1. Boston: James R. Osgood & Co., 1874.

"Buckland Shag." Surrey—Paranormal Database Records. Paranormal Database. https://www.paranormaldatabase.com/surrey/surrdata.php.

"Burgh, Suffolk." Shuckland. Accessed May 13, 2020. www.hiddenea.com/shuckland/burgh.htm.

Burne, Charlotte Sophia. *Shropshire Folk-lore, A Sheaf of Gleanings*. London: Trübner & Co., part 1, 1883 and part 3, 1886.

Burne, Charlotte Sophia. "Staffordshire Folk and Their Lore," *Folklore* 7 (1896): 366–386.

Burton, Robert. *The Anatomy of Melancholy*. London: Henry Cripps, 1621.

"Buxton-with-Lamas, Norfolk." Shuckland. Accessed May 13, 2020. www.hiddenea.com/shuckland/buxtonwithlamas.htm.

"B869, Between Stoer and Lochinver—Human-Faced Dog." Paranormal Database. Accessed May 25, 2020. https://www.paranormaldatabase.com/m/detail.php?address=1330.

C. T. C. S. "Popular Superstitions of Clydesdale," *Edinburgh Magazine* 3 (1818): 153–158.

"Cambridge, Cambridgeshire." Shuckland. Accessed May 26, 2020. https://www.hiddenea.com/shuckland/cambridge.htm.

Campbell, Archibald. *Records of Argyll: Legends, Traditions, and Recollections of Argyllshire Highlanders, Collected Chiefly from the Gaelic*. Edinburgh: William Blackwood and Sons, 1885.

Campbell, John Francis. *Popular Tales of the West Highlands Orally Collected with a Translation by the Late J. F. Campbell*. Vol. 4. Paisley: Alexander Gardner, 1893.

Campbell, John. *Popular Tales of the West Highlands Orally Collected with a Translation by J. F. Campbell*. Vol. 1. Edinburgh: Edmonston & Douglas, 1860.

Campbell, John. *Popular Tales of the West Highlands Orally Collected with a Translation by the Late J. F. Campbell*. Vol. 2. Paisley and London: Alexander Gardener, 1890.

Campbell, John. *More West Highland Tales*. Translated by John Mackay. Vol. 1. Edinburgh: Oliver & Boyd, 1940.

Campbell, John Gregorson. *Witchcraft and Second Sight in the Highlands and Islands of Scotland: Tales and Traditions Orally Collected by the Late John Gregorson Campbell*. Glasgow: James MacLehose & Sons, 1902.

Campbell, John Gregorson. *Superstitions of the Highlands & Islands of Scotland: Collected Entirely from Oral Sources by John Gregorson Campbell*. Glasgow: James MacLehose & Sons, 1900.

Campbell John L., and Trevor H. Hall. *Strange Things: The Story of Fr. Allen, Ada Goodrich-Freer and the Society for Psychical Research's Enquiry into Highland Second Sight*. Edinburgh: Birlinn Ltd., 2006.

Cargill Guthrie, James. *The Vale of Strathmore; Its Scenes and Legends*. Edinburgh: William Patterson, 1875.

Carmichael, Alexander. *Carmina Gadelica: Hymns and Incantations […]*. Vol 2. Edinburgh: Oliver and Boyd, 1900.

Celtic Magazine 12 (1887).

Celtic Monthly 5 (1892).

Chambers, Robert. *Book of Days*. Vol. 1. Edinburgh: W. & R. Chambers, 1869.

Chambers, Robert. *Popular Rhymes of Scotland.* Edinburgh: W. and R. Chambers, 1847.

"Chelmsford area, Essex." Shuckland. Accessed May 13, 2020. www .hiddenea.com/shuckland/chelmsford.htm.

Child, Francis James, ed. "42: Clerk Colvill." In *The English and Scottish Popular Ballads.* Vol. 1, 371–389. New York: Houghton, Mifflin & Co., 1886.

Choice Notes & Queries—Folklore. London, 1859.

Churchyard, T. *A Handful of Gladsome Verses,* 1592.

"Clopton (near Woodbridge), Suffolk." Shuckland. Accessed May 13, 2020. www.hiddenea.com/shuckland/cloptonnearwoodbridge.htm.

"Coastline-Dog with Glowing Eyes." Paranormal Database. Accessed May 25, 2020. https://www.paranormaldatabase.com/m/detail.php ?address=2416.

"Collecteanea," *Folklore* 27 (1916).

Cope, Elijah. "Some Local Fairies." In *Memorials of Old Staffordshire.* Edited by W. Beresford, 88–93. London: George, Allen & Unwin, 1909.

Couch, Jonathan, *The History of Polperro, A Fishing Town [...].* Truro: W. Lake, 1871.

County Folk-lore. London: The Folklore Society, 1901–1965.

Vol. 1: "Printed Extracts 1—Gloucestershire." 1895. Edited by E. S. Hartland.

Vol. 1: "Printed Extracts 2—Suffolk." 1893. Edited by E. C. Gurdon.

Vol. 1: "Printed Extracts 3—Leicestershire & Rutland." 1895. Edited by C. J. Billson.

Vol. 2: (Printed Extracts 4). "Examples of Printed Folklore Concerning the North Riding of Yorkshire and the Ainsty." Edited by E. Gutch, 1901.

Vol. 3: (Printed Extracts 5). "Examples of Printed Folklore Concerning Orkney and the Shetland Isles." Collected by G. F. Black and edited by N. W. Thomas, 1903.

Vol. 4: (Printed Extracts 6). "Examples of Printed Folklore Concerning Northumberland." Collected by M. Balfour and edited by N. W. Thomas, 1904.

Vol. 5: (Printed Extracts 7). "Examples of Printed Folklore Concerning Lincolnshire." Collected by E. Gutch and M. Peacock, 1908.

Vol. 6: (Printed Extracts 8). "Examples of Printed Folklore Concerning the East Riding of Yorkshire." Edited by E. Gutch, 1912.

Vol. 7: (Printed Extracts 9, 10 & 11). "Examples of Printed Folklore Concerning Fife, with Some Notes on Clackmannan and Kinross-Shires." Edited by J. E. Simpkins, 1914. .

Vol. 8: Somerset—see Tongue.

Croker, Thomas Crofton. *Fairy Legends and Traditions of the South of Ireland*. Part 3. London: John Murray, 1828.

Cromek, Robert Hartley, and Allen Cunningham. *Remains of Nithsdale and Galloway Song: With Historical and Traditional Notices Relative to the Manners and Customs of the Peasantry*. London: T. Cadell and W. Davies, 1810.

Crossing, William. *Tales of the Dartmoor Pixies: Glimpses of Elfin Haunts and Antics*. Newcastle upon Tyne: F. Graham, 1890.

Crowe, Catherine. "Chapter 14: Spectral Lights, and Apparitions attached to Certain Families." In *The Night Side of Nature*, 319–344. New York: Redfield, Clinton Hall, 1850.

Dalyell, John. *The Darker Superstitions of Scotland Illustrated from History and Practice*. Edinburgh: Waugh & Innes, 1834.

D'Arras, Jean. *Melusine*. Vol. 68. Edited by A. K. Donald. EETS edition, 1895.

Dathen, Jon. *Somerset Faeries and Pixies: Exploring Their Hidden World*. Milverton: Capall Bann, 2010.

Davies, Jonathan. *Folk-lore of West and Mid-Wales*. Aberystwyth: printed at the "Welsh Gazette" offices, 1911.

Day, J. Wentworth. *Here Are Ghosts and Witches*. London: B. T. Batsford, 1954.

De Lisle, P. "Tales & Traditions of Old Yarmouth," *Yarmouth Independent*, January 7, 1893.

Deane, Tony, and Tony Shaw. *The Folklore of Cornwall*. Stroud: The History Press, 2009.

Dempster, Miss. "Folk-lore of Sutherland-shire." *Folklore Journal* 6 (1888), 149–189.

Denham, Michael Aislabie. *The Denham Tracts.* Vol. 2. Edited by Dr. James Hardy. London: David Nutt, 1895.

"Denham Tracts." *Folklore Society* 35, London, 1895.

Dickins, Bruce, "Yorkshire Hobs," *Transactions of the Yorkshire Dialect Society* 7, part 13 (1942): 18–22.

Dieckhoff, Cyril H. "Mythological Beings in Gaelic Folklore," *Transactions of the Gaelic Society of Inverness* 29 (1918): 235–258.

Dixon, John H. *Gairloch in North-West Ross-shire: It's Records, Traditions, Inhabitants, with a Guide to Gairloch and Loch Maree, and a Map and Illustrations.* Edinburgh: Co-operative Printing Co., 1886.

"Dog That Isn't There." Dorset—Paranormal Database Records. Paranormal Database. Accessed May 15, 2020. https://www.paranormaldatabase.com /dorset/dorsdata.php?pageNum_paradata=10&totalRows_paradata=358.

"Donkey Faced Dog." Suffolk—Paranormal Database Records. Paranormal Database. Accessed May 25, 2020. https://www.paranormaldatabase .com/suffolk/sufpages/suffdata.php?pageNum_paradata=10&totalRows _paradata=336.

Douglas, George. *Scottish Fairy and Folk Tales: Selected and Edited with an Introduction by Sir George Douglas.* London: W. Scott, 1901.

Douglas, Mona. *"Restoring to Use Our Almost-Forgotten Dances": Writings on the Collection and Revival of Manx Folk Dance and Song.* Isle of Man: Chiollagh Books, 2004.

Dragstra, Henk. "'Bull-beggar': An Early Modern Scare-Word." In *Airy Nothings: Imagining the Otherworld of Faerie from the Middle Ages to the Age of Reason [...].* Edited by Karin E. Olsen and Jan R. Veenstra, 171–194. Leiden: Brill, 2013.

Drake, Joseph Rodman. "To a Friend." In *The Culprit Fay and Other Poems.* New York: George Dearborn. 1836.

Drayton. *Nymphidia.* 1627.

Duncan, Leland L. "The following extract from a letter," *Folklore* 8 (1897): 69.

"East Anglian Miscellany Upon Matters of History, Genealogy etc." Reprinted from the *East Anglian Daily Times*. Vol. 1. (1901).

"East Flegg Area, Norfolk." Shuckland. Accessed May 13, 2020. www .hiddenea.com/shuckland/eastflegg.htm.

Eberhart, George. *Mysterious Creatures: A Guide to Cryptozoology*. Santa Barbara, CA: ABC-CLIO, 2002.

Edmonston, Biot, and Jessie M. E. Saxby. *The Home of a Naturalist*. London: J. Nisbet, 1888.

Edmonston, Eliza. *Sketches and Tales of the Shetland Islands*. Edinburgh: Sutherland & Knox, 1856.

EST. "Shuck the Dog Fiend." *Notes & Queries* 2, no. 29 (1850).

Evans-Wentz, Walter Y. *The Fairy-Faith in Celtic Countries*. Oxford: Oxford University Press, 1911.

Fairfax, Edward. Translation of Torquato Tasso. *Godfrey of Bulloigne; or, The Recoverie of Jerusalem*, 1600, IX, xv, 162.

"Fairies in the Highlands," *Celtic Magazine* 4 (1879): 13.

"Fairy Tunnels." Fairies and Little People. Paranormal Database. Accessed May 26, 2020. https://www.paranormaldatabase.com/reports/fairydata .php?pageNum_paradata=6&totalRows_paradata=214.

"Finfolkaheem—The Ancestral Home." The Sorcerous Finfolk. OrkneyJar. Accessed May 8, 2020. www.orkneyjar.com/folklore/finfolk/heem.htm.

Fionn. "A Loohaber Hag: The Glaistig of Llanachan." *Celtic Monthly* 9 (1901): 189.

Fletcher. *The Faithful Shepherdess*.

Fletcher, John. *The Night Walker, Or, The Little Thief*. In *Beaumont and Fletcher*. Edited by. A. R. Waller (Cambridge: University Press, 1909), act 3.

Fletcher, John, and Francis Beaumont. *The Knight of the Burning Pestle*. 1607.

Folklore 27 (1916).

Folklore 63 (1952).

Forby, Robert. *The Vocabulary of East Anglia; an Attempt to Record [...]*. Vol. 2. London: J. B. Nichols and Son, 1830.

Fraser, Alexander. "Northern Folklore: Wells & Springs." *Celtic Magazine* 3 (1878): 18–31.

Garmonsway, G. *The Anglo-Saxon Chronicle* (February 1127). London: Dent & Sons, 1953.

Gascoigne. *The Buggbears,* in Richard Warwick Bond, ed., *Early Plays from the Italian: Edited, With Essay, Introductions and Notes by R. Warwick Bond,* 84–157. Oxford: Clarendon Press, 1911.

"Geldeston Area, Norfolk." Shuckland. Accessed May 25, 2020. https://www.hiddenea.com/shuckland/geldeston.htm.

Gervase of Tilbury. *Otia Imperialia: Recreation for an Emperor.* Edited and translated by S. E. Banks and J. W. Binns. Oxford Medieval Texts: Clarendon Press, 2002.

Gill, Walter. *A Manx Scrapbook.* London: Arrowsmith, 1929.

Gill, Walter. *A Second Manx Scrapbook.* London: Arrowsmith, 1932.

Gill, Walter. *A Third Manx Scrapbook.* London: Arrowsmith, 1963.

"Glashtin." Isle of Man—Paranormal Database Records. Paranormal Database. Accessed May 22, 2020. www.paranormaldatabase.com/isleofman/mandata.php.

Glyde, John Jr., comp. and ed. *The Norfolk Garland: A Collection of the Superstitious Beliefs and Practices [...].* London: Jarrold & Sons, 1872.

Goodrich-Freer, A. "The Powers of Evil in the Outer Hebrides," *Folklore* 10 (1899): 257–282.

Gordon Cumming, Constance F. *In the Hebrides.* London: Chatto and Windus, Piccadilly, 1883.

"Gorleston, Norfolk." Shuckland. Accessed May 13, 2020. www.hiddenea.com/shuckland/gorleston.htm.

Grainge, William. *The Vale of Mowbray: A Historical and Topographical Account of Thirsk and Its Neighbourhood.* London: Simpkin, Marshall & Co., 1859.

Grant, Katharine Whyte. *Myth, Tradition and Story from Western Argyll.* Oban: Oban Times Press, 1925.

Grant Stewart, William. *The Popular Superstitions and Festive Amusements of the Highlanders of Scotland.* London: Aylott & Jones, 1823.

"Great Yarmouth, Norfolk." Shuckland. Accessed May 18, 2020. www .hiddenea.com/shuckland/greatyarmouth.htm.

Greg, W. W., ed. *Wily Beguiled.* 1606.

Gregor, Walter. "A Sketch of Scottish Diablerie in General," *Fraser's Magazine,* vol. 25 (1842): 317–331.

Gregor, Walter. "Guardian Spirits of Wells and Lochs." *Folklore* 3 (1892): 67–73.

Gregor, Walter. "Kelpie Stories from the North of Scotland," *Folk-Lore Journal* 1 (1883): 292–294.

Gregor, Walter. *Notes on the Folk-lore of the North-East of Scotland.* London: Folk-lore Society, 1881.

Gregor, Walter. "Stories of faeries from Scotland" *Folk-Lore Journal* 1 (1883): 25–27, 55–58.

Grice, Frederick. *Folk Tales of the North Country: Drawn from Northumberland and Durham.* London: Nelson & Sons, 1944.

"Growing Hound." Devon—Paranormal Database Records. Paranormal Database. Accessed May 26, 2020. https://www.paranormaldatabase.com /devon/devodata.php?pageNum_paradata=15&totalRows _paradata=398.

"Gunton Park and House (partly destroyed by fire in 1882)—White Lady." Paranormal Database. Accessed May 11, 2020. www.paranormaldatabase .com/m/detail.php?address=7714.

Gurdon, Camilla. "Folk-lore from South-East Suffolk," *Folklore* 3 (1892): 558–560.

Gurdon, Eveline Camilla. *County Folk-lore, 37. Printed Extracts No. 2, Suffolk: Collected and Edited by the Lady Eveline Camilla Gurdon with Introduction by Edward Clodd.* London: D. Nutt, 1893.

"Gurt Dog," Black Shuck, Hellhounds, and Other Black Dog Reports. Paranormal Database. Accssed May 26, 2020. https://paranormaldatabase .com/reports/shuckdata.php?pageNum_paradata=13&totalRows _paradata=343.

Haddow, Grace, and Ruth Anderson. "Scraps of English Folklore, IX (Suffolk)," *Folklore* 35 (1924): 346–360.

Haldane Burgess, James J. "Some Shetland Folk-lore," *Scottish Review* 25 (January and April 1895): 91–103.

Halliwell-Phillipps, James Orchard. *Illustrations of the Fairy Mythology of A Midsummer Night's Dream.* London: Shakespeare Society, 1845.

Halliwell-Phillipps, James Orchard. *A Dictionary of Archaic & Provincial Words. […].* London: John Russell Smith, 1865.

Hardwick, Charles. *Traditions, Superstitions, and Folklore (Chiefly Lancashire and the North of England) […].* Manchester: Ireland & Co., 1872.

"Hare." Northumberland—Paranormal Database Records. Paranormal Database. Accessed May 26, 2020. https://www.paranormaldatabase.com /northumberland/nhumdata.php?pageNum_paradata=3&totalRows _paradata=86.

Harland, John, and T. T. Wilkinson, comps. *Lancashire Legends, Traditions, Pageants, Sports &c, […].* London: Routledge, 1873.

Harland, John, and T. T. Wilkinson, comps. *Lancashire Folk-lore.* London: Warne & Co., 1867.

Harris, J. Henry. *Cornish Saints & Sinners.* London: Clowes & Sons, 1907.

Harries, John. *The Ghost Hunter's Road Book.* London, Charles Letts, 1974.

Harrison, William. *Mona Miscellany: A Selection of Proverbs, Sayings, Ballads, Customs, Superstitions, and Legends, Peculiar to the Isle of Man.* Douglas, Isle of Man: The Manx Society, 1869.

Hartland, Edwin Sidney. *English Fairy and Folk Tales.* London: Walter Scott Publishing, 1890.

"Hatfield Peverel, Essex." Shuckland. Accessed May 13, 2020. www.hiddenea .com/shuckland/hatfieldpeverel.htm.

Haughton, William. *Grim the Collier of Croydon.* 1605. In J. Farmer. *Tudor Facsimile Texts.* 1912, 4, 1.

"Headless Hound." Black Shuck, Hellhounds, and Other Black Dog Reports." Paranormal Database. https://www.paranormaldatabase.com/reports /shuckdata.php?pageNum_paradata=1&totalRows_paradata=348.

Henderson, George. *Survivals in Belief Amongst the Celts.* London: Macmillan, 1861.

Henderson, George. *The Popular Rhymes, Sayings, and Proverbs of the County of Berwick; With Illustrative Notes.* Newcastle-on-Tyne: W. S. Crow, 1856.

Henderson, Mark. "The Bradwell Dog." In *Folktales of the Peak District.* Stroud: Amberley Publishing, 2013.

Henderson, William. *Notes on the Folk-lore of the Northern Counties of England and the Borders.* London: Folklore Society, 1879.

Herbert, Agnes. *The Isle of Man.* London: John Lane, 1909.

"Hevengham, Suffolk." Shuckland. Accessed May 26, 2020. https://www.hiddenea.com/shuckland/heveningham.htm.

Hewlett, Maurice. "The Secret Commonwealth." In *The Lore of Proserpine.* New York: Charles Scribner, 1913.

Hibbert, Samuel. *A Description of the Shetland Isles, Comprising an Account of Their Scenery, Antiquities, and Superstitions.* Lerwick: T. & J. Manson, 1891.

Hogg, James. "The Mermaid's Song." In *Songs by the Ettrick Shepherd: Now First Collected.* Edinburgh: William Blackwood, 1831.

Hogg, James. "Night The Second." In *The Queen's Wake: A Legendary Poem.* Edinburgh: Andrew Balfour, 1815.

Hogg, James. "The Wool-Gatherer." In *The Brownie of Bodsbeck; And Other Tales.* Vol. 2. Edinburgh: William Blackwood, 1818.

Hone, William. *The Every-day Book and Table Book [...].* London: William Tegg, 1878.

Hooper, J. "Demon Dogs of Norfolk & Suffolk." *Eastern Daily Press*, July 2, 1894.

Howitt, Mary. "The Carolina Parrot." In *Mary Howitt's Poems.* London: Nelson & Sons, 1872.

Hunt, Robert, comp. and ed. *Popular Romances of the West of England: Or, The Drolls, Traditions, and Superstitions of Old Cornwall: Collected and Edited by Robert Hunt.* London: Chatto & Windus, 1903.

Hutton, William. *The Beetham Repository, 1770.* Edited by John Rawlinson Ford. Kendal: T. Wilson, 1906.

Ian. "Llyn Cowlyd." Mysterious Britain & Ireland: Mysteries, Legends & The Paranormal. November 7, 2012. http://www.mysteriousbritain.co.uk /folklore/llyn-cowlyd/.

Ian. "The Written Stone, Dilworth." Mysterious Britain & Ireland: Mysteries, Legends & the Paranormal. January 30, 2013. www.mysteriousbritain .co.uk/folklore/the-written-stone-dilworth/.

Jacobs, Joseph. *More English Fairy Tales, Collected and Edited by Joseph Jacobs.* London: George Putnam, 1922.

James, M. H. *Bogie Tales of East Anglia.* Norwich: Pawsey & Hayes, 1891.

Jenkinson, Henry Irwin. *Jenkinson's Practical Guide to the Isle of Man.* London: Edward Stanford, 1874.

"Johnny Croy and His Mermaid Bride." OrkneyJar. Accessed May 8, 2020. www.orkneyjar.com/folklore/jcroy.htm.

Johnson, Marjorie. *Seeing Fairies: From the Lost Archives of the Fairy Investigation Society, Authentic Reports of Fairies in Modern Times.* San Antonio: Anomalist Books, 2014.

Johnson, Samuel. "Ostig in Skye." In *A Journey to the Western Islands of Scotland.* London: 1775.

Jonson, Ben. *Love Restored A Masque, 1612.* http://www.luminarium.org /editions/loverestored.htm.

Jonson, Ben. *The Devil Is an Ass.* 1616.

Jones, Edmund. *A Relation of Apparitions of Spirits in the County of Monmouth, and the Principality of Wales [...].* Newport: E. Lewis Etheridge, and Tibbins,1813.

Jones, J. ("Myrddin Fardd"). *Llen Gwerin Sir Gaernarfon.* Caernarfon: Gwmni y Cyhoeddwyr Cymreig, Swyddfa Cymru, 1908.

Jones, William. *Credulities of the Past and Present; Including the Sea and Seamen, Miners, [...].* London: Catto & Windus, 1880.

Kent, Charles. *The Land of the "Babes in the Wood," or The Breckland of Norfolk.* London: Chatto & Windus, 1910.

Kerven, Rosalind. *English Fairy Tales and Legends*. Swindon: National Trust, 2008.

King, Richard John. "The Folk-lore of Devonshire." *Fraser's Magazine* 8 (1873): 773–785.

Kipling, Rudyard. "Weland's Sword." In *Puck of Pook's Hill*. London: n.p., 1906.

Kruse, John. *British Fairies*. Street: Green Magic Publishing, 2017.

Kruse, John. *Faery: A Guide to the Lore, Magic & World of the Good Folk*. Woodbury, MN: Llewellyn Publications, 2020.

Leather, Ella Mary. *Folklore of Herefordshire*. Hereford: Jakeman & Carver, 1912.

Leney, I. H. *Shadowland in Ellan Vannin*. London: E. Stock, 1880.

Leslie, Forbes. *The Early Races of Scotland and Their Monuments*. Edinburgh: Edmonston and Douglas, 1866.

Leyden, John. *Journal of a Tour in the Highlands and Western Islands of Scotland in 1800*. Edited by James Sinton. Edinburgh: William Blackwood, 1903.

"Littleport, Cambridgeshire." Shuckland. May 18, 2020. www.hiddenea.com /shuckland/littleport.htm.

Longstaffe, William Hylton. *The History and Antiquities of the Parish of Darlington, In the Bishoprick*. London: J. Henry Parker, 1854.

Loveday, Ray. *Hikey Sprites: The Twilight of a Norfolk Tradition*. Norwich: R. Loveday, 2009.

MacCulloch, John. *The Highlands and Western Isles of Scotland [...]*. Vol. 4. London: Longman, Hurst, Rees, Orme, Brown, and Green, 1824.

MacCulloch, John. *The Misty Isle of Skye: Its Scenery, Its People, Its Story*. Edinburgh: Oliphant, Anderson & Ferrier, 1903.

MacCulloch, Mary Julia. "Folklore of the Isle of Skye." *Folklore* 33 (1922): 201–214, 307–317, 382–389.

MacCulloch, Mary Julia. "Folklore of the Isle of Skye." *Folklore* 34 (1921): 86–93.

MacDiarmid, James. "Fragments of Breadalbane Folklore." *Transactions of the Gaelic Society of Inverness* 21 (1896): 126–148.

Macdonald, Alexander. "Scraps of Unpublished Poetry and Folklore from Glenmoriston." *Transactions of the Gaelic Society of Inverness* 21 (1896): 22–36.

MacDougall James. *Folk Tales and Fairy Lore in Gaelic and English: Collected from Oral Tradition by Rev. James MacDougall.* Edited by George Calder. Edinburgh: John Grant, 1910.

MacGregor, Alasdair. *The Peat-Fire Flame: Folk-Tales and Traditions of the Highlands and Islands.* Edinburgh: Moray Press, 1937.

MacGregor, Alasdair. *The Ghost Book.* London: Robert Hale, 1955.

MacKenzie, Donald. *Scottish Folk-Lore and Folk Life: Studies in Race, Culture, and Tradition.* London: Blackie & Sons, 1935.

MacKenzie, Donald. *Tales from the Moors and the Mountains.* London: Blackie & Son, 1931.

Mackay, Charles. "The Kelpie of Corryvreckan." In *Legends of the Isles and Other Poems.* London: Charles Gilpin, 1851.

MacKenzie, W. M. *The Book of Arran.* Arran: Kilbrannan Publishing, 1914.

Mackinlay, James. *Folklore of Scottish Lochs and Springs.* Glasgow: W. Hodge, 1893.

MacLagan, R. C. "'The Keener' in the Scottish Highlands and Islands." *Folklore* 25 (1914): 84–91.

Macleod, Torquil. "The Mermaid of Colonsay." *Celtic Monthly* 6 (1897), 168–9.

MacPhail, Malcolm. "Folklore from the Hebrides." *Folklore* 7 (1896): 400–404

MacPhail, Malcolm. "Folklore from the Hebrides—II." *Folklore* 8 (1897): 380–386.

MacPherson, John. *Tales of Barra, Told by the Coddy.* Edinburgh: W. & A. K. Johnstone and G. W. Bacon, 1960.

MacRitchie, David. *The Testimony of Tradition.* London: Kegan Paul, Trench, Trübner & Co., 1890.

"Manchester Ghosts, Hauntings and Paranormal Activity." Paranormal Database. Accessed May 25, 2020. www.paranormaldatabase.com/hotspots /manchester.php.

Manning, Percy. "Stray Notes on Oxfordshire Folklore." *Folklore* 14 (1903): 65–74.

"Marshland Between Alderfen and Neatishead, Known as Heard's Holde— Heard's Lantern." Paranormal Database. May 26, 2020. https://www .paranormaldatabase.com/m/detail.php?address=7702.

Martin, Martin. *A Description of the Western Islands of Scotland Containing a Full Account [...].* London: A. Bell, 1716.

Marwick, Ernest. *The Folklore of Orkney and Shetland.* Edinburgh: Birlinn Ltd., 2011.

"Mary Queen of Scots," Derbyshire—Paranormal Database Records, Paranormal Database, accessed May 26, 2020. https://www.paranormal database.com/derbyshire/derbdata.php?pageNum_paradata=7&total Rows_paradata=268.

McKay, James. "The Evolution of East Lancashire Boggarts," *Transactions of the Burnley Literary & Scientific Club* 6 (1888), 113–127.

McPherson, Joseph. *Primitive Beliefs in the North-East of Scotland.* London: Longmans, 1929.

"Mer Children." Isle of Man—Paranormal Database Records. Paranormal Database. Accessed May 7, 2020. www.paranormaldatabase.com /isleofman/mandata.php.

Meynell, Laurence. *Bedfordshire.* London: Robert Hale, 1950.

Miller, Hugh. *Scenes and Legends of the North of Scotland; Or, The Traditional History of Cromarty.* Edinburgh: Johnstone and Hunter, 1835.

Milne, John. *Myths and Superstitions of the Buchan District.* R. Jack, 1891.

Milton, John. *L'Allegro.*

Milton. *Paradise Lost.*

"Monsters of the Deep." Orkneyjar. Accessed May 21, 2020. http://www .orkneyjar.com/folklore/mermaids.htm.

Moor, Edward. *Suffolk Words and Phrases; Or, An Attempt to Collect the Lingual Localisms of that County.* London: R. Hunter, 1823.

Moore, Arthur W. *The Folk-lore of the Isle of Man: Being an Account of Its Myths, Legends, Superstitions, Customs & Proverbs [...].* London: D. Nutt, 1891.

"Morag, the Monster of Loch Morar—1." The Carmichael Watson Project. University of Edinburgh. Blogger. December 22, 2011. http://carmichaelwatson.blogspot.com/search?q=morag.

"Morag, the Monster of Loch Morar—2." The Carmichael Watson Project. University of Edinburgh. Blogger. December 26, 2011. http://carmichaelwatson.blogspot.com/2011/12/morag-monster-of-loch-morar-2.html.

Morrison, Sophia. *Manx Fairy Tales.* London: D. Nutt, 1911.

Morrison, Sophia. "Dooiney-oie, The Night-Man: A Manx Folk-Tale." *Folklore* 23 (1912): 342–345.

Morrison, Sophia. "Buggane ny Hushtey, the Buggane-of-the-Water: A Manx Folktale." *Folklore* 34 (1923): 349–251.

Munday, A. *Fidele & Fortunio,* 1584.

Nares, Robert. *A Glossary or Collection of Words, Phrases and Names.* Stralsund, 1825.

"Near Castle Acre, Norfolk." Shuckland. Accessed May 13, 2020. www.hiddenea.com/shuckland/castleacrenear.htm.

"Near Ruins East of the Town—Wolfhound Howls and Doom Follows." Paranormal Database. Accessed May 25, 2020. https://www.paranormaldatabase.com/m/detail.php?address=542.

Newman, L., and E. Wilson. "Folklore Survivals in the Southern Lake Counties and in Essex: A Comparison and Contrast. *Folklore* 63 (1952).

Nicholson, Edward. *Golspie: Contributions to its Folklore [...].* London: D. Nutt, 1897.

Nicolson, James. *Shetland.* Newton Abbot: David & Charles, 1984.

Nicholson, John. *Folklore of East Yorkshire.* London: Simpkin, Marshall, Hamilton, Kent & Co., 1890.

Nimmo, William P. *Omens and Superstitions: Curious Facts and Illustrative Sketches.* Edinburgh: William P. Nimmo, 1868.

Norris, Edwin, ed. and trans. *Passio Domini.* In *The Ancient Cornish Drama.* Vol. 1. Oxford: University Press, 1859.

Northcote, Rosalind. "Devonshire Folklore, Collected Among the People Near Exeter Within the Last Five or Six Years." *Folklore* 11 (1900): 212–217.

"Northumberland—Paranormal Database Records." Paranormal Database. Accessed May 26, 2020. www.paranormaldatabase.com /northumberland/nhumdata.php;

Norway, Arthur. *Highways and Byways of Yorkshire.* London: Macmillan, 1899.

Norwich Mercury, January 25, 1860.

Notes & Queries 2, no. 61 (1850).

Notes & Queries, series 4, vol. 5.

Oliver, Stephen, the Younger [pseud.]. *Rambles in Northumberland, and On the Scottish Border [...].* London: Chapman and Hall, 1835.

"One Spared to the Sea." The Selkie-folk. Orkneyjar. Accessed May 7, 2020. www.orkneyjar.com/folklore/selkiefolk/spared.htm.

Opie, Amelia. *Memorials of the Life of Amelia Opie: Selected and Arranged from Her Letters, Diaries, and Other Manuscripts.* Composed by Cecilia Lucy Brightwell. Norwich: Fletcher & Alexander, 1854.

"Overstrand, Norfolk." Shuckland. Accessed May 26, 2020. https://www .hiddenea.com/shuckland/overstrand.htm.

Owen, Elias. *Welsh Folk-lore: A Collection of the Folk-Tales and Legends of North Wales.* Oswestry and Wrexham, Woodall, Minshall, and Co., 1896.

P. P., "Folklore of Lancashire." *Choice Notes & Queries—Folklore.* 188–189.

Palmer, Roy. *Folklore of Leicestershire and Rutland.* Wymondham: Sycamore Press, 1985.

Palmer, Roy. *The Folklore of Warwickshire.* London: Batsford, 1976.

Parkinson, Thomas. *Yorkshire Legends and Traditions, as Told by Her Ancient Chroniclers, Her Poets, and Journalists.* London: Elliott Stock, 1888.

Partridge, J. B. "Notes on Folk-lore." In *Folklore* 27 (1916): 307–311.

Peacock, Mabel. *Lincolnshire: Examples of Printed Folklore.* London: David Nutt, 1908.

"Phantoms of the Night." *Norwich Mercury.* January 28, 1944.

Phillips, John. *The Rivers, Mountains & Sea Coast of Yorkshire.* London: J. Murray, 1853.

Poole, Charles. *The Customs, Superstitions and Legends of the County of Stafford.* London: Rowney & Co., 1875.

Porter, Enid. *Cambridgeshire Customs and Folklore with Fenland Material Provided by W. H. Barrett.* London: Routledge & Kegan Paul, 1969.

R. J. K., "The Pool of the Black Hound." *Notes & Queries* 2, no. 61 (1850): 515.

R. R. "Barnby Fears Its 'Headless Hound'" *Eastern Daily Press,* January 17, 1968.

"Rabbit." Yorkshire—Paranormal Database Records. Paranomral Database. Accessed May 26, 2020. https://www.paranormaldatabase.com/yorkshire/Pages/yorkdata.php?pageNum_paradata=30&totalRows_paradata=753.

Radcliffe, Ann. "The Sea Nymph." In *The Mysteries of Udolpho, A Romance; Interspersed with Some Pieces of Poetry.* London: G. G. and J. Robinson, 1794.

Ralph of Coggeshall. *Chronicon Anglicanum, De Expugnatione [...]* (English Chronicle), 1197. Edited by J. Stevenson. London: Her Majesty's Stationery Office, 1875.

Ramsay, Allan. *The Gentle Shepherd.* In *Bell's British Theatre 9,* 1780.

"Ranworth, Norfolk." Shuckland. Accessed May 18, 2020. www.hiddenea.com/shuckland/ranworth.htm.

Ratcliffe, T. "Black Dogs: Gabriel Hounds." *Notes & Queries.* Series 11, vol. 5, no. 120 (1912).

Rawe, Donald. *Traditional Cornish Stories and Rhymes.* Padstow: Lodenek Press, 1971.

Reeve, Christopher. *A Straunge & Terrible Wunder: Story of the Black Dog of Bungay.* Wichita: Morrow & Co., 1988.

Reid, James. *Scotland, Past and Present.* London: Oxford University Press, 1959.

Rhys, John. *Celtic Folklore: Welsh and Manx.* Vol. 1. Oxford: Clarendon Press, 1901.

Rhys, John. *Celtic Folklore: Welsh and Manx.* Vol. 2. Oxford: Clarendon Press, 1901.

Rhys, John. *Manx Folklore and Superstitions.* Edited by Stephen Miller. Isle of Man: Chiollagh Books, 1994.

Richardson, Moses. *The Local Historian's Table Book, of Remarkable Occurrences, Historical Facts, Traditions, Legendary and Descriptive Ballads, &c., &c.,.* Newcastle upon Tyne: M. Richardson, 1844.

Ritson Joseph. "Dissertation II on Fairies." In *Fairy Tales.* London: Payne & Foss, 1831.

Robbins, Rossell Hope, ed. *Historical Poems of the XIVth and XVth Centuries.* New York: Columbia University Press, 1959.

Roberts, Kai. *Folklore of Yorkshire.* Stroud: History Press, 2013.

Robertson, William. *Historical Tales and Legends of Ayrshire.* London: Hamilton, Adams & Co., 1889.

Roby, John. *Traditions of Lancashire.* Vol. 1. London: George Routledge and Sons, 1872.

Roeder, Charles. *Manx Folk-Tales.* Edited by Stephen Miller. Isle of Man: Chiollagh Books, 1993.

Roeder, Charles. *Manx Notes & Queries, With an Account of [...].* Douglas: S. K. Broadbent & Co. Ltd., 1904.

Ross. *Scottish Notes & Queries.* 1893.

"Roudham, Norfolk." Shuckland. Accessed May 18, 2020. www.hiddenea .com/shuckland/roudham.htm.

Rowlands, Samuel. "Of Ghosts and Goblins." *More Knaves Yet? The Knaves of Spades and Diamonds,* 1612.

Rowll, John. *Sir John Rowll's Cursing (Heir Followis the Cursing of Sr. Johne Rowlis, Upoun the Steilaris of His Fowlis).* With an Introductory Note by David Laing. Aberdeen, 1822.

Rudkin, Ethel H. "The Black Dog," *Folklore* 49 (1938): 111–131.

"Running Hound." Black Shuck. Hellhounds, and Other Black Dog Reports. Paranormal Database. Accessed May 13, 2020. www.paranormaldatabase .com/reports/shuckdata.php.

Rye, Walter. *Eastern Counties Collectanea Being Notes and Queries [...].* In John L'Estrange, ed. Norwich: Thomas Tallack, 1872.

Rye, Walter. *The Recreations of a Norfolk Antiquary.* Norwich: Holt, Rounce & Wortley, 1920.

Saxby, Jessie. *Shetland Traditional Lore.* Edinburgh: Grant & Murray, 1932.

Scot, Reginald. *The Discoverie of Witchcraft.* Edited by B. Nicholson. London: Elliot Stock, 1886.

Scott, Walter. *Minstrelsy of the Scottish Border: Consisting of Historical and Romantic Ballads [...].* Vol. 1. Kelso: James Ballantyne, 1802.

"Shaggy Creature." Cryptozoology Reports from the Paranormal Database. Paranormal Database. Accessed May 18, 2020. www.paranormaldatabase .com/reports/cryptodata.php.

Shakespeare, William. *A Midsummer Night's Dream.* In *The Complete Works.* Edited by W. J. Craig. London: Oxford University Press, 1926.

Sharp, Cuthbert, comp. *The Bishoprick Garland: Or, A Collection of Legends, Songs, Ballads, &c, Belonging to the County of Durham.* London: Nichols, & Baldwin, & Cradock, 1834.

Shaw, Thomas. "Narrative of Shantooe Jest." In *Recent Poems, on Rural and Other Miscellaneous Subjects.* Huddersfield: J. Lancashire, 1824.

"Shorted Armed Mermaid." Argyll and Bute—Paranormal Database Records. Paranormal Database. Accessed May 8, 2020. www .paranormaldatabase.com/highlands/Argydata.php.

Sikes, Wirt. *British Goblins.* London: Sampson Low, Marston, Searle, & Rivington, 1880.

Spence, Lewis. *The Minor Traditions of British Mythology.* London: Rider & Co., 1948.

Spence, Lewis. *The Fairy Tradition in Britain.* London: Rider & Co., 1948.

Stewart, Alexander. *'Twixt Ben Nevis and Glencoe: The Natural History, Legends, and Folk-lore of the West Highlands.* Edinburgh: W. Paterson, 1885.

Stewart, George. *Shetland Fireside Tales; Or, The Hermit of Trosswickness.* Lerwick: T & J Manson, 1892.

"Somerset—Paranormal Database Records." Paranormal Database. Accessed May 26, 2020. https://paranormaldatabase.com/somerset/somedata.php.

Sugg, Richard. *Fairies: A Dangerous History.* London: Reaktion Books, 2018.

Sullivan, Jeremiah. *Cumberland & Westmorland: Ancient & Modern: the People, Dialect, Superstitions and Customs.* Kendal, John Hudson, Jos. Dawson, and Jas. Robinson, 1857.

Sutherland, George. *Folk-lore Gleanings and Character Sketches from the Far North.* Wick: John O'Groat Journal, 1937.

"Swanton Morley." Shuckland. Accessed May 18, 2020. https://www.hiddenea.com/shuckland/swantonmorley.htm.

T. T. W., "'Trash' or 'Skriker,'" *Notes & Queries.* Series 1, vol. 2, 1850.

Tarlton's News out of Purgatory. 1588.

The Ballad of Robin Goodfellow.

The Cobbler of Canterbury. 1608. "Robin Goodfellow's Epistle." In *Library of English Literature.* Vol. 2. Edited by F. Ouvry and H. Neville Davies. D. S. Brewer, 1976.

"The Fairy Man, or The Clan Donald's Last Struggle," *Celtic Monthly* 10 (1885): 211–212.

"The Gabriel Hounds: The Seven Whistlers as Bad Omens." *Notes & Queries.* Series 7, vol. 1, no. 11 (1886).

The Life of Robin Goodfellow, His Mad Pranks and Merry Jests. 1628.

"The Paranormal Gallery, Wiltshire, West Kennet Long Barrow." Paranormal Database. Accessed May 13, 2020. www.paranormaldatabase.com/zenphoto/index.php?album=wiltshire/west-kennet-long-barrow/.

The Sad Shepherd, 1637.

"The Water Nymph of the River Frome." Dark Dorset. Accessed May 11, 2020. www.darkdorset.co.uk/water_nymph.

The Wonders of this Windie Winter. By Terrible Stormes and Tempests, […]. London: G. Eld, 1613.

Thomas, Edward. *Collected Poems.* London: Faber and Faber, 2004.

Thornber, William. *An Historical and Descriptive Account of Blackpool and its Neighbourhood*. Blackpool: Smith, 1837.

Tickell. *The Guardian*. April 15, 1713.

Tongue, Ruth. *Somerset Folklore*. Edited by Kathleen Briggs. London: Folklore Society, 1965.

Tozer, Elias. *Devonshire & Other Original Poems; With Some Account of Ancient Customs, Superstitions, and Traditions*. Exeter: *Devon Weekly Times*, 1873.

Traill Calder, James. "The Mermaid of Dwarwick Head," in *Poems from John o' Groats*. 1–17. Wick: P. Reid, 1855.

Traill Dennison, Walter. "Orkney Folk-lore: Sea Myths." In *Scottish Antiquary* 6 (1891): 115–121.

Traill Dennison, Walter. "Orkney Folk-lore: Sea Myths." In *Scottish Antiquary* 7 (1892): 18–24, 112–120.

Train, Joseph. *An Historical and Statistical Account of the Isle of Man from the Earliest Times to the Present Date*. Douglas: M. A. Quiggin, 1845.

Trotter, Maria, and Bruce Trotter. *Galloway Gossip: Sixty Years Ago; Being a Series […]*. Edited by Saxon. Bedlington: George Richardson, 1877.

Trotter, Maria, and Bruce Trotter. *Galloway Gossip Eighty Years Ago*. Bedlington: George Richardson, 1901.

"Unknown Pool—Two Headed Dog." Paranormal Database. Accessed May 26, 2020. www.paranormaldatabase.com/m/detail.php?address=9084.

"Vanishing Hound." Black Shuck, Hellhounds, and Other Black Dog Reports. Paranormal Database. Accessed May 13, 2020. www.paranormaldatabase.com/reports/shuckdata.php.

"Village Square, Heading Out Towards the Hills—Dog That Still Isn't There." Paranormal Database. Accessed May 25, 2020. https://www.paranormaldatabase.com/m/detail.php?address=8702.

Waldron, George. *The History and Description of the Isle of Man: viz. Its Antiquity, History, Laws, Customs, Religion and Manners of Its Inhabitants […]*. Douglas: Manx Society, 1731.

Watson, E. C. "Highland Mythology," *Celtic Review* 5 (1908): 48–70.

Watt, Archibald. *Highways and Byways Round Kincardine.* Aberdeen, 1985.

"Welney, Norfolk." Shuckland. Accessed May 13, 2020. www.hiddenea.com /shuckland/welney.htm.

Westwood, Jennifer. "Friend or Foe? Norfolk Traditions of Shuck." In *Supernatural Enemies.* Edited by Hilda Ellis Davidson and Anna Chaudhri. Durham, NC: Carolina Academic Press, 2001.

Westwood, Jennifer, and Jacqueline Simpson. "Rutland." In *Haunted England: The Penguin Book of Ghosts.* Edited by Sophia Kingshill. London: Penguin, 2010.

Westwood, Jennifer, and Jacqueline Simpson. *The Lore of the Land: A Guide to England's Legends, From Spring-Heeled Jack to the Witches of Warboys.* Harmondsworth: Penguin, 2005.

Westwood, Jennifer, and Sophia Kingshill. *The Lore of Scotland: A Guide to Scottish Legends.* London: Random House, 2009.

Whitaker, Terence W. *Lancashire's Ghosts and Legends.* London: Robert Hale, 1980.

"White Dog," Black Shuck, Hellhounds, and Other Black Dog Reports, Paranormal Database. Accessed May 13, 2020. www.paranormaldatabase .com/reports/shuckdata.php.

"White Hare." Reports of Curses and Cursed Places in the UK and Ireland. Paranormal Database. Accessed May 28, 2020. https://www .paranormaldatabase.com/reports/curse.php.

White, John Pagen. *Lays and Legends of the English Lake Country, With Copious Notes.* London: John Russell Smith, 1873.

"White Rabbit." Haunted Churches and Other Myths & Legends. Accessed May 26, 2020. https://paranormaldatabase.com/reports/church .php?pageNum_paradata=26&totalRows_paradata=672.

White, Walter. *A Month in Yorkshire.* London: Chapman and Hall, 1861.

Whittock, Martyn. *A Brief Guide to Celtic Myths and Legends.* Philadelphia: Running Press, 2013.

"Wicken Area, Cambridgeshire." Shuckland. Accessed May 13, 2020. www .hiddenea.com/shuckland/wicken.htm.

Wilson, Thomas. *The Pitman's Pay and Other Poems.* Gateshead: William Douglas, 1863.

Wiltshire, Kathleen. *Ghosts and Legends of the Wiltshire Countryside.* Edited by Patrick M. C. Carott. London: Michael Russell, 1973.

"Winfarthing, Norfolk." Shuckland. Accessed May 13, 2020. www.hiddenea .com/shuckland/winfarthing.htm.

Witcutt, W. P. "Notes on Staffordshire Folklore," *Folklore* 52, no. 3 (1941): 236–237.

Withers, James Reynolds. "The Pond in the Meadow." In *Poems Upon Various Subjects.* Fordham, 1864, 117–118.

Wright, Elizabeth Mary. *Rustic Speech and Folk-lore.* London, H. Milford, 1913.

"Women with Child." Merfolk and Selkies. Paranormal Database. Accessed May 7, 2020. www.paranormaldatabase.com/reports/mermaid.php.

Word-Lore: The "Folk Magazine," (1926), 167.

Yarrell, William. "Gabriel Hounds." *Notes & Queries.* Series 1, vol. 5, 596.

Yeats, W. B. "The Mermaid." Section 3. From "A Man Young and Old." In *The Tower* (New York: Macmillan), 1928.

"Yellow Dog." Manchester Ghosts, Hauntings and Paranormal Activity. Paranormal Database. Accessed May 25, 2020. www.paranormaldatabase .com/hotspots/manchester.php.

Yn Lioar Manninagh; the Journal of the Isle of Man Natural History and Antiquarian Society, 1895–1905.

Young, Francis. *Suffolk Fairylore.* Norwich: Lasse Press, 2019. Citing Arthur Hollingsworth, *The History of Stowmarket, the Ancient County Town of Suffolk [...].* Ipswich: F. Pawey, 1844.

Young, Simon. "Folklore Pamphlet: The Sources for Jenny Greenteeth and Other English Freshwater Fairies." *Academia* (July 2019): 1–54. https:// www.academia.edu/39885284/Folklore_Pamphlet_The_Sources_for _Jenny_Greenteeth_and_Other_English_Freshwater_Fairies_Second _Edition

Young, Simon. "In Search of the Holden Rag." *Retrospect* 35 (2017): 3–10. https://www.academia.edu/38310291/Young_In_Search_of_Holden _Rag.

Young, Simon. "The Mysterious Rolling Wool Bogey." *Gramarye* 8 (Winter 2015): 8–17. https://www.academia.edu/24973729/Young_The_Mysterious _Rolling_Wool_Bogey.

Young, Simon. "The Reay Mermaids: in the Bay and in the Press," *Shima* 12, no. 2 (2018): 25–36. https://pdfs.semanticscholar.org/fd62/1ef9fc15857 f621e574f59ed77dd0ba44296.pdf?_ga=2.144243061.1393131365.15889 52007-252660946.1588713747.

Young, Simon, ed., and The Fairy Investigation Society. *Fairy Census 2014– 2017.* n.p., 2018. 1–401. www.fairyist.com/wp-content/uploads/2014/10 /The-Fairy-Census-2014-2017-1.pdf.

Young, Simon, and Ceri Houlbrook. *Magical Folk: British and Irish Fairies: 500 AD to the Present.* London: Gibson Square, 2018.